WILLIAM GOLDING

WILLIAM GOLDING

The Dark Fields of Discovery

by
VIRGINIA TIGER

MARION BOYARS
LONDON

A MARION BOYARS BOOK
distributed by
Calder & Boyars Ltd
18 Brewer Street
London W1R 4AS

First published in Great Britain in 1974
by Calder & Boyars Ltd

Reprinted in 1976
by Marion Boyars Publishers Ltd
18 Brewer Street
London W1R 4AS

© Virginia Tiger 1974

ISBN 0 7145 1012 2 Cased edition
ISBN 0 7145 2595 2 Paper edition

Printed and bound in Great Britain by
REDWOOD BURN LIMITED
Trowbridge & Esher

CONTENTS

General Editor's

FOREWORD

Since about the turn of the century and more so than at any other time in history, Western man has been preoccupied with the question of the 'modernity' of his culture. The 'modern' has for some while now been a term of praise or blame, depending on your point of view; and as an object of active investigation it has preoccupied, and continues to preoccupy, anyone trying to keep abreast of the frequently disturbing and disorientating achievements of our time.

This is particularly true of the writers, artists and thinkers who are the subject of this series, which is concerned primarily with the phenomenon variously known as 'neo-modernism' or 'post-modernism', i.e. work produced roughly since World War II which explores media in a more or less radical way. Earlier writers are not of course excluded, but they will only be considered if they can still be shown to exert a cultural influence on our contemporary world. In other words, the series will concentrate on present-day innovators of one kind or another working in the tradition of the great moderns, now dead, such as Joyce, Proust and Thomas Mann. It will not concern itself with the ups and downs of the volatile avant-garde, but only with such contemporary writers, artists, works, genres and movements as can be said to satisfy at least one of the following criteria:

(1) that they have affected in a perceptible way current styles or attitudes;
(2) that they already present an appreciable opus or corpus of creativity;

(3) that they are demonstrably 'masterly' in the sense of having made a real impact on the contemporary arts and stayed in the forefront of cultural endeavour.

The series aims, in fact, to offer a fresh and original way of approaching the works of our contemporaries, and to render accessible what is challenging and often difficult. Although the stress will fall mainly on creative writing, there will also be a place for artists working in other media and in fields generally considered peripheral to literature proper. All forms of contemporary artistic endeavour hang together so much that none can be scrutinized in isolation, and the series as a whole will urge the organic nature of art in a period of rapid and often disconcerting change.

Twenty years of literary prominence hardly account for the uncanny resonance, that appalled delight that William Golding's fiction has provoked in so many countries. From *Lord of the Flies* to the recent *The Scorpion God*, his novels have spoken to the private imagination of the private reader with immediacy and certainty. Yet his is a remote and dreadful world which, unpopularly, insists on the spiritual. The novels themselves are difficult and demand unremitting attention. How has Golding constructed a myth so pungently relevant to contemporary man?

Provocations such as this are described and responded to in this study by Virginia Tiger. She argues that Golding's view of man is essentially religious; for him it contains a mystery or darkness. Dr. Tiger examines the fiction's preoccupation with the proverb's puzzle that 'Where there is no vision, the people perish.' She holds that in the novelist's view contemporary man lacks vision; he experiences mystery only as malignancy, not holiness. So how is he not to perish?

In the complex techniques of the novels, Virginia Tiger sees not deliberate obscuration but Golding's chemistry to make the life of the spirit a reality, at least in the imaginative realm. *The Dark Fields of Discovery* explores, in particular, the unusual structure which each novel possesses, a structure involving two apparently contradictory perspectives. Towards the end of each novel the reader moves from the protagonist's point of view and enters abruptly another character's point of view on the same situation. Golding intends that the two perspectives are to be linked; the bridge between the apparently contradictory perspectives is to be built by the reader who is driven by the paradoxical structure to accept paradoxes of existence which are to Golding symptoms of the spiritual world.

The study is based on an analysis of a definitive bibliography of critical works on Golding and conversations conducted by Dr. Tiger with Mr. Golding over a period of years.

John Fletcher
General Editor
1974

ACKNOWLEDGMENTS

Any critical book has perhaps more elaborate need than otherwise to contain its author's statement of intellectual debts owed and personal ones unrepayable. Primarily, I must record my gratitude to Mr. William Golding for his generous commitment to the ambience of literature which stimulated a private man to discuss his works in conversations and letters over a period of years. Mr. Golding, despite his passionate avowal of the hermetic nature of imaginative work, suspended this principle to read—and note—his detailed response to an earlier version of this manuscript. It is, of course, important to say that he is not to be held responsible for my analyses and interpretations; only the words attributed to him in quotations are his own. For these irreplaceable comments it is a serious statement to thank him.

My first introduction to the grip of literature, and the pleasures and dilemmas of understanding this, occurred as an undergraduate at Trinity College, University of Toronto; the farther away from that provocation I am in time, the more singular and important I know it was. The particular adventure of this project began at the University of British Columbia where I was tutored and encouraged by a demanding group of scholars. While there were others too, I am most clearly aware of my debt to Professors John Hulcoop, D. G. Stephens, and M. W. Steinberg.

I am happy to acknowledge my gratitude to the Canada Council and the Rutgers University Research Council for their financial support of this project. Libraries become part of the blood stream of literary critics and for their unfailingly congenial transfusions I am grateful to the Library of the University of British Columbia, the Reading Room of the British Museum, the British Museum's Newspaper Library, Colindale, and Dana Library at Rutgers University, Newark.

I wish also to thank the following for permission to quote from Golding's works. Excerpts from William Golding's *Lord of the Flies* are reprinted by permission of Faber and Faber; copyright © 1954 and Coward McCann, Inc.; copyright © 1955 by William Golding. Excerpts from William Golding's *Free Fall*, *The Hot Gates*, *The Inheritors*, *Pincher Martin*, *The Pyramid*, *The Scorpion God*, and *The Spire* are reprinted by permission of Faber and Faber; copyright © 1955, 1956, 1959, 1964, 1965, 1967, 1971 by William Golding and by permission of Harcourt Brace Jovanovich, Inc.; copyright © 1955, 1956, 1957, 1959, 1964, 1965, 1966, 1967, 1971 by William Golding. Excerpts from William Golding's *Poems* are reprinted by permission of Macmillan; copyright © 1934 and William Golding copyright © 1964.

Personal debts may be the most preposterous to try to acknowledge in formal terms since they are themselves, by definition, so outside formality. Steven M. L. Aronson was the first person to read this manuscript who had no professional connection with it; his spirited commitment to the adolescences of books, even before he became a publisher of them, was a generous ingredient of this book's life. But finally, most books are written in houses; I have shared one with my husband, Lionel Tiger. His complex engagement, passionate intelligence, and wackily proportioned wit have always permitted me to celebrate energies, energies which have their source in our household but then have firmly grown to become my own.

Virginia Tiger
New York City, New York

BIOGRAPHICAL NOTE

William Gerald Golding's response to considerable literary prominence since the 1954 publication of *Lord of the Flies* has been to shun personal publicity. Further, he has requested that no literary biography be written. One must honour the spirit of this request; what follows is a brief summary of his life since his birth at St. Columb Minor, Cornwall, in 1911.

The son of Mildred and Alec Golding, he received his secondary education at Marlborough Grammar School where his father was Senior Assistant Master. In 1930 Golding entered Brasenose College, Oxford and after reading science and then English Literature he graduated in 1935. Following the publication of a book of verses in 1934, he was a writer, actor, and producer in a provincial theatre company; he began teaching at Bishop Wordsworth's School, Salisbury and married Ann Brookfield, daughter of E. W. Brookfield in 1939. They have two children: a son and a daughter.

Golding joined the Royal Navy in 1940 as an ordinary seaman and became connected with Lord Cherwell's Research Establishment; later in World War II he saw active duty at sea as lieutenant on a rocket-launching craft and participated in the sinking of the *Bismarck* and the landings in Normandy on D-day.

In 1945 he returned to Bishop Wordsworth's School and taught English and Philosophy there until 1961. Following the outstanding success of *Lord of the Flies*, his first novel, and the rapid publication of three more novels—*The Inheritors*, *Pincher Martin*, and *Free Fall*, he was a frequent contributor of essays and reviews to the BBC, *The Spectator*, and *Holiday Magazine*. A play, *The Brass Butterfly*, was produced at the Strand Theatre starring Alastair Sim.

After spending 1962 as writer-in-residence at Hollins College, Virginia and numerous lectures that year at American universities, he published *The Spire*. Since then, Golding has devoted himself solely to writing and travelling—particularly in Greece—and to his many hobbies: classical Greek, archaeology, Egyptology, music, and sailing. In 1955 he was made a Fellow of the Royal Society of Literature; MA Oxon, 1961; Honorary Fellow of Brasenose College, 1966; CBE, 1966; and Hon. D. Litt., Sussex, 1968. Following the publication of *The Pyramid* in 1967, his most recent book was *The Scorpion God*, published in 1971.

INTRODUCTION

I

Far away and beyond reach of anything but random shot, the Liar had climbed out of the water to the top of a wall that, like a narrow path, led onward beneath the heads of palms to the central current of the flood. He turned back to the terrace, arms gesticulating, miming silently, but staunchlessly, the mechanics, the necessity of survival.

—Golding, 'The Scorpion God'

William Golding's fiction plays with the puzzle of Proverbs xxiii. 18 that 'Where there is no vision, the people perish.' This is, in the widest sense, a religious exploration and without stating so explicitly, all the fiction embodies this dictum for it deals in the primordial patterns of human experience. The fiction—unlike most contemporary novels—is preoccupied with what is permanent in man's nature, looking not at men simply in relation to a particular society but at man in relation to his cosmic situation: his evil in *Lord of the Flies*, his origins in *The Inheritors*, his destiny in *Pincher Martin*, his guilt in *Free Fall*, his vision in *The Spire*, his heart's meanness in *The Pyramid*, and his heady inventiveness in *The Scorpion God*. In the fiction, Golding consciously tries to construct a religious mythopœia relevant to contemporary man since he agrees generally with the anthropological notion that it is through myth that the imaginative substance of religious belief is expressed, communicated, and enhanced. As he has remarked in conversation: 'Myth is a story at which we can do nothing but wonder; it involves the roots of being and reverberates there.' In Golding's view, contemporary man lacks vision. How is he not to perish? In each of the novels, there is the effort of bridgebuilding between the physical world which contemporary man accepts and the spiritual world which he ignores but which—in Golding's view—does not ignore him. In a century of disbelief and formidable violence, Golding's mythopœia contends, mystery is experienced only as malignancy, not as holiness or wholeness. It is as though the spiritual is experienced not as individual or transcendent mercy, but as personal and universal guilt. Man abstracts from his violence—something his nature possesses in Golding's view—and projects it as fear of a demon which will destroy him. He seldom abstracts from his goodness, something his nature also possesses. Thus, in the early fiction, the central symbol for the spiritual dimension is 'darkness' and the central symbolic episode involves the nightmare world where character undergoes atavistic reordering or, as in the case of Pincher Martin, death itself.

It will be my argument throughout that seen with other eyes, Golding's eyes, the life of the spirit becomes a reality, at least in the imaginative realm. This Golding accomplishes through the use of an unorthodox structure in each of the five novels (fragments of the technique are noticeable in *The Pyramid* and *The Scorpion God* as well). I call this structure an ideographic structure so as to suggest specifically the following features: first, the ideographic structure consists in two narrative movements, the second of which is a coda. Following the plot's major movement there is in all the novels a coda ending. Secondly, the ideographic structure involves two different perspectives on the same situation: that emerging from the first movement and that emerging from the coda. In the first narrative movement events are seen from one character's point of view while in the coda events are seen either from another character's point of view or (as in the case of *The Spire*) from the enlightened consciousness of the novel's protagonist. The ideographic structure moves the reader outside the world of sensation he has been inhabiting and puts him abruptly into another world of sensation. Thirdly, the ideographic structure seems, at first reading, to create two contradictory perspectives on the same circumstance since the coda reverses the expectations which the first movement has built up. It is interesting that, though superficially contradictory, the two perspectives can be linked together by the reader. For Golding intends that the two perspectives are to be complementary, not contradictory. Fifthly and finally, in forcing the reader to build the bridge between contradictory perspectives, the ideographic structure forces the reader to accept—at least in the imaginative realm— paradoxes of existence which the novel's characters are represented as being unable to perceive or accept. The bridge between the two perspectives is there to be built by the reader who is driven by the paradoxical structure of each novel to accept paradoxes of existence which are to Golding symptoms of the spiritual world. As a character in *Free Fall* comments: the spiritual is three times more real than the material.

In each of these novels, we, the readers, are the inheritors of the new conjunction, a conjunction that cannot be located in the fictional world except in so far as we, by hints collected and assembled, imaginatively construct the wider view. Related to this emphasis on the reader's discovery is another feature of Golding's fiction—its subversion of popular literary models. But this is an area perhaps altogether familiar to readers. In varying degrees, each of the novels has its genesis in another writer's view of the same situation. It is Golding's intention that the reader judge the moral distance between Ballantyne's view of small boys in *Coral Island* and Golding's own recasting of that situation in *Lord of the Flies*. Similarly, the reader construes *The Inheritors'* ironic sublation of Wells's *The Grisly Folk* and *Free Fall*'s sensual inversion of the spiritual values of Dante's *Vita Nuova*. This strategy of indirection informs other technical features: the limitations of points of view, the metaphoric weight of certain image-clusters, the mannered asides of various characters, the symbolic density of certain passages where the reader feels as though he is, against his will, being pushed through fog. Its purpose is to make the reader encounter, by the imaginative impact of words, those experiences that conventionally words do not reach, formulate, communicate, or control: the primacy of spiritual experience itself. So when Golding records the assault on the senses of facts, the moment of confrontation between 'thing' and 'darkness', he not only describes terror and awe, he creates them. 'I don't simply describe something. I lead the reader round to discovering it anew.'[1] Golding would have his readers see in the world of unresurrected fact what in an essay he calls the 'thumbprint of mystery'[2] where reality freed from learnt meanings and dreary systems occurs as a spiritual event: close, incommunicable—'like the taste of potatoes'.[3]

Another fictional technique derives from Golding's concern with the spiritual realm and this I call the confrontation scene. Simon is before the Head, Lok peering down at the reflection of himself in water and Pincher prostrate before the Dwarf; Sammy is hunched before a monstrous 'thing' and Jocelin shrieks at the crossways and then stares at a church spire; Oliver before a music teacher's grave: each is a massively sculpted episode which functions in the novel as a single crystallization of that novel's total structure. The confrontation scene brings about the kind of conjunction between the two worlds which I earlier described in structural terms above. In the confrontation scene, the protagonist is forced through some fearful but ambiguous purgation—often in darkness, often in water—to encounter his own Being, 'the thing' in the centre of his 'darkness', that which is his internal landscape. For example, in the case of Simon the encounter with the Lord of the Flies Head transforms his innocent view of himself, by making him confront his own capacity for evil. And yet this confrontation permits him, even stimulates him, to act without evil. On the other hand,

Sammy Mountjoy is incapacitated by the unwholesomeness of his deepest self. As Simon puts it, man is both 'heroic and sick' and the confrontation scene dramatizes this opposition in the darkness between what in conversation Golding calls the 'My Godness' of man, that original spirit, the *Scintillans Dei* which flashes as suddenly as does the kingfisher in *The Spire* and the pervasive brutality in man which constantly overcomes but never quite completely destroys him.

It is in this kind of context that I want to examine the novels and other Golding fiction up to and including his most recent publication to date: *The Scorpion God*. Though the novels interest me most deeply, Golding's thematic consistency is such that minor and occasional pieces demand to be absorbed into a general argument. For this reason, essays from *The Hot Gates*, passages from the unpublished plays, 'Miss Pulkinhorn' and 'Break My Heart', allusions to 'The Anglo Saxon' and 'Our Way of Life' often preface discussion in the chapters which follow. The difficulty I found in achieving a relatively intense examination of Golding's fiction was that a more extensive elaboration of Golding's position in contemporary English and European literature had to be precluded. The reader's attention is drawn to those few pamphlets and articles which have touched on this matter. Furthermore, like all figures of critical controversy, Golding invites the most varied commentary; another problem one discovers in discussing his work is assessing judiciously the huge bibliography which has been spawned over the last twenty years. This is the place, in fact, to note the other books which treat Golding exclusively. Bernard F. Dick's *William Golding* (New York 1967) is useful as a general introduction to the minor works; he argues as does James R. Baker in *William Golding, A Critical Study* (New York 1965) that Golding adapts the techniques of Greek tragedians. Bernard S. Oldsey and Stanley Weintraub's *The Art of William Golding* (New York 1965) treats Golding's fiction in terms of what is taken to be its 'reactive' nature. Finally, there are two careful studies—Ian Gregor and Mark

Kinkead-Weekes: *William Golding, A critical Study* (London 1967) and Howard S. Babb: *The Novels of William Golding* (Ohio State University Press, 1970)—which ground their discussion of Golding's achievement in an exploration of his narrative and prose style.

For my part I would like to explore some propositions about Golding's fictional technique. After this chapter's general introduction, the chapters which follow will examine the novels in terms of their initial critical reception; the thematic use of the notion of darkness; the consistent use of the technical features which I describe above; point of view; the inversion of literary models; the confrontation scene; the ideographic structure. During my discussion the last term, ideographic, is used to describe Golding's apparently intentional use of a specific and unusual structural form to make an essentially religious, though not necessarily Christian, statement in an historical time when such statements cannot be made explicitly. For our purposes, then, the term 'religious' has misleading theological overtones; in the pages which follow it refers to that ambiguous area of belief: the magical, mysterious, powerful, terrible, dangerous, awesome.

As a synthetic summary of the argument throughout, in the conclusion I view briefly the last two published works, *The Pyramid* and *The Scorpion God*. There seems to be a most marked evolution, from externally wrested structures where pattern sublates pattern in the manner described above, to internally realized structures. I believe one can see a parallel thematic development from the awful darkness of man's heart as represented in *Lord of the Flies* through its opacity in *The Spire* to its inventive but humorous ineptitude in *The Scorpion God*.

II

. . . it is in some ways a melancholy thought that I have become a school textbook before I am properly

dead and buried. To go on being a schoolmaster so
that I should have time to write novels was a tactic I
employed in the struggle of life. But life, clever life,
has got back at me. My first novel ensured that I
should be treated for the rest of my days as a
schoolmaster. . . .

—Golding, 'Fable'

William Golding's fiction has received—indeed suffered—
widespread critical attention and acclaim. At first its reception
was tentative, although most of the first reviews of *Lord of the*
Flies, in 1954 for example, were favourable. By the end of the
year E. M. Forster had chosen it as book of the year. Six years
later, after the publication of four more novels, a play:
The Brass Butterfly, an adaptation based on his novella 'Envoy
Extraordinary', two obscurely published short stories: 'Miss
Pulkinhorn' and 'The Anglo Saxon', and two BBC plays: 'Miss
Pulkinhorn' and 'Break My Heart', it had become a critical
commonplace that Golding was a most significant writer.

Thus ten years ago, in the early 1960s, Golding's reputation
had become quite firmly established and when post-war
British fiction was dominated by the neo-realism of Doris
Lessing, Kingsley Amis, Anthony Powell, and C. P. Snow,
Golding's effort seemed unique:

. . . it is in this engagement to what is constant in man's
nature and in the correlative belief that a writer can
make valid generalizations about the whole meaning of
life that Mr. Golding stands most apart from his time—
he is a writer who has designs on us, a moralist in an
unmoralist age.[4]

Even in the international context of contemporary fiction—
Lawrence Durrell, Philip Roth, Norman Mailer, Graham
Greene, Jean-Paul Sartre, Alain Robbe-Grillet, Albert Camus,

Samuel Beckett, and Jorge Luis Borges—he was granted a position of conspicuous excellence.

Consequently, in their 1965 study, Oldsey and Weintraub had no doubts about nominating him 'dean' of his generation of writers and a 1962 BBC Third Programme broadcast, one of several productions which dramatized and discussed his work, concluded that he should be considered the outstanding novelist of the day. Predictably, a literary myth was launched which saw Golding mired in a pessimism and morbidity so intense that it approached the gloom and doom of a Calvinist seer. Partially attributable to Golding's personal retreat from publicity, it reflected for the most part, the relentlessness of American journalism's effort in dozens of interviews conducted during his year on a lecture engagement in the United States. Baker terms it appropriately a 'newspaper fable' but the insight does not seem to prevent him from contributing to the myth; he writes: 'Product of wartime disillusionment, Golding retreated from modern problems to the art of allegory.'[5] The British press and Sunday supplement world was quick to pick up the American image; thus, one finds Anthony Burgess describing Golding as 'a baroque bearded mythic visionary, frowning at some terrible landscape of the mind.'[6] Not the least interesting side of a study of a contemporary writer seems to me to be the window it opens on literary cults in the making as well as the *mafiosa*-like connectedness of the mass media and the academic world.

Yet in the last ten years there have been real uncertainties about his reputation; opinion has by no means agreed about Golding's ultimate literary status or even his popular position. Despite ever increasing academic attention—one critic remarked acidly that Golding had attained a type of pedagogic Valhalla in being catalogued in the PMLA Annual Bibliography —and the kind of public approbation indicated by such awards as a CBE, there is considerable divergence of critical and public opinion regarding the work. In fact in the seventies there seems to have developed a modish reaction against his achievement. *Lord of the Flies* has been, and remains, the most popular of the novels. The critical reception of the fourth novel *Free Fall* (1959) was on the whole hostile; that of its predecessor *Pincher Martin* (1956) uncomprehending; that of the second novel *The Inheritors* (1955) as indulgent as it was superficial. *The Spire* (1964) stimulated a good deal of controversy in the year that also saw the publication in England of works by Beckett and Elizabeth Bowen, but determined attacks started to appear. As praise has mounted, so has adverse criticism. The reception of *The Scorpion God* (1971) recapitulated all those critical clichés which had by this time accumulated about Golding's work. While recognizing the collection's scrupulous literary merit, most reviewers found Golding's territory too limited: a pre-adolescent and pre-historical world which promised a good deal more than it fulfilled.

Now Golding's reputation is based on a number of critical hypotheses about the earlier novels. Thus a review of *The Pyramid* (1967) in *The London Magazine*, for example, makes the familiar assumption that each novel necessarily has literary origins in another writer's view of a similar situation and claims that there is a marked resemblance to Sherwood Anderson's *Winesburg, Ohio*. In my opinion, a much more fruitful approach to this novel is to see its relationship to the plays 'Break My Heart', *The Brass Butterfly*, and the essays of childhood reminiscence, 'Billy the Kid' and 'The Ladder and the Tree' from *The Hot Gates* (1965). It is then clear that in this particular novel another method of narration is present, a tragicomic mode in which comedy casts its ironic colour yet does not entirely wipe away the tragic shadow. Similarly in the two new novellas of *The Scorpion God*, the subject is the familiar serious one—a crucial stage in two sorts of social development—but the tone is more abundantly and abidingly humorous, even urbane.

III

Even a very brief discussion of the critical reception that has already been accorded to Golding's novels will have made it clear that certain terms, such as 'allegory', 'fable' and 'parable' have frequently been applied to the novels. Since these terms may well be referred to as my examination continues, it might be convenient to define them here.

Golding's fiction eludes easy categorization. It has been called, for example, both allegory and parable. Understood as modalities of fiction, allegory and parable are both symbolic narratives but whereas allegory traditionally employs four levels of meaning to imply correspondences between its fictional scheme and the wider conceptual truth it seeks to demonstrate, parable has only the one level of plot which brings out the parallel between its elements and a lesson. Both allegory and parable are didactic in intention. Thus, allegory converts a thesis—often a theological doctrine—into a narrative sequence whose agents are abstract personifications and whose setting represents as well a general concept. Parable, on the other hand, consists in what Louis MacNeice in *Varieties of Parable* (1965) calls 'an enigmatical or dark saying'; it is predisposed to paradox and ambiguity rather than to drawing systems of correspondence between orders of reality. Nevertheless, in parable, character does not determine incident; rather incident is moral *exemplum*. In other words, in parable the whole action of the plot has significance only in the light of the moral idea it embodies. The story, then, becomes a direct and universal image of the content of the moral idea.

Fable has also been applied as a term to Golding's fiction and I propose to use it with Golding's conception in mind. He writes: 'With all its drawbacks and difficulties, it was this method of presenting the truth as I saw it in fable form which I adopted for the first of my novels which ever got

published.'[7] Fable is a protean fictional device. In its broadest
sense it is a story whose characters—traditionally animals as in
Aesop's fables—all serve a moral design which shows itself
in fictional terms by marked formal clarity and coherence. In
terms of such a patterned blueprint, fable is obviously akin to
allegory, with its specific relationship between different levels
of meaning. In the latter, however, the counterpointing of
literal narrative and a set of controlling abstractions is
usually detailed, precise, and extremely arbitrary. In its
element of moral didacticism fable is obviously akin to
parable. 'By the nature of his craft,' Golding has remarked,
'the fabulist is didactic, desires to inculcate a moral lesson.'
In parable, however, the moral image is primary, while in
fable the dramatic situation is primary.

No narrowly exclusive stipulated definition of fable is
useful, for my purpose, however desirable such formal
precision is. The term should be elastic enough to suggest
similar elements in very dissimilar works and writers themselves as dissimilar as Bunyan, Faulkner, Orwell, Kafka,
Borges, Burgess, and Donald Barthelme Perhaps it is best to
look at it not as an exclusive fictional form but as an imaginative
direction which fiction may take. Thus it can range from very
schematized stories such as Wells's *The Island of Doctor Moreau*,
Aldous Huxley's *Brave New World*, or cautionary tales like
Beatrix Potter's *Tale of Johnny Town Mouse*, to the rich
exploration of ambiguous situation in such novels as Doris
Lessing's *Briefing for a Descent into Hell*. As a fictional tendency
rather than a strict modality, the peculiar nature of the fable
lies in the intellectual effort to bring together generalized
significance and a direct rendering of life.

Two points must be made about the fabulist's effort: first,
he always tries to make his dramatic situation serve as an
analogue of the world at large. Secondly, the fabulist always
tries to let his dramatic situation be open to vitality and
imaginative resonance in its own right. Two limitations of the
fabulist's art follow directly from this: fable often suffers from

narrowness of range since the subtler possibilities of dramatic
and character development must be eliminated to allow an
internally consistent intellectual distillation. Otherwise, the
fable may, in Golding's phrase, imaginatively, 'burst at the
seams'. The vitality of the life presented may well distort the
arbitrary design. In 'Fable' Golding puts the danger this way:

> Fable, as a method, depends on two things neither of
> which can be relied on. First the writer has to have a
> coherent picture of the subject, his picture is likely to
> get a little dim at the edges. Next a fable . . . like the
> small scale model cannot be exact in every·detail. It is
> because every sort of life, once referred to, brings up
> associations of its own within its own limits which may
> have no significant relationship with the matter under
> consideration. . . . In other words, the fable must be
> under strict control. Yet it is at this very point that the
> imagination can get out of hand.

The last sentence in this passage is, I think, entirely in keeping
with Golding's use of the fabulist's method and his attitude to
this contentious matter of the role of the imagination in the
fabulist's art. In our conversations over a period of time,
Golding sometimes referred—I thought rather too gnomically
—to a general aesthetic continuum consisting of allegory,
fable, and myth in which (as far as I can see) the critical
terms signified aesthetic possibilities, directions or trends
rather than discrete modes.

In the first case, the idea of this aesthetic continuum
emerges from the author's firm belief that 'intellectualism is
the enemy of living mythology'; a familiar enough dictum to
anyone who knows his Plotinus. Golding also shares some of
the English Romantic poets' conceptions of the mind and the
imagination. Coleridge's definition of allegory, for example,
makes possible the distinction between 'organic' and
'mechanic' form, a distinction with which Golding apparently

agrees. Coleridge writes in his *Essays and Lectures on Shakespeare and Some Other Old Poets and Dramatists*:

> The form is mechanic when on any given material we impress a pre-determined form, not necessarily arising out of properties of the material—as when to a mass of wet clay we give whatever shape we wish it to retain when hardened. The organic form, on the other hand, is innate; it shapes, as it develops, itself from within, and the fulness of its development is one and the same with the perfection of its outward form. Such as the life is, such is the form.

For Golding, each of the imaginative tendencies of fiction (allegory, fable and myth) represents one step away from intellectual fabrication towards imaginative recreation. Allegory is first and basic: 'it is an invented thing,' he commented. The poet here arbitrarily chooses to represent a set of circumstances by a certain set of signs; since the meaning of allegory can easily be sifted out from its story as a set of intellectual correspondences, 'allegory is nothing more than exegesis.' Didactic lesson is primary, story secondary.

Fable, in turn, depends for its success on a similar strict intellectual control and is most successful when the literary parallels between image and moralized world are as exact as possible. But it is the dilemma of the fabulist's art that a dramatic situation brings up its own associations. This Golding calls 'achieving passion', by which I would take it he means apparently the force of primeval reality which infuses any story, but which the allegorist often is under strict laws not to tap. When a writer's imagination is liberated from intellectual bonds, however, and allowed to proceed according to its own logic, all sorts of private and communal reverberations may enter a story. These falsify the simplicity of the fable's situation but they do not falsify the human nature depicted. It is an experience excellent for the novel that does not claim to be a fable Golding argues in 'Fable', but it leads to a distortion of the fable *per se*. 'Yet,' he remarks, 'is it not the experience which we expect and hope the novelist to have?' Finally, the fabulous world is an invented thing; for Golding, it differs from allegory in that certain situations and significant figures cease to serve an analytic design. These figures— Golding here cites Simon in *Lord of the Flies*—defy critical analysis since their personalities reverberate meaningfully on various levels. To the author himself they are discovered, not invented. Look at these remarks, for example: 'The point of the fable under imaginative consideration does not become more real than the real world, it shoves the real world on one side. The author becomes a spectator, appalled or delighted, but a spectator. At this moment, how can he be sure that he is keeping a relationship between the fable and the moralized world, when he is only conscious of one of them.' This imaginative process which involves, Golding goes on to explain, 'merciless concentration' and a willed brooding on an impenetrable target results in something which has (he has said in conversation) its own 'off beat life and we [reader and author] cling to this without really understanding why.' Symbolic action, such as this, when described at length becomes myth.

I find Golding's use of this term 'myth' extremely difficult to fix. In an interview with Frank Kermode back in 1959 he commented that he would prefer to have his novels considered as myths rather than fables. Again he talks not of the aesthetic product but the imaginative process:

> . . . I think a myth is a much profounder and more significant thing than a fable. I do feel fable as being an invented thing on the surface whereas myth is something which comes out from the roots of things in the ancient sense of being the key to existence, the whole meaning of life, and experience as a whole.[8]

I take the term as one made to describe (and eulogize) both a superior mode of perception akin to Coleridge's Secondary Imagination which 'dissolves, diffuses, dissipates in order to recreate', and to indicate an aesthetic landscape where the unchangeable patterns of human nature may be celebrated. Golding, then, would agree with Aristotle's prescription that the fundamental myth is the dramatic human tale, for he believes that 'Myth is a story at which we can do nothing but wonder'. But Golding is not so much interested in myth as an aesthetic device (those recurrent irreducible 'archetypal' patterns such as the dragon-slaying myth which Jung isolates in *The Archetypes of the Collective Unconscious*), but rather in the myth-making and myth-responding proclivity of the human imagination. Myth, then, is not a distinct fictional mode or form. Myth is simply an imaginative tendency or 'mode of perception to which all art struggles'. Thus—and I think this is central to his own type of religious vision—myth cannot simply be invented or made; it must be discovered. Both a novel like Lawrence's *The Rainbow*, or a parable like Samuel Beckett's *How It Is*, reach into a similar mythic landscape, and both defy analysis into equations; there is no philosophizing or explanation which is not absorbed, digested, and subdued by the story-spell. Understood in this way, myth carries its own powerful imaginative resonance, ambiguities, religious overtones, adaptations, and modulations 'wrapped up within itself'. Such a story can move in and out of overt reality (as for example, in Odysseus' adventure when he grapples with the whirlpool monsters of Scylla and Charybdis) without distorting life or meaning. And, Golding concludes, its power and meaning ultimately reside in and derive from the expectations people have of it.

At one pole in Golding's aesthetic continuum allegory exists, and at the other pole, myth.[9] When allegory translates abstract notions into narrative episodes, the latter recreates or discovers eternally familiar human actions by finite concrete tales. Emphasis in the former rests on divergence and distinction—for its weapon is the intellect. In the latter, coalescence and reconciliation occur, for its wand is the imagination. Depending on their participation in invention or discovery, individual stories lean towards one fictional landscape or the other. Fable in Golding's view apparently sits in the centre of the continuum, sharing in part one landscape and the other. Thus, in terms of my earlier discussion of fable as a fictional mode, it is both intellectual analogue and dramatic situation.

IV

Despite all the evident enthusiasm of criticism for labelling aspects of his work, Golding himself distrusts theoretical categories and discursive reasoning as crude impositions upon what is an essentially mysterious, magical and ambiguous reality. 'The job of the novelist', he commented to Owen Webster, a journalist, 'is to scrape the labels off things . . . to show the irrational where it exists'; ultimately he must offer a 'recognizable picture of the mystery.' Logical categories, particularly the scientific sort contemporary man uses, cannot by themselves comprehend reality; at best, they dismiss its confusions, as the boy in the essay 'The Ladder and the Tree' discovers, making mystery into muddle, 'looming terror' into 'absence of light'. Empirically, discursive reasoning, on its own, is the instrument of those systems that strive to net down the world and explain away its wonder. Morally—and this is often where Golding's fiction probes most intensely—such reasoning erects itself into stubborn dogmas which codify and thus insulate the essentially ambiguous nature of the moral life. Logical scientists correspond to archaeologists, for example, who may publish diagrams of digs, 'statistical analysis of pottery fragments and photographs of sections of the earth with each stratum labelled',[10] but who do not tell us anything about the past. For 'history', Golding writes in an essay 'Digging for Pictures', 'is not diagrams—however accurate—but pictures.' The antiquarian, for whom 'the land is aglow with every kind of picture' declines such denotative thinking: for him 'there is a glossy darkness under the turf and against that background the people of the past play out their actions.' It follows from this that the moral man must similarly try to repudiate merely conceptual categories when he examines the lessons of the past. It should be his brooding effort (we are told in a companion essay: 'Egypt from My Inside') to penetrate by a 'one-pointedness of the will' and a vast act of imagination temporal boundaries and credit such historically interred creatures as the past holds with humanity.

Golding is much preoccupied with history and pre-history and in many of The Hot Gates essays (as well as in The Scorpion God) there is just such a plea for the use of the moral imagination; it is almost as though Golding believes any deliberate exercise of logic can dissociate person from place, or perceiver from perceived. For contemporary man, who lacks vision, such a breakdown holds profound religious and moral implications. Clearly it is Golding's conviction that our analytical consciousness—whose vigour he does not deny—can sever us from our responsibility; instead of acknowledging in history our own humanity—and possible depravity—we put an objective diagram there. 'Perhaps, then, . . . the parallelism between intelligence and evil comes out in my books because it is our . . . particular sin—to explain away our own shortcomings rather than remedy them,' he remarked to Kermode. At the same time Golding sees that this very act of naming is man's passion and his despair, just in the way that the Neanderthals are doomed in The Inheritors to yearn for the New People, or just as Pincher's formidable power to endure is rooted in his daemonic ego. Indeed, in Golding's world, the point at which man acts triumphantly from his consciousness is precisely the point at which he can fall. The sources and gestures of power and dynamic creation may also be the sources and gestures of destruction.

There is another way of knowing dramatized in Golding's work. Though it is depicted as interpenetrating with self-consciousness, this mode of perception is marked by instinctiveness as it penetrates and encounters the mystery of things. Even in the essays Golding employs wholly symbolic terms to describe this intuitive mode and that primordial and undifferentiated ultimate to which it is drawn. He is obviously trying to restore a lost dimension to the contemporary human understanding when there are no longer shared terms or relevant images for what Sophocles' Electra calls the All-seeing, what Plotinus calls the Fountain, what Aristotle calls the Mind, or what the Christian calls God. And, insofar as there is any shared intellectual climate now it is psychological in persuasion. Thus the metaphors Golding uses to depict contemporary spirituality have to do with an isolated creature's sense of his innermost self. And throughout the fiction the metaphors remain consistent and deliberately non-specific.

Here it is useful to locate this one last term which I will use primarily in the discussion of *Pincher Martin* and *Free Fall*. I have been suggesting that, in Golding's view, contemporary man experiences his spirituality as 'darkness'. His interior landscape contains 'a central not comprehended dark' which is accessible but elusive. The 'darker dark' or 'centre' inhabiting that darkness constitutes the *ding an sich*, the ineradicable entity, or 'isness' of the unique character, his central organizing principle or Being, and it controls the character as it itself may be controlled by a 'pattern' suspended there. Here Golding remains deliberately ambiguous, suggesting at one time the excessive isolation of the 'thing' while, at other times, stressing the necessary interconnectedness of the microcosmic 'thing' to the macrocosmic universe. One element remains constant throughout the six fables: darkness itself is morally significant. As the protagonist of *Free Fall* puts it:

It is the unnamable, unfathomable and invisible darkness that sits at the centre of him, always awake, always different from what you believe it to be, always thinking and feeling what you can never know it thinks and feels, that hopes hopelessly to understand and to be understood. Our loneliness . . . is the loneliness of that dark thing.

But such darkness cannot examine itself; it resists any concentration on the darkness that is itself. Further, something in the darkness sometimes threatens submersion of that simple, physical, and psychic identity that the individual, the 'you' of the *Free Fall* passage above, asserts about its 'dark thing'. Golding then constructs an occasion when a character's centre breaks away from its internal landscape, resisting something in its own nature and directs itself to an external and commonplace landscape which it appropriates by intellectual patterns and controls. From such a germinal dislocation other kinds of polarities evolve. All the fiction is directed at understanding why this loss of wholeness has occurred and in what remote societies it was lost. In turning away from their given essential Being, contemporary individuals over and over again, in differing ways, posit some menacing demon there, the 'thing' in the darkness becomes for them horrible. 'God is the thing we turn away from into life, and therefore we hate and fear him and make a darkness there,' Golding wrote.[11]

To present such a mythopœia, Golding creates moments of extreme psychic and physical danger in each of the novels. A direct confrontation is made to occur between a character's centre (roughly intelligence or 'consciousness') and his darkness. What an adult remembers as a childhood terror of darkness he may experience at such moments as a threat posed by nonbeing to his 'carefully hoarded personality.' In such a confrontation, all that ostensibly makes a particular man a man—especially language and thought—are purged until only a bar of identity remains. It is here that Golding's imagination departs from a modernist context, for he holds

2

that man has a choice between two alternatives, each—Golding implies—causally determined yet free. He may like Christopher Martin resist the darkness and suffer a slow but inevitable annihilation that, as the case of Pincher Martin demonstrates, the guilty will inflict upon themselves. Or he may in extremity rush through and down the darkness and emerge, like Sammy Mountjoy, momentarily into transfigured totality, or like Jocelin into the beatific vision that prefaces his death.

For contemporary man Golding claims that darkness holds the promise and danger of wholeness. Of course, as any mystic will declare this wholeness implies extinction as well as completeness since it transcends mere self-consciousness, that particularly modern strategy of survival. Only the saints, the Nathaniels and Simons, can embrace darkness and discover its 'lighted centre.' At a communal level Golding sees such saints playing a purgative role, purging a particular society of its ills. By their death as scapegoats they release in that community regenerative powers once again. For ordinary men who must build some kind of new society—the Liar, for example, in *The Scorpion God*—there is another ideal that consists in a tension, a state of uneasy suspension between the landscape of darkness and that of self-consciousness, which tension is then the point at which the 'dark centre' endures an antique rhythm. Compelled to communicate, such a dark centre is forced to act and control, to move outward from itself. The compulsion removed, it sinks back into what is still its darkness, or guilt. This is the free fall which contemporary men inherit, a suspension between the worlds of wonder and fact: an admixture of past and present that Ralph, Tuami, Sammy, and Roger Mason share. It is not the innocence of Ma, the Neanderthals, and Beatrice where the centre is a 'neutral point of observation', 'a gap in the middle', 'a negative personality', any more than it is the solely rapacious ego of the evil Philip and Pincher. As *Free Fall* concludes: 'The innocent and the wicked live each in one world. . . . But we are neither the innocent nor the wicked. We are the guilty. We fall down.' The saintly condition so defined differs from the innocent, the wicked, and the guilty condition. Since the saint overwhelms his evil by recognizing it, he has found the 'lighted centre' of his darkness. Spirituality is, in consequence, no longer dark but light. The saint lives in the condition of sanctity, and is proof, Golding insists, to the 'illiterate of the existence of God.'

V

In what follows, I try to build on the critical works which Golding's fiction has stimulated by exploring some of the central points of tension between the author's conception and realization of his work and those of his critics. Towards this analysis, the author's own writing about his novels and material from/interviews with Mr. Golding have been assembled in the context of the critical material and employed in a relatively detailed probing of each of the novels. Inevitably, I must touch on the question of the author's approach to fiction, reality, and to rather more philosophical issues. Inevitably, I must admit to a certain degree of concern that this book is adding to the proliferating burden of some twenty year's commentary; when is fog dispelled and when, in fact, is it perpetuated? The general technical point I want to make is that I wish to elucidate the relationship between the structure of fictional works and the wider world view of the writer, Golding. My critical method throughout is to analyse in detail matters of prose style in order to explore how the verbal resonances of language itself contribute to a novel's imagined world. Inevitably, one is drawn to confront the problem throughout posed by the apparent paradox which David Lodge identifies in *Language of Fiction*: 'It is the irony of our position as critics that we are obliged, whatever kind of imaginative work we examine, to paraphrase the unparaphrasable.'[12] In this regard, it was with considerable pleasure that I read the remarkable critical investigation of modern fiction by Gabriel Josipovici: *The World and the Book* (1971)—one of his chapters treats Golding's fiction. In his view, modern fiction is forced—because of contemporary uneasiness about communication—to herald its own fictiveness. In other words, writers now use the refractive potential of fiction itself to suggest the refractive world we actually live in. Fiction, like the cocaine sniffing actor-artistes in Gelber's *The Connection*, deliberately interrupts the flow of its action to call attention to itself—somehow this self-conscious chagrin makes the mad act of mimesis more real, more potent, than any direct, frank representation of life.

For these reasons, my effort here has been to locate clues about the intention of a work in its relatively impersonal and austere structure—to discover the religious dimension towards which the technical devices of the structure, as well as other fictional features, are always directed.

INTRODUCTION—NOTES

1 Golding's comments in an interview with Owen Webster, 'Living with Chaos', *Books and Art* (March 1958), p. 16.
2 Golding, 'Egypt from My Inside', *The Hot Gates* (London: Faber and Faber, 1965), p. 81.
3 Golding, *Free Fall* (London: Faber and Faber, 1959), p. 6.
4 [Samuel Hynes], 'The Cost of a Vision', *Times Literary Supplement* (April 16, 1964), p. 310.
5 J. R. Baker, *William Golding, A Critical Study* (New York: St. Martin's Press, 1965), p. xvii.
6 Anthony Burgess, 'Golding Unbuttoned', *The Listener* (November 4, 1964), p. 717.
7 Golding, 'Fable', *The Hot Gates*, p. 86. For a full discussion of Golding's fiction as fabulation, two early articles are frequently helpful: John Peter, 'The Fables of William Golding', *Kenyon Review* (Autumn, 1957); Margaret Walters, 'Two Fabulists: Golding and Camus', *Melbourne Critical Review*, (1961).
8 Golding to Kermode in 'The Meaning of It All', *Books and Bookmen* (August, 1959), p. 10. This transcript of a BBC Third Programme discussion contains extremely useful information.

9 Another Romantic poet's conception of this analytic/synthetic continuum seems entirely relevant here: William Blake writes: 'the last Judgment is not Fable or Allegory but Vision. Fable or Allegory are a totally distinct and inferior kind of Poetry. Vision or Imagination is a Representation of what Eternally exists, Really and Unchangeably. Fable or Allegory is Form'd by the Daughters of Memory. Imagination is surrounded by the daughters of Inspiration, who in the aggregate are call'd Jerusalem. Fable is Allegory, but what Critics call The Fable, is Vision itself. The Hebrew Bible & the Gospel of Jesus are not Allegory, but Eternal Vision or Imagination of All that Exists. Note here that Fable or Allegory is seldom without some Vision.' *Complete Writings*, ed. Geoffrey Keynes (London, 1957), pp. 604–605.

10 Golding, 'Digging for Pictures', *The Hot Gates*, p. 62.

11 Golding, in John Peter's 'Postscript', *William Golding's Lord of the Flies, A Source Book* (New York, 1963), p. 34.

12 David Lodge, *Language of Fiction* (New York, 1966), p. 34.

LORD OF THE FLIES

I

*I would like to make a point about the writing of
Flies and its position in the world of scholarship.
I said to Ann [Mrs. Golding] in about 1953,
'Wouldn't it be a good idea to write a book about
real boys on an island, showing what a mess they'd
make?' She said, 'That is a good idea!' So I sat
down and wrote it. You see, neither I nor she nor
anyone else could dream of the sheer critical firepower
that was going to be levelled at this mass of words
scribbled in a school notebook. Then, carried away by
the reverence of exegetes, I made the great mistake of
defending the thing. . . . It's astonishing that any of
the book still stands up at all. It has become painfully
and wryly amusing to me when people throw things
like the Summa at my poor little boys. Of course,
that trick works. How not? Dialetic has always
clobbered rhetoric, from Socrates down. But—remembering the words scribbled in the school note book—is
the journey really necessary? Isn't it cracking an
opusculum with a critical sledgehammer?*

—Golding, Letter, 1970 (unpublished)

Lord of the Flies, still Golding's most popular fiction, is not
nearly so long as the critical commentary it has spawned.
After some twenty years of narcissistic, repetitive exegesis, it
cannot be the author alone who suffers blank, wearisome
boredom with the packets of pamphlets and articles on its
source, meaning, and symbolism. A mixture of hurt and

jeering guilt is triggered in me, for example, when I inspect such recent essay titles as 'An Illiberal Education: William Golding's Pedagogy' or 'The Decline of *Lord of the Flies*', and compare these with a 1965 issue of the British radical journal, *Anarchy*, wholly devoted to reverent assessments of the novel, or *Time Magazine*'s 1962 quip that the book was 'Lord of the Campus'. Learning now that *Lord of the Flies* is not used as once it was to introduce students to good fiction, one cannot help being relieved. Perhaps the novel can start to state its own strengths, free of those sticky hands in the academic community intent on titillating bored adolescents: that portion of the intellectual community committed to the commercial exploitation of the relevant.

Yet over the two decades, the novel has also received superb, sustained attention; to judge from recent criticism, it continues to demand critical vigour and, best of all, aesthetic frankness. As is the case with Doris Lessing's fiction, serious readers seem compelled to account for their initial astonishment and appalled recognition that finally a novelist was confirming what had only been privately understood about human behaviour. For just as Lessing's *Golden Notebook* made public the private tone of female grievance, so Golding's *Lord of the Flies* tugged at one's private hunch that males—even small boys—enjoyed aggression, group hierarchies, and the savour of blood.

Powerful thematic conceptions like these govern the narrative action throughout. As many of us now realize, much of the book's persuasive resonance comes from its strong structural shape. While this form has eluded easy categorization—terms such as allegory, parable, fable, science fiction, romance, have been variously suggested[1]—its element of arbitrary design obviously makes it akin to allegory. Judging from his comments in the essay 'Fable' in *The Hot Gates*, Golding's own preference is the term fable, which he once defined for me as 'allegory that has achieved passion.' I take this gnomic clue to imply the peculiar conjunction of

contrived pattern and fictional freedom which is a characteristic feature of Golding's work. As readers we sense strongly
our own freedom from complete iconographic control, yet
we judge as pertinent the author's intellectual effort to bring
together generalized significance and a direct rendering of
life. In protean fictional modes like this, the story's conceptual
machinery antedates its imaginative expression; nevertheless,
such a fable must be distinguished from parable (Orwell's
Animal Farm, for example), the purpose of which is wholly
didactic and the agents and adjuncts of which are more often
than not supernatural or preternatural. Gregor and Kinkead-
Weekes put the matter rather more cleanly in their introduction to the school edition (Faber and Faber, 1962) when
they described *Lord of the Flies* as 'fable and fiction simultaneously'.

Another persistent classification has attended to the book's
intellectual schema—its affinity to neither romance nor
realism, its definition as neither parable nor fable, but its
relation to the Christian apologia. Frederick Karl's discussion
in *A Reader's Guide to the Contemporary English Novel* was first
to suggest that Golding wrote 'religious allegories' whose
conceptual machinery undermines the 'felt life' of the tale:
'the idea . . . invariably is superior to the performance
itself.'[2] The notion that *Lord of the Flies* in particular was
somehow intellectually or philosophically contrived became,
in fact, one of the major critical assumptions about the rest of
his work. Ignoring the fictional landscape altogether, many
commentators constructed explications of 'meaning' more
relevant to social and literary history than the analysis of
fiction; teacup controversies raged in religious journals such
as *Commonweal* and *America*, for example. A passage from one
critic neatly sums up all the pertinent critical attitudes of this
type in one sentence:

It is, in fact, a cannily constructed—perhaps contrived—
allegory for a twentieth century doctrine of original sin

and its social and political dynamics and it conforms
essentially to a quite orthodox tradition not really more
pessimistic than the Christian view of man.[3]

Despite the numerous interpretations, religious, political,
psychological, anthropological, the story itself seems rather
simple. And it would seem that one of the main reasons for
the many contradictory critical interpretations of this fable is
that while the meaning of the fable is coherent at so many
different levels critics have isolated for discussion only one or
two of these levels. Against this we must put Golding's own
statement to Kermode that 'it was worked out very carefully
in every possible way, this novel.'

Since *Lord of the Flies* has incited so many internally consistent but contradictory interpretations in the twenty years of
its critical treatment, it seems to me relevant to consider
several of these before examining what particularly interests
me: the formal matter of the fable's ideographic structure and
the dramatization of that thematic juxtaposition in the confrontation scene. In the section which directly follows, I have
collated and arranged critical analyses in an effort to show the
wide range of explanation the story's rhetorical density has
suggested yet not wholly endorsed. A thorough presentation of
critical estimations of *Lord of the Flies* in these terms may provide
sufficient background to discussion of the fables in later
chapters. For it is a significant fact that Golding's reputation
has been established on the basis of *Lord of the Flies*; judgments
of the other books—even *The Scorpion God*—always adopt the
first fable as the single prototype for excellence or failure.
Readers uninterested in the relatively arcane matter of the
building of an author's critical reputation may ignore this and
move to Section III of the Chapter.

II

. . . a fable can only be taken as far as the parable, the

2*

*parallel is exact; and these literary parallels between
the fable and the underlying life do not extend to infinity . . . the fable must be under strict control. Yet it
is at this very point, that the imagination can get out
of hand.*

Golding, 'Fable'

Lord of the Flies tells a totally absorbing adventure story but
like another sort of island story, *Robinson Crusoe*, it seems
susceptible of various interpretations. It has been read as a
moral fable examining personal disintegration, a social fable
which explores social regression, and a religious fable which
offers a variant account of the Fall of Man. As a moral fable,
Lord of the Flies seems capable of endorsing a number of
mechanico-psychological theories of behaviour, or at least
commentators have argued so—and in discussion these have
ranged from Aristotle's *Ethics* through Jung's *Psychological Types*.

It is possible to view the boys as representatives of various
instincts or elements of the personality. 'The catastrophe
occurs because the qualities of intelligence, address, bravery,
decency, organization, and insight are divided among Piggy,
Jack, Ralph, and Simon. Each of them lacks some vital gift;
none of them is a complete person.'[4] E. M. Forster declares
that it is just this fragmentation that is responsible for their
regression.[5] One critic argues that the fragmentations correspond to Plato's division of the human soul: 'Golding is careful
to point out that it is Ralph's administrative duties—an image
of the soul's balance and power when governed by reason—
that enable him to keep the anarchy that resides in his heart
under control.'[6] Offering a variant *schema*, E. L. Epstein
believes Freudian psychoanalytical theory is relevant: 'The
Devil is not present in any traditional religious sense; Golding's
Beelzebub is the modern equivalent, the anarchic amoral,
driving force that Freudians call the Id.'[7]

If seen as a moral fable, *Lord of the Flies* appears to emphasize
the inadequacy not the depravity of the solely human. In this

light, the power and potential of individual human responsibility becomes a workable index for moral actions, and a legitimate abstraction from this is that people are governable inasmuch as they can be the responsible authors of their own actions. Simon is a 'saint'—Golding's term for the boy—precisely because he tries to know comprehensively and inclusively; he possesses a quality of imagination which forces an 'ancient, inescapable recognition.'[8] Before the obscene decapitated pig on the spike he comes to acknowledge the existence of his own evil. In contrast, Ralph because of a failure of moral imagination exhibits only a 'fatal unreasoning *knowledge*' (226, italics added) of his approaching death which is directed towards his own survival not that of the community's.

Such a moral account of the fable posits the duality of man: man is, in Swiftian terms, not *animale rationale* but only *rationis capax*. Individual recognition of unreason is symbolic of order; failure is symbolic of decay. A legitimate inference, one that Piggy and Ralph keep voicing, is that society—the *Noumos*—does not confine and deform but is man's only proper habitat: its influences, however faulty, are the bonds that free him from unreason and disorder.

Viewed from another perspective, which concerns itself generally with social correspondences, *Lord of the Flies* might be seen to shift from moral fable to social fable. Here it becomes what some commentators call an anti-Utopian satire. For the island society is microcosmically a human society, related all too ironically to the 'grown-up' society that occasioned the original fall from the skies. Anthropologically the society is a mirror of the first, primitive societies of prehistoric man; its progress illustrates a biological maxim now fairly well discredited: that the development of the individual recapitulates in capsule time the development of the species (ontogony recapitulates phylogeny). It alludes implicitly 'as Golding, I think could never do explicitly,'[9] to Frazer's *Golden Bough*, Freud's *Totem and Taboo* and *Moses and Monotheism*: 'Denied the sustaining and repressing authority of parents, church, and state, they form a new culture the development of which reflects that of the genuine primitive society, evolving its own gods, and demons (its myths), its rituals and taboos (its social norms).'[10]

The critical danger in discussion of this sort is again to start treating the boys as men, since in their terms they appear less as autonomous characters than as images of social ideas. Thus one critic sees the tale in social psychological terms and decides it 'shows how intelligence (Piggy) and common sense (Ralph) will always be overthrown in society by sadism (Roger) and the lure of totalitarianism (Jack).'[11] Seen in political terms it is a dramatization of 'the modern political nightmare' in which responsible democracy is destroyed by charismatic authoritarianism: 'I hope', writes V. S. Pritchett, 'this book is being read in Germany.'[12]

If seen as a social fable, Lord of the Flies appears to stress not the capabilities of the boys but their depravity and man's apparent inability to control aggression within a workable social order. Seen from the perspective of the moral fable, morally speaking Piggy and Ralph do exercise good will and judgment; from the angle of the social fable they are inadequate politically. Much more damaging is their participation in the murder of Simon, a murder effected by the tribal society which Jack leads.

Many of the accounts of Lord of the Flies place the fable in a mythic frame, rather than the social or moral one, for ultimately 'it derives from—displaces—a familiar myth, that of Earthly Paradise which it handles ironically.'[13] Here the Christian tradition has been by far the most popular mythic framework cited by critics, though the fable itself makes no immediate or direct allusion to orthodox Christianity. Many critics write that Lord of the Flies dramatizes the Fall of man. As Adam unparadised, the boys cradle within themselves the beast of evil, 'Beelzebub' (the Hebraic original for its English translation, lord of the flies [II Kings i.2]; 'the chief of the devils' in Luke ii.15). They turn the Edenic island into a fiery hell. When he discussed his notion of the morally diseased creation in 'Fable', Golding himself admitted that in 'theological terms' man is a 'fallen being'. 'He is gripped by original sin. His nature is sinful and his state perilous.' Such a statement merely describes metaphorically a general condition, it does not place it within a constricting metaphysic, a constricting scheme of theology. It is interesting here to note in passing that the epigraph to *The Pyramid*—'If thou be among people make for thyself love, the beginning and end of the heart'—was taken from a deliberately non-Christian context, the *Instructions of Ptah-Hotep*, to show that while the Christian explanation may have diagnosed man's condition correctly, the condition itself obviously predates the Christian apologia. Ultimately the conceptions of innocence and original sin and guilt are great commonplaces, central to man's conception of himself in more than one culture.

Other mythic contexts seem equally relevant to the image of evil in *Lord of the Flies*. One such commentary sees the titular lord of the flies as a primary archetype for the destructive element, a Dionysian irrationalism that Jack celebrates and Piggy ignores. Baker regards Piggy in what he takes as a Promethean aspect and argues Piggy's empirical disavowal of the 'beastie'—'Life . . . is scientific, that's what it is. In a year or two when the war's over they'll be travelling to Mars and back. I know there isn't no beast . . .' (105)—is evidence of intellectual *hubris* which must be punished. Greek myth is invoked: 'The final punishment of those who denied the god of nature is to render them conscious of their awful crimes and to cast them out from their homeland as guilt-stricken exiles and wanderers upon the earth.'[14]

Suggestive analogies have also been seen in variant anthropological myths: thus the dead man is not so much an ironic parody of the Crucifixion as a parody of the fertility god of Frazer, the Hanged or Sacrificial god. As Claire Rosenfield suggests, Simon is the ritual hero who is metaphorically swallowed by a serpent or dragon 'whose belly is the underworld; he undergoes a symbolic death in order to gain the elixir to revitalize his stricken society, and returns with his knowledge to the timid world as a redeemer.'

III

For the poor man [Daniel Defoe] did not know he was a significant bit of Eng. Lit. or that there was, indeed, something called Eng. Lit. in which he would be examined as severely as any pirate. He did not know that he was inventing the English novel and providing plunder for whole shiploads of academics. He was busy trying to catch up with his creditors and turning and twisting through the eighteenth century like a hunted hare.

—Golding, 'The Scum of the Sea'

Conceptual analyses of the sort reconstructed above obscure— even destroy—the primary strength of Golding's fable. For *Lord of the Flies* is first and foremost a gripping adventure story: '. . . it falls well within the main stream of several English literary traditions. It is a 'boy's' book as are *Treasure Island*, *The Wind in the Willows*, *High Wind in Jamaica* and other books primarily about juvenile characters which transcend juvenile appeal; it is in the tradition of the survival narrative, along with *Robinson Crusoe*, *The Swiss Family Robinson*, and even Barrie's *Admirable Crichton*.'[15] It is related ironically to various literary conventions: science fiction, Utopian fantasy, boys' south-sea adventure, survival narrative, and desert island tale. Readers now are familiar with the most important source, R. M. Ballantyne's *Coral Island* (1858), a nineteenth-century Victorian boys' story which Golding has admitted has a 'pretty big connection.'[16] Golding chooses the same situation as Ballantyne's; his main characters are, like Ballantyne's, named Ralph and Jack—though Ballantyne's third character, Peterkin, is recast into two boys: Peter and Simon. Whereas Ballantyne's

boys lead noble, even ennobling lives—for they are 'Britons', a
term with which they compliment one another throughout—
Golding's boys progressively deteriorate. When at the end a
naval officer, surveying the hideous children before him,
remarks: 'I should have thought that a pack of British boys—
you're all British aren't you?—would have been able to put up
a better show than that—I mean. . . . Like the *Coral Island*'
(248), Golding defuses Ballantyne's conception of the
civilized child and by extension civilized man. *Lord of the Flies*
represents in its recasting of the situation not only an inversion
of a popular literary model—a strategy of reversal which
Golding adopts in the three subsequent fables—but a refutation
of *Coral Island* morality which Golding obviously regards as
unrealistic.

Ballantyne's island is a nineteenth-century island inhabited
by English boys in the full flush of Victorian smugness, ignorance, and prosperity. Carl Niemeyer's sketch of the book is
useful here. He writes:

> Ballantyne shipwrecks his three boys—Jack, eighteen;
> Ralph, the narrator, aged fifteen; and Peterkin Gay, a
> comic sort of boy, aged thirteen—somewhere in the
> South Seas on an uninhabited coral island. Jack is a
> natural leader, but both Ralph and Peterkin have abilities
> valuable for survival. Jack has the most common sense
> and foresight, but Peterkin turns out to be a skilful killer
> of pigs and Ralph, when later in the book he is separated
> from his friends and alone on a schooner, coolly navigates
> back to Coral Island by dead reckoning. . . . The boys'
> life on the island is idyllic; and they are themselves with-
> out malice or wickedness, though there are a few curious
> episodes in which Ballantyne seems to hint at something
> he himself understands as little as do his characters. . . .
> Thus Ballantyne's story raises the problem of evil . . .
> which comes to the boys not from within themselves but
> from the outside world.

And Niemeyer continues:

> Tropical nature to be sure, is kind, but the men of this
> non-Christian world are bad. For example, the island is
> visited by savage cannibals, one canoeful pursuing
> another, who fight a cruel and bloody battle, observed by
> the horrified boys and then go away. A little later, the
> island is again visited, this time by pirates (i.e., white men
> who have renounced or scorned their Christian heritage)
> who succeed in capturing Ralph. In due time the pirates
> are deservedly destroyed, and in the final episode of the
> book the natives undergo an unmotivated conversion to
> Christianity, which effects a total change in their nature
> just in time to rescue the boys from their clutches. Thus
> Ballantyne's view of man is seen to be optimistic, like his
> view of English boys' pluck and resourcefulness, which
> subdues tropical islands as triumphantly as England
> imposes empire and religion on lawless breeds of men.[17]

By now the *Lord of the Flies'* story is all too familiar. A group
of schoolboys, stamped through with Britishness like seaside
rock and educated by public schools in a system designed to
overwhelm an empire,[18] are dropped on an Eden-like island
in the Pacific or Indian Ocean. There, they are confronted
with the task of survival. First the boys proceed to set up a
rational society based on a 'grown-up' model. They establish a
government and laws; shelters are constructed, plumbing
facilities and food supplies are arranged. Yet almost immediately the society disintegrates under two pressures—aggression
and superstition. Their signal fire becomes a defensive hearth
stoked by the matronly Piggy's twins, and then a ritualistic
pig's spit fed by Jack's braves; the dark unknown which
descends at night assumes a monstrous identity and is pro-
pitiated by totemic pig heads as a 'beast'. Hunting becomes
killing as Jack's hunters break away from Ralph's fire-keepers
to form a tribal society with gods, rituals, and territory at the

island's end. When two of the boys from the original tribe invade this territory they are killed, one (Simon) ritually as a totemic beast and the other (Piggy) politically as an enemy or what Erik Erikson has called a pseudo-species. Finally, a sacrificial victim (Ralph) is hunted down in order to offer his head to the god ('Pig's head on a stick' [177]) when the adult world intervenes in the person of a British naval officer. The fable concludes with the pathetic image of Ralph crying for 'the end of innocence, the darkness of man's heart, and the fall through the air of the true, wise friend called Piggy' (248).

Now obviously Golding's island is a twentieth-century island, inhabited by English boys just as smug about their decency, just as complacent and ignorant as the boys in Ballantyne's story. Talking about its genesis in *Coral Island*, Golding explained to Kermode: 'What I'm saying to myself is "don't be such a fool, you remember when you were a small boy, how you lived on that island with Ralph and Peterkin", who is Simon by the way, Simon called Peter, . . . I said to myself finally "Now you are grown up, now you are adult . . . you can see that people are not like that, they would not behave like that if they were God-fearing English gentlemen, and they went to an island like that, their savagery would not be found in natives on an island. As like as not they would find savages who were kindly, and uncomplicated, that the devil would rise out of the intellectual complications of the three white men." '

It is Golding's intention in *Lord of the Flies* to tell a true story —to cite the beast within and tell a realistic story—'a book' as he put it, 'about real boys on an island, showing what a mess they'd make.' Ballantyne's children are children free of Original Sin. They epitomize the optimism, the certitude, and perhaps even the pomposity of the Victorian Age; they not only play at being empire-builders: they are. Consider, for example, the following passage from *Coral Island*:

I have made up my mind that it's capital—first rate—the

best thing that ever happened to us, and the most splendid
prospect that ever lay before three jolly young tars.
We've got an island all to ourselves. We'll take possession
in the name of the king; we'll go and enter the service of
its black inhabitants. Of course, we'll rise, naturally, to
the top of affairs. White men always do in savage
countries.[19]

Instead of Ballantyne's unshaken faith in the superiority of
the white race, Golding questions civilization itself; against
man's innate savagery it seems contemptibly weak. While in
Coral Island the natives' faces 'besides being tattooed, were
besmeared with red paint and streaked with white', in *Lord of
the Flies* it is the choir boys, Jack's hunters, who colour their
faces so their primitive selves can be released from shame.
'Jack began to dance and his laughter became a bloodthirsty
snarling . . . the mask was a thing of its own, behind which
Jack hid, liberated from shame and self-consciousness' (80).
To qualify Ballantyne's pastoral evocation of life on a tropical
island where everything is glamorous, Golding stresses such
things as the diarrhoea of the 'littluns', who 'suffer untold
terrors in the dark and huddle together for comfort' (74); the
densely hot and damp scratching heat of a real jungle; the
remote and 'brute obtuseness of the ocean' (137) which
condemns the boys to the island; of the filthy flies which drink
at the pig's head; and the hair grown lank: 'with a convulsion
of the mind, Ralph discovered dirt and decay; understood how
much he disliked perpetually flicking the tangled hair out of
his eyes' (96). Perhaps the most important recasting of *Coral
Island* optimism is Golding's inversion of Ballantyne's cheerful
notion of the psychology of the child. One evening, Ballantyne's
boys hear a distant but horrible cry; at the suggestion that it
might be a ghost, Jack answers:

I neither believe in ghosts nor feel uneasy. I never saw a
ghost myself and I never met anyone who had; and I have

generally found that strange and unaccountable things have always been accounted for, and found to be quite simple, on close examination. I certainly can't imagine what *that* sound is; but I'm quite sure I shall find out before long. . . .

Golding's boys, of course, do grow frightened of the unknown. In fact, it is just the fear of a beast—and its ambiguous existence on the island—which forms the dramatic and symbolic core of *Lord of the Flies*.

IV

Ralph found himself understanding the wearisomeness of this life, where every oath was an improvisation and a considerable part of one's waking life was spent watching one's feet. He stopped . . . and remembering that first enthusiastic exploration as though it were part of a brighter childhood, he smiled jeeringly.

—Golding, *Lord of the Flies* (95)

Had Golding simply recast *Coral Island* morality, *Lord of the Flies* might well be a derivative fable along the lines of Richard Hughes' *High Wind in Jamaica* demonstrating a twentieth-century belief that, without the discipline of adults, children will deteriorate into savages. No such rigorous allegory emerges, it seems to me. To the initial source reversal, Golding has sewn a structural reversal which makes the fable question even its own ground. A superb coda elevates *Lord of the Flies* above diagrammatic prescription to something like 'an allegory which has achieved passion.' There is no essential difference between the island world and the adult one and it is the burden of the fable's structure—what I call its ideographic structure—to make it clear that the children's experiment on the island has its constant counterpart in the world outside. Both the occasion of the boys' landing on the island and the parachutist remind us that 'the majesty of adult life' is another childish delusion. As the narrative progresses the reader is lulled into the unguarded belief that adults may save the situation; yet, one detects certain ironic clues which the coda will confirm. Take the reiteration of motifs—for example the phrase 'Let's have fun' that Ralph as liberal leader introduces and which later the Head obscenely throws back at Simon— these force one to reconsider what earlier seems innocuous. The heaving of logs by Sam'eric, the rolling of larger and larger stones, the several gifts to the sea, the several pig hunts, the two desperate races by Ralph—these sequences of repeated actions, placed at intervals during the story, intensify the ambiguous threat and give the illusion of a vastly speeded-up dénouement. The cumulative effect on the reader is to create a vague yet familiar threat, a sense of doom which cannot be adequately located in the narrative's thrust until its confirmation in the coda.

In *Lord of the Flies* the ideographic structure consists in two movements; in the first, the story is seen from the point of view of the childish protagonist, Ralph, as he gradually grows more and more aware of the island's disintegration. In the second movement, the coda which concludes the fable, we see events from a new point of view, that of the adult naval officer, who is completely unaware and largely indifferent to the suffering. The coda, in conjunction with such symbols as the parachutist, indicates that adulthood is also inadequate to prevent destruction. The dead parachutist shows man's inhumanity to man; he is a legacy of barbarism in both ancient and contemporary civilization who, Golding says, represents history;[20] thus he haunts the boys, a haunting appropriately represented by his uncanny position and motion: 'the figure sat on the mountain-top and bowed and sank and bowed again' (119).

The children reveal the same nature as the grown-ups whom some invoke and try to emulate. In fact the child's world on the island is a painful microcosm of the adult world, for the ruin they bring upon themselves is universal—recall that it is atomic warfare in the air that brings about their initial descent to the island. The cruel irony of the matter is made all the stronger by the sudden switch in perspective. Here the officer's dismal failure to comprehend the 'semi circle of little boys, their bodies streaked with coloured clay, sharp sticks in their hands' (246) is itself testimony to 'the infinite cynicism of adult life' (170) and silent witness to the Lord of the Dung's general sway. It is as though he has sailed straight from the pages of *Coral Island*, moments after we have witnessed the consequences of that novel's banal optimism.

In fact, the story is more striking precisely because Golding chooses wonderfully real children as protagonists, children who yank up socks, stamp feet, and quarrel over sand castles. The arrival of the officer at the end with its sudden shift from Ralph's agonized eyes to the benign view of the adult throws the story back into grotesque miniature. The children are dwarfed to children again. The officer sees Jack this way:

> A little boy who wore the remains of an extraordinary black cap on his red hair and who carried the remains of a pair of spectacles at his waist, started forward at the question, 'Who's boss,' then changed his mind and stood still. (247–8)

Throughout the narrative's first movement—and with appalling momentum—the children appear to have been adults dealing with adult problems. Now they are whining little boys held in control by the presence of an adult. Yet the reader cannot forget the cruelty of what has gone before. For the conch of order has been smashed; the spectacles of reason and rescue have been used to destroy the island. A tribal society has hunted down and killed two individuals. Nor can we forget that Ralph's piteous weeping at the end transcends the smug cynicism of the rescuer, for Ralph knows the real nature of the 'pack of British boys' (248).

Ralph is saved only because the adult world intervenes; yet his rescuer is on the point of returning to 'adult' war, a nuclear war which is in numerical terms infinitely more extravagant in its potential disaster. Given the barbaric chaos the boys have been reduced to, the officer appears to them (to us) as order. It is only on reflection that the reader remembers that the officer is involved in a nuclear war and yet is still 'order'. This brings up Golding's own explication of the thematic content of his fable:

> The whole book is symbolic in nature except the rescue in the end where adult life appears, dignified and capable, but in reality enmeshed in the same evil as the symbolic life of the children on the island. The officer, having interrupted a man-hunt, prepares to take the children off the island in a cruiser which will presently be hunting its enemy in the same implacable way. And who will rescue the adult and his cruiser?[21]

The meaning of *Lord of the Flies* is not, then, allegorically simple but instead ideographically suggestive. The moral operation on the reader of the fable's ideographic structure—when the two patterns clash—makes such a symbolic density possible. For *Lord of the Flies* suggests a large scale of human values, social, political, moral and mythic which are relevant in both universal and contemporary terms, but it isolates and roots these concerns in a boy's world, a world where real boys make a mess of things. Finally, that child's educated view of things is crossed by an adult's uneducated view and the reader must join the two perspectives and probe the question Golding poses above: 'who will rescue the adult and the cruiser?'

Perhaps a useful elaboration on the contrast between what I am implying about an ideographic response and an allegorical one would be to examine here one allegorical feature of the fable upon which no doubt is cast. In Golding's view, the innocence of the child is a crude fallacy, for *homo sapiens* has by nature a terrible potentiality for evil. This potentiality cannot be eradicated or controlled by a humane political system no matter how respectable. Thus, in 'Beast from the Water', one of the fable's most allegorical chapters, the fundamental inadequacy of parliamentary systems to deal with atavistic superstition is portrayed. In this episode, the scene's physical and psychological atmospheres are as schematically constructed as the major characters' different pronouncements on the 'Beast'.

A parliamentary assembly begins at eventide; consequently the chief, Ralph, is merely 'a darkish figure' (96) to his tribe. Light is, at first, level and only Ralph stares into the island's darkness; his assembly before him faces the lagoon's bright promise. But light gradually vanishes, accompanied by increasing spiritual blindness and fear. The place of assembly on the beach is described as 'roughly a triangle; but irregular and sketchy, like everything they made'(96). Obviously it is like a receding boat, a kind of mirror image of the island-boat itself; Ralph remarked at the outset the island was 'roughly boat-shaped' (38); because of the tide's configuration he felt 'the boat was moving steadily astern' (38).

Since Ralph sits on 'a dead tree' (96) that forms the base, no captain occupies the boat's rightful apex: where 'the grass was thick again because no one sat there' (97). Like the island that appears to move backward, the assembly-boat is pointed to the darkness of the jungles not the brightness of the navigable lagoon behind. Hunters sit like hawks on the right of Ralph; to the left Golding places the liberals, mostly children who giggle whenever their assembly seat, 'an ill-balanced twister' (97), capsizes. And Piggy stands outside the triangle, ironically showing the moralizing ineffectuality of the liberal: 'This indicated that he wished to listen but would not speak; and Piggy intended it as a gesture of disapproval' (98). Darkness descends on the shattered assembly, and for the first of many times the 'beastie' is ritually appeased. Island boat, assembly boat, and the ship of civilization itself, rational government, all drift bleakly into blackness. The wail of Percival Wemys Madison of the Vicarage, Harcourt St. Anthony, turns into an inarticulate gibber, the 'dense black mass' (115) of mock hunters swirls and the 'three blind mice' (116), Piggy, Ralph, and Simon sit 'in the darkness, striving unsuccessfully to convey the majesty of adult life' (117).

V

> What was that enemy? I cannot tell. He came with the darkness and he reduced me to a shuddering terror that was incurable because it was indescribable. In daylight I thought of the Roman remains that had been dug up under the church as the oldest things near, sane things from sane people like myself. But at night, the Norman door and pillar, even the flint wall of our cellar, were older, far older, were rooted in the darkness under the earth.
>
> —Golding, 'The Ladder and the Tree'

In the passage above, drawn from an autobiographical essay, Golding dramatizes an atavastic quest through darkness which is central to all his fiction. Pondering over the church graveyard at the foot of his garden, the child, Billy, grows terrified of some enemy he imagines is lurking there to harm him. A similar mythopœia of a beast is central to Lord of the Flies though its implications are by no means fully worked out in this fable. They are dramatized in the crucial confrontation scene where two apparently irreconcilable views of one situation are brought slap up against each other.

Ultimately, the meaning of the fable depends on the meaning of the beast—the creature which haunts the children's imagination and which Jack hunts and tries to propitiate with a totemic beast. Simon's quest, then, is the fable's major pursuit, for he is used as a mouthpiece for what Golding, in conversation, has called 'one of the conditions of existence, this awful thing.' Simon, the strange visionary child, encounters and recognizes the beast. In this confrontation scene he recognizes his own capacity for evil as well as his ability to act without evil. He is thus able to release the parachutist and try to tell the boys below about 'mankind's essential illness' (111): 'Whenever Simon thought of the beast, there arose before his inward sight the pictures of a human at once heroic and sick' (128). The confrontation scene brings about a single crystallization of the fable's total structure since it brings together the concepts of evil-and-innocence as does the ideographic structure.

At the heart of the fable's mythopœia is the visual hieroglyphic[22] or symbol of the severed Head of the pig, to which Simon turns in distaste and awe, and from which he first tries to escape. Grinning cynically, its mouth gaping and its eyes half-closed, the Head is placed on a rock in a sea-like clearing, before Simon's cabin-island.[23] The Head here is like an island surrounded by sea. It is, of course, a symbol[24] which operates macrocosmically as well as microcosmically. A larger macrocosm, the Castle Rock, at the island's end is like a severed head too—it mirrors the pig's head. Described as a 'rock, almost detached' (38), this smaller landmass is separated—a point, it should be noted, which Golding makes repeatedly—from the island's main body, by a 'narrow neck' (130). 'Soon, in a matter of centuries' (130), this Head will be severed too. At the story's conclusion giggling black and green savages swarm around and over it as the black and green flies swarm around the Lord's head.

Piggy's death occurs at this Head; it is the slaughter of a pig for he is decapitated by 'a glancing blow from *chin* to knee' (222, italics added). Travelling through the air, with a grunt he lands on the square red rock in the sea, a sacrificial table. And the monster-sea sucks his body, which 'like a pig's after it has been killed, twitched' (223). Presumably the emblematic name of the character is now pretty obvious. His head is smashed and Ralph, running along the rocky neck, jumps just in time to avoid 'the headless body of the [sacrificial] sow' (223). The preparation is clear; a Head is needed.

From a traditional point of view, this symbolism suggests that the Head—the centre of reason—is destroyed with the death of Piggy and, as the island society regresses, the 'bridge' (134) between rationality and irrationality is cut. But rationality is, for Golding, a suspicious concept. The severed Head of the sow is not the Lord of the Dung either; it does not symbolize an evil external to the individual. Rather, it is a symbol of corrupt and corrupting consciousness. It is a symbol for the malaise of the human consciousness which objectifies evil rather than recognizes its subjectivity: the kind of moral distancing the officer commits. This intellectual complication is 'mankind's essential illness' which Simon discovers in the severed Head; it prospers on the island's Head, Castle Rock.

Three ambiguous confrontation scenes formulate the mythopœia: Simon before the Head; Ralph before the skull of the pig; Ralph before a savage. However, the scenes function by symbolic cluster on a symbolic level and they have little dramatic necessity. Golding himself, in 'Fable', suggests a reason for this fragmentation: 'I don't think the fable ever got right out of hand; but there are many places I am sure where the fable splits at the seams and I would like to think . . . they rise from a plentitude of imagination'. Clearly he cherishes these 'splits' for he adds warmly: 'May it not be that at the very moments when I felt the fable to come to its own life before me it may in fact have become something more valuable so that where I thought it was failing, it was really succeeding?' And significantly he quotes the passage of Simon before the Head to illustrate these comments.

Simon alone recognizes the real Beast and like Moses with the tablets of the law brings the truth down from the mountain. What is the truth? Simon broods before the totemic sow's Head, having witnessed the anal rape and decapitation. Suddenly the pig's head speaks in 'the voice of a schoolmaster' (178) and delivers 'something very much like a sermon to the

boy.' It insists that the island is corrupt and all is lost: ' "This
is ridiculous. You know perfectly well you'll only meet me
down there—so don't try to escape!" ' (178). Shifting by the
ironic motif of 'fun' into schoolboy language, the Head assures
him: ' "*We* are going to have fun on this island" '(178),
(italics added) even though 'everything' is 'a bad business'
(170). Such counselling of acceptance of evil is 'the infinite
cynicism of adult life' (170), the cynicism of the conscious
mind, the cynicism that can ignore even 'the indignity of
being spiked on a stick' (170), the cynicism that 'grins' at the
obscenities that even the butterflies must desert; recall that the
butterflies 'danced preoccupied in the centre of the clearing'
(178) during the sow's mistreatment—the Head then represents something a great deal more obscene than simple blood-
lust. It is the cynicism and easy optimism of the naval officer at
the end who '*grinned* cheerfully at the obscene savages while
muttering "fun and games" ' (247, italics added).[25]

But this Lord of the Dung *is* Simon: the Head that counsels
acceptance is his own strategic consciousness. Evil exists but
not as a Beast. To interpret incorrectly the Head as an
objective symbol for evil, independent of consciousness,
would be to make the same mistake as Jack of externalizing
and objectifying one's own evil. The identity of the two is
worked out very carefully indeed. Speaking in schoolboy
language, the Lord's head has 'half-shut eyes' (170) and Simon
keeps 'his eyes shut, then sheltered them with his hand' (171)
so that his vision is partial. He sees things 'without definition
and illusively' (171) behind a 'luminous veil.' Simon feels his
own savagery: he 'licks his dry lips' and feels the weight of his
hair. Later, after his epileptic fit, the blood 'dries around his
mouth and chin' (180) in the manner of the 'blood-blackened'
(170) grinning mouth of the Head. The flies, now that the
butterflies have dismissed them, detect the identity and—
though they are sated—leave the guts and 'alight by Simon's
runnels of sweat' (171) and drink at his head. The Head grins
at this indignity. By a profound effort of will, Simon forces

himself to penetrate his own loathing and break through his own consciousness: 'At last Simon gave up and looked back; saw the white teeth and dim eyes, the blood—and his gaze was held by that ancient, inescapable recognition' (171).

It is himself he is looking at. His face (i.e., the Head) grins at the flies of corruption and he acknowledges it as himself. Rather like Golding's Egyptian mummy, he prepares 'to penetrate mysteries' and 'go down and through in darkness'. He looks into the vast mouth of hell, and thereby submits to the terror of his own evil.

> Simon found he was looking into a vast mouth. There was blackness within, a blackness that spread. . . . He fell down and lost consciousness (178).

He penetrates here his own evil. Returning from non-being, he awakens next to 'the dark earth close by his cheek' (179) and knows that he must 'do something'. He approaches the beast on the hill to discover that 'this parody', ringed as well by green flies, is nothing more 'harmless and horrible' (181) than the Head. Both are man as he is. In releasing the figure 'from the rocks and . . . the wind's indignity' (181) he frees himself.

Twice Ralph is confronted with just such a primal confrontation, face to face, eye to eye. We earlier see that he cannot connect with primal nature. For example, standing at the island's rocky shore 'on a level with the sea' (136), he follows 'the ceaseless, bulging passage' (136) of the waves and feels 'clamped down', 'helpless,' and 'condemned' (137) by a 'leviathan' (131) monster with 'arms of surf' and 'fingers of spray' (137). Nor can he accept Simon's intuitive and correct faith, when the latter whispers 'you'll get back all right' (137), that man can escape the 'brute obtuseness' (137) of nature. Much later, after the deaths of Simon and Piggy, Ralph stands in the clearing confronted by the same offensive Head. He looks steadily at the skull that 'seemed to jeer at him cynically' (227). Once again the darkness is depicted as resting 'about on a level with his face' (228) and the skull's 'empty sockets seemed to hold his gaze masterfully and without effort' (228). But unlike Simon, he turns away from acknowledging his own nature and makes a monster there:

> A sick *fear* and *rage* swept him. Fiercely he hit out at the filthy thing in front of him that bobbed like a toy and came back, still grinning also into his face, so that he lashed and cried out in loathing. (228, italics added)

And no more than Jack can recognize his own image behind the 'awesome stranger's' (80) mask of warpaint when he looks into the water-filled coconut, can Ralph recognize his own face, though he keeps 'his face to the skull that lay grinning at the sky' (228).

For Ralph cannot penetrate this 'parody thing' which in its motion amalgamates the parachutist's bowing, the 'black ball['s]' (180) bobbing, and the sea's 'breathing' (131). All three motions are those of an ancient primal rhythm that does not so much 'progress' as endure 'a momentous rise and fall' (137). It is the rhythm of man's darkness, 'this minute-long fall and rise and fall' (131), and man's history. It is the rhythm that transfigures Simon in death, that engulfs the parachutist on its way to sea: 'on the mountain-top the parachute filled and moved; the figure slid, rose to its feet, falling, still falling, it sank towards the beach . . .' (189) and the rhythm that imparts to Piggy some beauty: the water becomes 'luminous round the rock forty feet below, where Piggy had fallen' (234). Yet for Ralph, the ordinary man, it is a terrifying rhythm, 'the age-long nightmares of falling and death' (235) that occur in darkness, intimating the 'horrors of death' (228).

Golding seems to be indicating that once atavistically in contact with this dark rhythm, at the centre of the self, man will no longer be, in Ralph's words, 'cramped into this bit of island, always on the lookout' (125). If man is prepared to face his face, he may escape (in symbolic terms) the Island.

Ralph, in fact, is given just such an opportunity. In his last desperate race (depicted in the penultimate scene where many of the earlier symbols are recapitulated) Ralph hides himself in Simon's cell, 'the darkest hole' (242) of the island. Like Simon he connects in terror with primal nature: 'He laid his cheek against the chocolate-coloured earth, licked his dry lips and closed his eyes' and feels the ancient rhythm: 'Under the thicket, the earth was vibrating very slightly' (243). Jerking his head from the earth, he peers into the 'dulled light' and sees a body slowly approaching: waist, knee, two knees, two hands, a spear sharpened at both ends.

A head. Ralph and someone called a 'savage' (244) peer through the obscurity at each other repeating in their action Simon's scrutiny before the Head:

> You could tell that he saw light on this side and on that, but not in the middle—there. *In the middle was a blob of dark* and the savage wrinkled up his face, *trying to decipher the darkness.* (245, italics added)

Just at the moment his eyes connect with those of the savage, Ralph repeats Simon's early important admonition 'you'll get back' (245) and with this partial acknowledgment of his own savagery he breaks through the cell. Expecting nothing he strikes out, screaming:

> He forgot his wounds, his hunger and thirst, and became fear; hopeless fear on flying feet, rushing through the forest towards the open beach. (245)

Rushing, screaming through the fire that undulates 'forward like a tide' (245), screaming and rushing and '*trying to cry for mercy*' (246, italics added), he trips, and fallen on the ground, sees, before him, the officer. In a manner of speaking he is saved; in a manner of speaking he is given mercy.

VI

For I have shifted somewhat from the position I held when I wrote the book. I no longer believe that the author has a sort of patria potestas over his brain-children. . . . Once they are printed . . . the author has no more authority over them . . . perhaps knows less about them than the critic who . . . sees them not as the author hoped they would be, but as what they are.

—Golding, 'Fable'

A germinal eschatology of the scapegoat/sacrificial victim seems to be emerging here. Simon's recognition of evil—and all mankind's complicity—occasions his ritual death. He meets the fate of those who remind society of its guilt; man prefers to destroy the objectification of his fears than recognize the dark terrors and evil of himself. In 'Fable' Golding declares this a 'failure of human sympathy' which amounts to 'the object-ivizing of our own inadequacies so as to make a *scapegoat*' (94, italics added). It is, by the way, the only time he has mentioned the term. Thus the ritual enacts the confinement and destruction of the boys' own terrors. They kill Simon as a beast, yet paradoxically his death exorcizes (for a short while at least) their fears. Piggy is killed on the other hand because he is an alien, a pseudo-species. And his death marks the essential inadequacy of the rational, logical world; the conch is smashed as the blind Piggy falls into the sea. But Ralph, the ordinary man, can only operate within the community's pattern; he cannot exorcize it. There is no way for him to release fully the fear even in himself. He can weep 'for the end of innocence, the darkness of man's heart' (248).

Now while this eschatology is implicit in the narrative texture, little of it is explicit in the narrative plot. True, Simon's encounter with the airman brings about his death, while unravelling the mystery of the bobbing figure. Ralph's foray with the savage does release the dénouement; the fire sweeps through the island thus signalling the naval ship—a not implausible arrival given the earlier ship—and the ultimate ironic rescue. Nevertheless, charges of 'gimmickry', some technical manipulation, obscurity, and inconsistency seem not ill-considered. Such lengthy and tonally weighted episodes as those before the Head do not contribute directly to the drama nor do they adequately suggest the rather simple dictum that mankind is evil.

Experienced at the level of sensation, however, these episodes seem to me to be extremely significant. By their density and ambiguity, and yet familiarity, these confrontation scenes all draw the reader into the imaginative act the characters themselves make. For the confrontation scenes here construct a parallel between the focusing of the individual character's vision and the focusing of the reader's vision. Point of view is so skilfully handled that what Simon recognizes, when he affirms his face, the reader is forced to recognize. The fable's total structure brings about a similar fusion in the readers' focusing of events. By means of its ideographic structure, Lord of the Flies portrays its thematic meaning.

LORD OF THE FLIES—NOTES

1 An extensive survey of critical pronouncements on this matter can be found in Virginia Tiger's 'An Analysis of William Golding's Fiction,' (unpublished Ph.D dissertation, University of British Columbia, 1971).

2 Frederick Karl, 'The Novel as Moral Allegory, The Fiction of William Golding', A Reader's Guide to the Contemporary English Novel (New York, 1962), pp. 244–261.

3 George C. Herndl, 'Golding and Salinger, A Clear Choice', Wiseman Review (Winter 1964–1965), p. 310.

4 Philip Drew, 'Second Reading', The Cambridge Review (October 27, 1956), p. 78.

5 E. M. Forster, 'Introduction', Lord of the Flies (New York: Coward McCann, 1962), pp. ix–xii. In his essentially sympathetic account, it is interesting that Forster prefers Piggy to the others, seeing him as

symbolic of 'the human spirit, aware that the universe has not been created for his convenience.'

6 Robert J. White, 'Butterfly and Beast in *Lord of the Flies*', MFS (Summer 1964), p. 165. This article was the first to suggest that *Lord of the Flies* is built on Greek sources, in particular *The Republic*, and Euripides' *Bacchae* where Simon like Pentheus is a scapegoat. Baker's article, 'Why It's No Go: A Study of William Golding's *Lord of the Flies*', *Arizona Quarterly*, XIX (Winter 1963), pp. 293–305, is a fuller account of the *Bacchae* source and its relation, in particular, to Simon's death. In fact, the argument of Baker's *Study* is that Golding is more influenced by Greek literature than Christian; 'taken collectively', the Greeks 'represent the most potent force in shaping . . . Golding's conception of human psychology and human fate'. p. xvii. Robert C. Gordon's discussion of Homeric and Euripidean elements is very suggestive: '. . . the ending of *Orestes* throws light on one of Golding's characteristic and most controversial devices—the gimmick ending'. *Orestes* provides the prototype for the naval officer; Apollo's entry is 'one of the most flatly unprepared for uses of the *deus ex machina* in the history of drama'. 'Classical Themes in *Lord of the Flies*', MFS (Winter 1965–1966), pp. 424–427. See finally Bernard F. Dick's chapter in the Twayne English Author Series, 1967.

7 E. L. Epstein, 'Notes on *Lord of the Flies*', *Lord of the Flies* (New York: Capricorn Books, 1959), p. 190.

8 William Golding, *Lord of the Flies* (London: Faber and Faber, 1958), p. 171. All subsequent quotations will be taken from this edition and be indicated by textual parentheses.

9 Kermode, 'The Case for William Golding', *The New York Review of Books* (April 30, 1964), p. 3.

10 Claire Rosenfield, 'Men of Smaller Growth, A Psychological Analysis of William Golding's *Lord of the Flies*', *Literature and Psychology*, XI (Autumn 1961), p. 93.

11 C. B. Cox, '*Lord of the Flies*', *Critical Quarterly* (Summer 1960), p. 112.

12 V. S. Pritchett, 'Secret Parables', *New Statesman* (August 2, 1958), p. 146.

13 Kermode, p. 3.

14 Baker, p. 8.

15 Oldsey and Weintraub, *The Art of William Golding* (New York: Harcourt Brace & World, 1965), p. 16.

16 Carl Niemeyer, in 'The Coral Island Revisited', *College English* (January 1961), pp. 241–245, makes full use of this hint and an earlier discussion of the parody features of the two books by Frank Kermode: 'Coral Islands', *The Spectator* (August 22, 1958), p. 257. These two essays and Golding's comment on the genesis of *The Inheritors* have given rise to a plethora of source articles, among which appears the suggestion by S. Sternlicht, 'A Source of Golding's *Lord of the Flies, Peter Pan?*' *English Record* (December 1963), pp. 41–43. The possible parallel is based on the similarity between the rape of the sow and that of Wendy [sic].

17 Niemeyer, p. 242.

18 No one has drawn the rather obvious allegorical correspondence between the island-ship with the island England and her traditional associations with sea-faring. The island-ship is gliding backwards just as post-Imperialist England is reverting to its nineteenth-century character under the guidance of Jack. The most contemporary character is Piggy, the fat boy with the short-sightedness of the caricature-scientist, and he is more classless than the others. But his wounds, his asthma, his matronly body, and his balding head disqualify him from captainship, just as the pre-World War I tolerant rationalism disqualify Ralph from taking the seat of power.

19 R. M. Ballantyne, *Coral Island* (London and Glasgow), p. 23.

20 Golding writes in 'Fable': 'What the grown-ups send them is a sign . . . that arbitrary sign stands for off-campus history, the thing which threatens every child everywhere, the history of blood and intolerance, of ignorance and prejudice, the thing which is dead and won't lie down . . . it falls on the very place where the children are making their one constructive attempt to get themselves helped. 'It dominates the mountaintop and so prevents them keeping a fire alight there as a signal'. pp. 95–96.

21 Golding, 'Biographical and Critical Notes,' *Lord of the Flies*, ed. E. L. Epstein, p. 189.

22 Golding's term in 'Egypt from My Inside', p. 71. His imagination is engaged by 'pictures', which by their physical suggestiveness evoke certain relevances. He tells us: 'I . . . started to learn hieroglyphics; so that I cannot now remember when those sideways standing figures, those neat and pregnant symbols, were not obscurely familiar to me. My inward connection with Egypt has been deep for more than a generation.'

23 Simon's canopied bower is described in terms of the ship/island symbol. On the island/boat this bower is, ironically, the captain's 'little cabin' (72), its 'creepers dropped their ropes like the rigging of floundered ships' (71) with its centre occupied by a 'patch of rock' (71) on which the foundered ship will strike. (Recall that on this rock a demonology not a church is built: Jack instructs his braves to 'ram one end of the stick in the earth. Oh—it's rock. Jam it in the crack' [169].) With the advance of evening, Simon's cabin/island/ship is submerged by the sea: 'Darkness poured out, submerging the ways between the trees till they were dim and strange as the bottom of the *sea*' (72, italics added).

24 'Golding's symbols are not in fact clear, or wholly articulate, they are always the incarnation of more than can be extracted or translated from them'. Gregor and Kinkead-Weekes, *William Golding* (London: Faber & Faber, 1967), p. 19. Consider, for example, the initial symbol of the Island. It is a ship at sea, a civilization threatened with submergence, a tooth in a sucking mouth, a body dissociated from primal nature, consciousness divorced from the brute passivity of the subconscious. On it the boys are islanded by an ineluctable sea to which they turn in awe and distaste. The dominant symbol is woven into the narrative texture at various places, and by a technique of clustering suggestion engenders

suggestion. By gathering to itself other images it evolves a logic of association, the organizing principle being recurrence with variation. Thus, Ralph's isolation at the tail-end of the Island—'He was surrounded on all sides by chasms of empty air. There was nowhere to hide, even if one did not have to go on' (130)—is the isolation of the despairing hero as well as the rupture of the self-conscious mind. And when Piggy is described as 'islanded in a sea of meaningless colour' (91) while he embraces the rock with 'ludicrous care above the sucking sea' (217), the microcosmic/macrocosmic resonances are extremely rich. Since individual symbolic clusters are associative rather than syntactical or logical, at its best, meaning often hovers over several referrents, thought is in continuous dynamism. The whole book seems built on shapes that shift and resettle, like cells under a microscope, stars at the end of a telescope.

25 Fragments of the confrontation scene between Simon and the Head inform 'Egypt from My Inside', where a small boy broods on the face of an Egyptian mummy and a red-faced, smug scientist looks on with 'an eternally uncheerful grin'. 'Egypt from My Inside', p. 76. Another such primal encounter is dramatized in 'Digging for Pictures'. Excavating for ruins in the chalk hills of Wiltshire, the Golding-persona discovers a victim of prehistoric murder, in a 'dark and quiet pit': its 'jaws were wide open, *grinning* perhaps with *cynicism*'. 'Digging for Pictures', p. 60, italics added.

THE INHERITORS

I

*We stand, then, on the shore, not as our Victorian
fathers stood, lassoing phenomena with Latin names,
listing, docketing and systematizing. Belsen and
Hiroshima have gone some way towards teaching us
humility. . . . It is not the complete specimen for the
collector's cabinet that excites us. It is the fragment,
the hint. . . . We pore, therefore, over the natural
language of nature. . . . We look daily at the appalling mystery of plain stuff. We stand where any
upright food-gatherer has stood, on the edge of our
own unconscious, and hope, perhaps, for the terror
and excitement of the print of a single foot.*

—Golding, 'In My Ark'

Much more explicitly than *Lord of the Flies*, *The Inheritors*
endorses Golding's view that the proper end of literature is
imaginative discovery; it is not the level of knowledge that
literature can raise, but the level of knowing. Here, Golding
explores the possible origins of man's guilt and violence in the
evolutionary appearance of *homo sapiens* but the fable, mythic
in impulse, consciously tries to construct a mythopœia relevant
to contemporary man by using anthropological conventions in
the same way as *Lord of the Flies* used the literary convention of
the desert island narrative. This fable presents its version of
the loss of Eden not by a full and rich creation of life but by
exactly the opposite technique: there is a tight funnelling of
character, episode, image, and motif. Furthermore the
rigorous ideographic structure, by its contradictory perspectives, illustrates imaginative truths which are themselves
complex, mysterious, even incomplete.

As is the case with *Pincher Martin*, what we initially experience in reading *The Inheritors* is a severe formalism of structure,
where every superfluous gesture has been removed. Both fables
are rigorously restrictive in mood, tone, and setting, for
Golding's imagination works away at a single focus—an island,
a droning fall—yet it discovers, as its spirit shapes, and
scrapes, and polishes the mystery of that single focus how that
focus must be translated from coherence into incoherence.
Both fables construct 'an uncountry', a landscape only
archetypally connected to the overt world; each seems to be a
discrete independent universe with laws provided by the
author—and perhaps most significantly—by the verbal
resonances of language itself. Looking in *The Inheritors* at the
origins of man and in *Pincher Martin* at his end, the two fables
reveal important fragments of Golding's personal mythopœia,
a mythopœia he intends to be relevant to contemporary man.

In *The Inheritors* as well as in *Pincher Martin* an initial narrative
pattern is imposed and, by the abrupt conjunction with the
coda's other pattern it is released, reformulated and in its re-
interpretation transcended. We, the readers, build the bridge
between the two views, and thus we are the inheritors of the
new conjunction. It is the reader, not either of the characters
Tuami or Lok, who sees in the confrontation of the 'pre-
lapsarian' People and the 'post adamite' (Golding's phrase)
New People the inadequacies of both species of consciousness.
Point of view is handled throughout in such a way that we
construct the wider view. We know both people; within the
protagonist, Lok's mind and limited point of view, we gradually
lose our innocence, but throughout the loss we experience,
almost as an after-image, the abstractions of guilt of the
antagonist, Tuami. We knit up the two perspectives, seeing
from the inside and the outside simultaneously, until the two
fragmentations merge in the wider perspective of what
Golding would call myth. Here in *The Inheritors* mythic
reconciliation involves the integration of such opposites as
fire and water, light and dark, forest and plain. The bridge

which the ideographic structure directs us to build is between innocence and guilt, just as in *Pincher Martin* the fable's ideographic structure bridges the spiritual and physical worlds.

What is genuinely new about the fable, *The Inheritors*, is that the ability to focus opposites in this way is the vision not of Lok, though he longs towards it in bafflement and love, nor that of Tuami, though he as artist does capture intimations of it as he starts to sculpt the death-weapon into a new shape at the story's close. It is discovered by the reader as we take hold of the complexity of the total experience and understand that the downward path of the innocent and the upward path of the guilty are essentially related.

II

> . . . *We know very little of the appearance of the Neanderthal man, but this* . . . *seems to suggest an extreme hairiness, an ugliness, or a repulsive strangeness in his appearance over and above his low forehead, his beetle brows, his ape neck, and his inferior stature.* . . . *Says Sir Harry Johnston, in a survey of the rise of modern man in his* Views and Reviews: '*The dim racial remembrance of such gorilla-like monsters, with cunning brains, shambling gait, hairy bodies, strong teeth, and possibly cannibalistic tendencies, may be the germ of the ogre in folklore.* . . .'
>
> —Wells, *The Outline of History*

Prefixed to *The Inheritors* is the passage above from *The Outline of History*; as Golding himself remarked to a BBC commentator, the epigraph was the initial springboard for his own fable about the encounter between Neanderthalis and his immediate descendant Cro-Magnon man. *The Outline* seems first to have been a source of information and narrative detail. The geographical setting of *The Inheritors* as well as the physical characteristics of the two species—with some modifications—

derive from Wells's account.[1] However, as earlier in *Lord of the Flies*, Golding intended another ironic rebuff to nineteenth-century smugness and explicated to Kermode the ironic inversion at length:

> Wells's *The Outline of History* is the rationalist gospel *in excelsis*. . . . It seemed to me to be too neat and too slick. And when I re-read it as an adult I came across his picture of Neanderthal man, our immediate predecessors, as being these gross brutal creatures who were possibly the basis of the mythological bad man . . . the ogre. I thought to myself that this is just absurd. What we're doing is externalizing our own inside.

Obviously, Golding rejects Wells's 'furtive optimism'[2] that the 'fact' of evolution presumed a similar ethical evolution in man; he suggests instead that the coming of *homo sapiens* represented a falling away from a state of comparative innocence. Recent evidence indicates that contrary to Wells's hypothesis, Neanderthal man might well have been a gentle creature. Petrified flowers, for example, were discovered in Iraq beside skeletal fragments in a newly excavated Neanderthal grave. Skulls placed in a cuplike position seemed to indicate a libation ritual and a concern for the individual and his life after death. In Golding's view, man's biological and evolutionary superiority in consciousness is an incalculable asset gained at an enormous price. Guilt and human consciousness—as both Kermode and Josipovici comment—are true handmaidens. (Ethologists have recently proposed, in fact, that a critical factor in the enlargement of man's brain was a development of higher-brain inhibitions of lower-brain patterns. This 'development of tameness is the suggested basis upon which co-operative social life can emerge in hunting communities', M. R. A. Chance argues, and such an inhibiting pattern has been termed guilt.[3]) Like others, then, Golding sees that guilt is the result of technological and linguistic power.

Taking its plot in large measure from Wells's semi-documentary adventure story, 'The Grisly Folk', *The Inheritors* re-explores the encounter between two species. And in so doing it reverses the moral values of *The Outline* as in *The Aeneid*, for example, when Virgil similarly recasts the Homeric adventure with the Cyclops by deepening the pathos of the one-eyed giant and coarsening Odysseus' craftiness. First, the moral natures of the two species are exchanged; Wells portrays the Neanderthals as monsters easily conquered by a clever species. Golding's People are a gentle and harmonious tribe, unable to conceive of the New People's violence, rapaciousness, and corruption.

Early criticism tended to see the novel as fairly exciting pre-history—see, for example, Avrom Fleishman, *The English Historical Novel* (1971)—as pseudo science fiction, or as bad anthropology. I have had conversations with several anthropologists who reluctantly dismiss the book because modern palaeontology does not support Golding's picture of Neanderthal man's relation to Cro-Magnon man. Apparently, there is no evidence that the second race exterminated the first and it is more likely that Neanderthalis was overevolved and over-specialized for the peculiar conditions of the late Pleistocene. Against this criticism one must put Golding's 1970 comment in *Talk* that he had read everything there was to read on Neanderthal man and contradictions which have now emerged may be the result of new evidence.[4]

The first and final preoccupation of *The Inheritors*, certainly, is with the nature of evolution. In this sense, *The Inheritors* shares the wide mythic sweep of *The Spire*, for both fables explore not simply the loss of one way of life, the fall of one kind of perception, but the loss-and-gain, the fall-and-rise as one form of life takes over from another, willy nilly, despite itself and just because that is the nature of the cosmos: to change. This is not to say that Golding is restating the smug

Myth of Progress; neither is he endorsing the rival myth of unregenerate evil. Somewhere, in the ideal world of the imagination—the golden land Golding calls myth—the whole truth of the two partial views is accessible and discoverable. What resides here is not in competition with historical or scientific truth; it derives from them and is supplementary to them. To this end, it seems to me unimportant that *The Inheritors'* picture of Neanderthal man may be technically inaccurate; it does matter that the fable gives a translucent image of that possible time.

The fable itself exhibits the characteristic ideographic structure; it is built in two unequal sections: Chapters I–X and XI–XII. The first part makes up most of the novel's action while the slighter final coda section is, in part, a meditation on the preceding drama. In the first part, events are viewed from the limited perspective of the Neanderthal mind, a mind that cannot reason beyond sense data. We participate as readers in a world in which ideas and communications are a series of images, not a function of speech and causality. Thus *The Inheritors* differs dramatically from *Lord of the Flies*, where the island is viewed at first through the comparatively broad scope of Ralph's rational mind, and then seen from a more and more restricted angle as the 'curtain' of memory drops and Ralph fumbles for rationality. In *The Inheritors*, rather than shrink, understanding expands; gradually and simultaneously with the Neanderthal protagonist the reader is made aware of Other People occupying the Neanderthals' territory. In fact, narrative interest derives solely from this gradual intrusion. There is a scent, then an obscurely familiar sound which Lok cannot place, 'from the foot of the fall, a noise that the thunder robbed of echo and resonance'[5] then a horrifying shape moves up a tree, and finally white boned figures with tufted heads appear. In these figures we gradually recognize ourselves.

Towards the conclusion of Chapter XI a shift from the Neanderthal angle of vision to that of the Cro-Magnon occurs.

This remarkable transition is brought about by tonal alterations as the style modulates into a scientific cum objective rhetoric. Third person singular is abandoned at exactly the moment when the last Oa-priestess drops over the fall caught in the dead tree. The omniscient author seems to retreat away from the figure of Lok who becomes, in the distance, simply an impersonal creature: 'The red creature stood on the edge of the terrace and did nothing. . . . Water was cascading down the rocks beyond the terrace from the melting ice in the mountains. . . . It was a strange creature, smallish, and bowed. The legs and thighs were bent and there was a whole thatch of curls on the outside of the legs and the arms' (216–219). It is the first time we have seen Lok as an animal; the description recalls Wells's epigraph. But divesting Lok of his human-ness paradoxically deepens his pathos. He becomes a tiny bent creature overwhelmed by the immensity of his loss, and the immensity of gloom, cold moonlight, and the long curved fall of water that heralds the Ice Age's end and the end of his species.

Emotional understatement is superbly used in the whole transition section and is coupled with quite extraordinary visual stillness and linguistic precision; one passage, for example, describes the physical business of weeping water, but not by denoting that the red creature is crying. The reader becomes simply the observer of a natural occurrence—until the point in the rhythmic repetition where the reader imparts meaning and thus pain to the action. 'The lights increased, acquired definition, brightened, lay each sparkling at the lower edge of a cavern. Suddenly, noiselessly, the lights became thin crescents, went out, and streaks glistened on each cheek. The lights appeared again, caught among the silvered curls of the beard. They hung, elongated, dropped from curl to curl . . . one drop detached itself and fell in a silver flash, striking a withered leaf with a sharp pat' (220). The passage is character-istic of the best of Golding's style—one thinks of the poetic description of Simon in death here—where things are anthropomorphized, while that to which we normally impart humanity is figured in non-human architectural/natural terms. *Pincher Martin* makes especially successful use of this device.

In *The Inheritors'* final chapter a coda brings about a dramatic reversal (James Gindin, the devil's advocate in these matters, thinks the reversal breaks the fable's unity without adding a relevant perspective.[6] But quite the contrary is true; the reversal is vital both to the dramatic outcome of the narrative and to the larger mythopœia *The Inheritors* constructs.) Suddenly we are placed in the pragmatic minds of the Cro-Magnons, the opposing tribe, and the tone shifts from emotive lyricism to nautical gruffness: 'A fair wind, steerage-way, and plenty of water all round—what more could a man want. . . . Forrard there under the sail was what looked like lower land, plains perhaps where men could hunt in the open, not stumble among dark trees or on hard, haunted rocks' (224), Tuami mutters to himself as he broods on the 'devils' which have hindered the passage of his people from island and fall to the lake's upper regions. The subtle effect is to make us now revise our unsympathetic assumptions about the wholly evil nature of the New People, and by an act of imaginative extension, to understand their part in the week's furor.

III

I'd say I'm passionately interested in description, the exact description of a phenomenon. When I know what a wave looks like or a flame or a tree, I hug that to me or carry the thought agreeably as a man might carry a flower round with him.

—Golding, 'Personal Communication'

Onyx marsh water, hard haunted rock, the shock head of a dead tree, a droning fall, the prolonged harsh bellow of a rutting stag, the sea white bitter smell of salt: the world of *The Inheritors* is anchored, like its statement on the

Fall, in the substantial world. Its inception resulted, Golding told me, from a vision of such a fact: 'when I discovered Lok running in I was able to introduce the rest of the characters and the thing wrote itself—in a month.' The fable begins and ends in utterly solid surfaces, and sensuous shapes, smells, sounds, sights. Partly because, so delimited, its landscape—the physical patch of the land itself with beech trees, stepping stones, two paths, sheer cliffs from a terrace, an island, a river, and a fall, and the relationship between the parts—become intimately known. The reader seems to lie with the character up against the face of real things, confusedly caught in these things: stationary with these things.

> By his face there had grown a twig: a twig that smelt of other, and of goose, and of the bitter berries that Lok's stomach told him he must not eat. This twig had a white bone at the end. There were hooks in the bone and sticky brown stuff hung in the crooks. His nose examined this stuff and did not like it. He smelled along the shaft of the twig. The leaves on the twig were red feathers and reminded him of goose. He was lost in a generalized astonishment and excitement. (106)

Though the point of view here is technically omniscient, as in *Lord of the Flies*, sustaining for three-quarters of the book primitivistic, anthropomorphic descriptions and perspectives, the formal mode consists in something very different, a technical feat that Frank Kermode has hailed as wholly original. For we see most events, the activities of *Homo sapiens*, over the shoulder of a pre-rational mind. In *Lord of the Flies*, *Pincher Martin*, *The Spire*, even *Free Fall*, we enter rational minds which gradually grow obscured and a-rational—there to be upset by the coda's reversal; here the reader shares Lok's perspective, inhabiting at times a creature whose sensory equipment perceives, but does not understand. In the other fables, the protagonists 'understand' as it were but they do

not 'perceive'; this is especially true of *The Spire* where
Jocelin must learn, with a new clarity of eye: 'What's this
called? And this?' (147). But in *The Inheritors* there is an
interesting variation for 'Perception is itself, no more; not
what we normally expect it to be, a stepping stone to an idea
rapidly transferred from the eye to the mind.'[7] Everything,
the part by part shape of the arrow sunk in the tree beside
Lok's face, is rendered through the physical sensations, about
which he is wholly unconscious. As he is bombarded by arrows,
smells, associating in his first fall the smell of the island with
the fire and old woman, Lok attends scrupulously to the
concrete, and can no more abstract from a twig to an arrow
than import hostility to the New Men shooting an arrow at
him: 'Suddenly Lok understood that the man was holding the
stick out to him but neither he nor Lok could reach across the
river. He would have laughed if it were not for the echo of the
screaming in his head' (106). Lok's senses merely report a
series of inexplicable events: an ominously missing log, the
old woman's bundle that mysteriously moves to the island,
yet remains—he discovers when he falls at the terrace—in her
hands beside him, a smell without a 'picture' which brings
him 'blank amazement' (62). Lok's senses simply report a
dislocation of self that not only tears him from the People but
fragments him between an inside-Lok with a 'tidal feeling'
and an outside-Lok that grows tight fear like another skin,
and finally, gruesomely, a New People with bone faces, log
bodies, bird-fluttering language who 'walked upright . . . as
though something that Lok could not see were supporting
them, holding up their heads, thrusting them slowly and
irresistibly forward' (144).

The plot, a dramatic account of the extermination of one
species by another, is extremely simple. We follow the
migration of a small band of 'People' (31) from their winter
quarters by the sea to their summer quarters in coastal mountains at the edge of a river and waterfall. For a long time, the
epigraph from Wells's *Outline* remains the only clue to the

identity of the story's actors. The band of eight is the only
Neanderthal group to have survived a Great Fire. Coming to a
marshy stretch of water, they discover a log-bridge is missing—
an ominous fact since in the past it has always been there and
should still remain: 'To-day is like yesterday and tomorrow'
(46), they console themselves. But this faith is to be bitterly
shattered. The leader of the band, Mal the old man with all
the memories of sweeter times, falls into the dreaded water.
The tribe tortuously climbs up a cliff, forced to make a new
passage to their ancient overhang. They set about finding food,
but it gradually becomes clear that for some inexplicable
reason Mal has miscalculated the seasons and they have
arrived at their summer quarters too early. Then Ha falls
victim to some unknown calamity—in swift succession Mal
dies of over exposure: Nil and the old woman are killed,
perhaps by some creature, the two children, Liku and the
new one, are kidnapped. Only Lok and Fa remain, frantically
trying to rescue the children whose kidnapping they simply
cannot understand.

The narrative now turns to the activities of the New People;
the starving tribe is gradually introduced: the charismatic
magician Marlan and the beautiful Vivani;[8] the artist Tuami;
Pine-tree, Chestnut-head, Bush, Tuft, the four braves; Twal
and her daughter, Tanakil. We watch from the summit of
the dead tree through Neanderthal eyes the mysterious
gestures of this tribe, their mimetic rituals, their rapacious
orgies, their terrified brutal efforts to escape from some
unknown danger. A last crucial episode occurs at the over-
hang; the New People are confusedly trying to accomplish
the portage of their canoes past the waterfall: 'There was an
hysterical speed in the efforts of Tuami and in the screaming
voice of the old man. They were retreating up the slope as
though cats with their evil teeth were after them', as though
'the river itself were flowing uphill' (209). A variation of this
verbal paradox of falling upward closes *The Spire* when
Jocelin glimpses the tower as an 'upward waterfall.' Lok and

Fa make one last desperate effort to rescue the children, Fa distracting attention so that Lok can rush for the new one. The attempt fails; several of the New People fall over the fall while Tuami draws a savage totemic figure. 'It was some kind of man. Its arms and legs were contracted. . . . There was hair standing out on all sides of the head as the hair of the old man had stood out when he was enraged or frightened' (215).[9] A confused scuffle ensues and Fa is chased to a log. The log spills over the cascading waters of the fall and she is carried as the other People were to her death-by-water.

At just this point the objective transition is placed: we watch Lok's dumb pain as he scurries back and forth looking for Liku; finally he unearths her Oa-doll and with this folds himself into a foetal position at the ancient grave in the over-hang. At the fable's close one solitary canoe is seen carrying the tormented New People upward towards some new camp. Tuami broods on the change and his bedevilled irrational grief, 'as though the portage of the boats . . . from that forest to the top of the fall had taken them all onto a new level not only of land but of experience and emotions' (225). As he studies the tribe before him, their history is swiftly reviewed. They too have been overcome by water; Tuami thinks: 'I am like a pool . . . some tide has filled me, the sand is swirling, the waters are obscured and strange . . .' (227). And *The Inheritors* ends with Tuami staring out at a 'line of darkness' (233) apparently without end.

Both Lok's primitive perspective and the omniscient authorial descriptions deliberately limit any formulation or deduction or interpretation of events. The latter Golding contrives to make work by concealing familiar elements in anthropomorphic images. Thus the cliff is described as leaning out 'looking for its own feet in the water', the island 'rearing' against the fall is a 'seated giant' whose 'thigh that should have supported a body like a mountain lay in the sliding water of the gap' and the river 'sleeps' and 'fell over on both sides of the island' (23). The reader becomes, through these sorts of metaphors, immersed in reality, with the trick of abstraction blanked out.

The first four chapters of *The Inheritors* where we follow the 'People' in their movement upstream from their winter quarters to their summer quarters in the overhang, directly adjacent to the fall, are static, propelled not by action but through description, a mode fundamental to the growth of the fable. For what is encountered, indeed discovered, by the reader in these chapters—the tree by the clearing where Lok swings Liku, the ice cavern beyond the waterfall, where 'the drone of the fall diminished to a sigh' (81), the fall itself with logs slowly descending—these physical phenomena assume a dramatic then a symbolic role as the tale proceeds. As substantial phenomena they are, first of all, points in the actual narrative scene which, by introduction and reintroduction during the course of the developing narrative, begin to assume a symbolic import, much in the way I argued the island and the Head did in *Lord of the Flies*. Furthermore, they absorb verbal echoes as they grow out of the fabric of each event. The use of trees is an example of this : not only do falling trees, falling over the fall, result, at each point, in disaster, but the New People are made to resemble, in the People's view, their awful nature. Lok thinks that they are trees and calls one Chestnut-head. Of course, people can in no way be identified with trees, but if they share in the food of the Dead Tree, if they send the old woman over the fall like a log, if they in turn utilize trees to get beyond what for them is the terror of the dark forest and the ringing fall, then they participate in the nature of the Fallen Tree. In all Golding's fables dramatic structure, imagery, and the created language operate in this way; they are both their literal selves and the symbolic embodiment of an idea.

Basically, then, our sense of the People[10]—their code of ethics, their solicitous community, their common emotions, their deep reverence for and awe of life—is a matter of accumulated physical sensation. Moreover the symbolic nature of the fable's first movement becomes our immersion in their substantial world and through it in a very real sense, unique to this fable, we may be said to enact the return of the characters with them. An ingenious device and integral unit in this regard is 'the picture', for it allows Golding to move away from the immediate and constant present. The People communicate by 'sharing pictures' or imagining simultaneously images of events. Through these 'pictures' the reader has access to the Neanderthals' past and tradition. Mal has a memory, what he calls a 'picture' of a time of perpetual summer 'and the flowers and fruit hung on the same branch' (35), an Edenic myth that was destroyed by a 'Great Fire', a nightmare of which begins to recur in Lok's mind, when he hears the droning of the fall and its hated water. Lok's only picture, 'a picture of finding the little Oa' (33), introduces us to the People's religion, a concept of the numinous, the power dwelling in the caverns of the glacier—the loins of the ice woman—and in the blackened woman-shaped root cuddled by the child Liku:

> There was the great Oa. She brought forth the earth from her belly. She gave suck. The earth brought forth woman and the woman brought forth the first man out of her belly (35).

Likewise, we learn of the old woman's dreadful but unfearful sanctity. Oa's earthly representative, she carries the fire, breathing into the clay like her Greek counterpart and 'awakening' the flame—the ruddy sunset, and those points of fire-love in the People's eyes. To Lok her own eyes are those of the visionary; she wraps things in understanding, compassion, and remote stillness. 'He remembered the old woman, so close to Oa, knowing so indescribably much, the door-keeper to whom all secrets were open. He felt awed and happy and witless again' (61).

Together the People share emotions, perhaps even sexual partners; they either share a picture spontaneously or exert themselves to get another to share a picture. This becomes the major device for Lok's characterization and it is a mark of the tragedy that Lok, the witless but innocent clown, as the last surviving adult male, has many words but few pictures. Words, however—and this is central to the book's exploration of our linguistic inheritance—are indefinite; some members occasionally emit them more or less at random to express excitement, joy, or terror. But before the old woman's hearth, they sink into a kind of undifferentiated darkness, a communal whole without speech, without identity, without thought. Golding wonderfully visualizes this slow bonding in both microcosmic and macrocosmic terms. As the flame wavers, nursed by a creature of 'mixed fire and moonlight' (72), their skins grow ruddy 'and the deep caverns beneath their brows' are inhabited 'by replicas of the fire and all their fires danced together' (33). The scene is one of the most poignantly realized in the book; significantly, it relates to Golding's own pictorial conception of the origins of myth where he sees a tribe sitting before a fire, joined in and tied to one story that is sifted and resifted, told and retold, adapted through successive stages of rejection and coalescence, in his word 'mulching' down in the very fabric of the community's existence.

The 'pictures', say Gregor and Kinkead-Weekes, 'are visualizations not conceptualizations, telepathic snapshots not of an idea but of an entire event.' Significance mysteriously resides in them inasmuch as they represent some rounded aspect of a whole truth, unfragmented and unabstracted. Thus for Lok even a smell is accompanied by a picture, 'a sort of living but qualified presence' (74); alternatively he can, at great expense of energy, evolve a new picture 'not by reasoned deduction but because in every place the scent told him—do this!' (77). Such intuition amounts to a comprehensive understanding of a new, viz. unexperienced, phenomenon; unlike deduction from a thing to its essential nature, this mode of consciousness makes the knower, in knowing, become that which is known:

> . . . the scent turned Lok into the thing that had gone before him. He was beginning to know the other without understanding how it was that he knew. Lok-other crouched at the lip of the cliff and stared across the rocks of the mountain. . . . He threw himself into the shadow of a rock snarling and waiting (77). [11]

Technically the 'picture' is a fine instrument for revealing the Neanderthals' incapacity for abstract thought, thus distinguishing them from the more advanced evolutionary species.

But most importantly the 'picture' renders, as no other device could, the life of the senses and instinct since the impression the reader receives of the outside world is of a series of still images. Thus we are confused and frightened in a way which we cannot quite grasp. For example, fearsome suspense and tension are built into the description of the New People's last activity on the terrace as they try to escape, precisely because—though there is intense and concentrated action—it is pictured by Lok as a series of stills, each devoid of motion like moments caught in past-time. They appear to be random events without the causality of one action leading to another. 'The fat woman was screaming. . . . The old man was running. . . . Chestnut-head was coming from where Lok was' (210). Each short sentence conveys the impression of arrested speed, yet each operates like the beginning of a tale—an action caught immediately; in fact, they recall the beginning of *The Inheritors* itself: 'Lok was running as fast as he could' (11). One action is apart from another; each is finishing and static; none is connected to another, not even by the simple connective 'and'. So there is nothing Lok can imagine to do to either connect the actions together or stop them. Thus Tanakil is dropped by Lok. Chestnut-head is travelling through the air, 'fitting the delicate curve of the descent' (211) over

the fall. Marlan is flinging an arrow. Fa is jumping at the gully.
A canoe is falling and splitting in two.

Of course, all the actions are related but lacking the rational
perspective that makes a pattern of random events they impress
the reader as individual assaults. As the Neanderthals slowly
begin to formulate—and, as we shall see, this is most wonderfully done during the ritual stag dance—Golding can depict,
by making us bring into focus the foreground of the story, the
nature of innocence. For Golding sees the alogical, undifferentiated mentality—what Sammy Mountjoy has in abundance
as a child—as essentially innocent. We not only experience a
consciousness that twentieth-century man has lost in which
instinct, intuition, and pictorialization predominate; we
participate in its loss.

The Inheritors' total effort is to implicate the reader in the
experience of and responsibility for this loss of innocence; in
this way the fable's ideographic structure forces the reader to
know that the innocence lost is our own innocence, just as in
Pincher Martin we will come to know the Purgatorial state.
We proceed within the innocent's consciousness until the
penultimate chapter where, after the objective anthropological
transition, we enter the New People's minds. This brings pain.
For the knot binding the people together 'by a thousand
invisible strings' (104) has been supplanted by the 'strips of
skin' (208) tying the groaning men to their log/canoes and by
the 'long piece of skin' (159) which leashes Liku to Tanakil.
And in the fragmentations between inside-Lok and outside-Lok
which so intensifies his alienation both from himself and Fa we
recognize the very image of our own dissociated and pluralized
sensibilities. The change to Cro-Magnon man's point of view,
with its gain in intellectual grasp and apprehensive imagination,
involves the painful loss of Neanderthal man's intuitive if
disconnected thinking.

Point of view, then, is employed so as to depict the ironic
evolution from People to Men, from pre-lapsarian to post-
adamite, from a primitive to contemporary mentality. Not

only does the reader's mentality emerge from Lok's mind to
Tuami's, it comes with the Neanderthals to the 'place of the
Fall'; it leaves with *Homo sapiens*. From the point of view of
innocence, the biological evolution is a moral devolution, as
ironic a turning as the Wells epigraph or the Beatitude referred
to in the title that the 'meek shall inherit the earth'. The
departure is a departure from innocence; the light of dawn
that touches the sailors, like the new spring and new age that
the melting ice hails, seems essentially bleak.

IV

*But I quite agree that the parallelism between intelli-
gence and evil does come out in my books because it is
our . . . particular sin—to explain away our own
shortcomings rather than remedy them.*

—Golding

A new kind of darkness shadows the world; as the epigraph
above suggests with manipulative intelligence comes the
capacity to avoid our essential selves, or what lies in our
'darkness'. Thus, in *The Inheritors* 'Lok felt himself secure in
the darkness' (185) while the new creatures are terrified of it.
The point is fundamental, I think, to Golding's moral diag-
nosis: man abstracts from his own evil—something his nature
possesses—and projects it as a fear of something Other which
will haunt or destroy him. In the second fable, the mythopœia
is often developed imagistically. As Vivani stands fearfully
stroking the new one, the others attempt to placate their own
fear by stroking the new one, whom they regard as a totemic
figure, and stoking the fire which is already excessive; they all
face '*outward* at the darkness of the forest' (185, italics added).
But their Promethean fire itself metamorphoses darkness,
makes the island so impenetrably dark that the night-sight of
Lok and Fa is temporarily lost. In Lok's mind the fire and the
fall become associated so that the clearing below the tree is

beaten with a 'fountain of flame' (171), not warm light but 'fierce, white-red and blinding' (171). The firelight, symbolically intelligence, intensifies the darkness, and in fact, makes it hideous. Precisely the same light/dark image is repeated at the fable's close. The New People's canoes sail forward on shining water, viz., water that is imagistically associated with light, yet it also seems hemmed in by darkness. In fact, it is projecting outward the moral darkness of the sailors. In the fable's very last line, Tuami is made to remark that 'there was such a flashing from the water' (233) that he 'cannot see if the line of darkness had an ending' (233). Obviously Golding is making, by the symbolic extension of optical illusion, the point that intense light obscures—man's intelligence projects its own internal darkness outward. Man's mind, Golding is saying, deceives itself; man imagines devils who 'live in darkness under the trees' (233) and then tries to destroy the fantasies he has himself created. Yet this fear of 'tree-darkness' drives man forward—it is, in fact, the very basis of his strength, as Lok understands when he knows 'the impervious power of the people in the light' (185). 'Haunted, bedevilled, full of strange irrational grief' (225), man carries his fear with him.

From a stasis of calm description at the fable's opening to the frantic and confused dramatic action at its close, the reader comes gradually to experience imaginatively the loss of innocence and the genesis of guilt. First, Lok's incomprehension is our incomprehension; then, Tuami's doubt is our doubt. In the book's central confrontation—where Lok sees a 'thing' in the water—Golding dramatizes the sudden conjunction of this innocence and its perfect opposite: consciousness. Reading the moment, in a sense, we actively participate in the first emergence of the mythological ogre in the primitive mind.

Hanging from what will be the tree of knowledge, having already learned a new knowledge from that tree, Lok leans out over the dreaded water, trying to reach out towards the

island and the kidnapped Liku. He strains and balances,
noticing that the water under him darkens as he stretches
forward. Just as his ears hear the water-fall, the branches
begin to bend under him. Gibbering in fright, he sinks and a
'Lok-face' (107) comes up at him as the water appears to rise.
It is the moment when the unknown, something dark and
autonomous, confronts Lok's mind. The entire episode is
projected through a technique whereby we are locked in the
primitive mind and hence without the interpretation that
attends the similar scene in, for example, *Lord of the Flies* where
Simon confronts the Head of the pig. 'Pictures', even fear,
disappear, yet he cannot connect the Lok-face with himself; it
is simply some dark spectre—released from his mind—and now
compulsively, independently, capable of harming him. Lok
sees something foreign which we know is also himself, but to
him it is a threatening image of 'teeth grinning in the water'
(108). It gradually fuses with a new terror—the result of the
water-fall and its implicit Fall:

> The weed-tail was shortening. The green tip was with-
> drawing up river. There was a darkness that was con-
> suming the other end. The darkness became a thing of
> complex shape, of sluggish and dreamlike movement.
> Like the specks of dirt, it turned over but not aimlessly.
> It was touching near the root of the weed-tail, bending
> the tail, turning over, rolling up the tail towards him.
> The arms moved a little and the eyes shone as dully as the
> stones. They revolved with the body, gazing at the surface,
> at the width of deep water and the hidden bottom with
> no trace of life or speculation. A skein of weed drew
> across the face and the eyes did not blink. The body
> turned with the same smooth and heavy motion as the
> river itself until its back was towards him rising along the
> weed-tail. The head turned towards him with dreamlike
> slowness, rose in the water, came towards his face.
> (108–109)

Lok sees the old woman, like one of the logs that keeps falling off the fall, drifting towards him, in the water from the fall. The body is a nightmarish thing in dark water and its knowing eyes are scraped and affronted by the weed-tails. The eyes sweep across his face, 'looked through him without seeing him, rolled away and were gone'; the eyes that once saw into the mystery of things no longer have any power in the technological world *Homo sapiens* has created. And innocence, which before had been characterized by wholeness, becomes aware of deepwater within itself, some part of the self inescapably fragmented from itself and uncontrollable. The encounter, then, results in a psychic fragmentation not unlike similar confrontation scenes in *Lord of the Flies* and *Free Fall*, which, however, bring about psychic unification.

While there are similarities between this and other confrontation scenes, here the episode reverberates, for the reader, with a kind of energy and terror that seems rationally inexplicit. For something horrendous happens in Lok, in us, as well as to him. Gregor and Kinkead-Weekes suggest that it is as though a 'formless thing disengages itself from the depths of the mind, becomes a dark spectre, rises with dreadful slowness . . . reveals sudden intimations of terror; hides them. Then slowly, relentlessly, it turns towards us the full horror of its face.' Certainly we respond primarily to the rhythm of nightmare—recall that same disturbing motion was used to describe the bowing corpse and the bouncing Head in *Lord of the Flies*. In *Pincher Martin* there is a toy doll, a 'Cartesian Diver', whose motion is similar, in *The Spire*, Jocelin atop the spire waves left and right with the same dreadful slowness.

The entire episode seems a radically compressed account of the book's theme since it connects the two psychic conditions of innocence and guilt, and shows how the latter emerges from the former, as indeed Cro-Magnon man emerges from Neanderthal man. But its resonance functions at a level not analytically obvious. Certain motifs, simple physical phenomena, inhabit the scene: 'wetness down there, myster-

ious and pierced everywhere by the dark and bending stems'
(107), the pillars of spray from the fall, the rising water—
Lok's weight pulls the tree to the water but his experience is
that the water comes to him—the fluttering weed tails that
regularly 'eclipse', the stuff rising towards the surface, turning
over and over, floating in circles as his own teeth grin in the
water. 'He experienced Lok, upside down over deep water
with a twig to save him' (108). But each of these motifs
operates with a kind of total recall because it has been pre-
figured in the narrative texture and will be repeated throughout, in an endless interwound dance. Actual phenomena—
river, tree, water, weed—are invested and charged with an
energy that operates at a synaesthetic and symbolic level
though they still maintain physical credibility.

Lok's incomprehension becomes finally our comprehension;
if like the presentation of the Pharoah in Golding's short story
'The Scorpion God', the presentation of the New People is by
indirection, that indirection is dehumanizing. We see them
less ambiguously as the tale proceeds until finally we are ripped
out of the Neanderthal perspective in the coda. Thus we look
at inexplicable events from the inside and from the outside; as
he goes along, I have been arguing, the reader is expected to
deduce significance and to connect details into meaningful
constructs which the simplified Lok is incapable of formulating.
Thus, as Lok and Fa stare incredulously, we deduce—in what
is perhaps the most obscure chapter of the book—the magic-
religion of the New People, the totem religion of the Stag.
We begin to appreciate that though we discover the rituals of
the totemic Stag cult, in particular the sacrifice of a brave's
finger to that magic, here from the vantage point of 'tree-
bound innocence' by way of the passive uncorrupt senses of
Lok and Fa, our proper station is below; our corrupt consciousness's place is at the Dead Tree's base. The entire long episode
from the tree, with the fall droning in Lok's ears, the wood
pigeons pecking, the light of the fire blinding, the water
shivering, has an imaginative power unsurpassed in Golding's

fiction. At a very basic level there is a simple wonder in the concrete—since it is Lok's screen—rendering of sensuality: 'She lifted her arms to the back of her head, bowed, and began to work at the pattern in her hair. All at once the petals fell in black snakes that hung over her shoulders and breasts. She shook her head like a horse and the snakes flew back till they could see her breasts again' (154). Then, in turn, the point of view is so realized that we can discover ourselves below and understand both the sour-smelling 'wobbling animal' and the complicated and engrossing pleasure 'hunted down' by the Bacchanals. Using our corrupt consciousness, we even guess the most shocking event in the book: Lok smells Liku all around the campfire because she has been killed and eaten.

Golding himself takes the putting to sleep of Lok just at this juncture of the narrative as an example of his own ability to make the best he can out of the limitations of the fabulist's art. It seems to me to be much more than a fabulist's intellectual trick, however. For inasmuch as we guess from Fa's 'dead eyes' what has occurred, we in a sense share in the act of murder by discovering the act. The point is fundamental to Golding's moral scheme: knowledge makes one participate in responsibility. The guilty may make a darkness, some blank fear or some totem of fear but knowledge is recognition and it brings with it the necessity to acknowledge in our own nature, the Beast. The problem that *The Inheritors*, *Lord of the Flies* and *The Spire* raise is the contemporary gap between such knowledge and that knowledge put into action, the whole impulse of a creature who transforms darkness of the unknown into a threatening ogre, or devil, or external system of evil.

V

*What nonsense to say that man is reduced to insigni-
ficance before the galaxies. The stars are a common
brightness in every eye. What 'out there' have you
that does not correspond to an 'in here.' The mind of*

man is the biggest thing in the universe, it is through-
out the universe. . . . We are a foolish and ignorant
race and have got ourselves tied up in a tape-measure.

—Golding, 'All or Nothing'

With the single exception of *The Pyramid*, *The Inheritors* is the one novel of his own Golding will reread: it is his 'favourite' and 'my finest'. For me the curious history of its invention brings into radical question the notion of Golding as an allegorist, writing only from moral hypotheses which deter- mine the shape of his fiction. For *The Inheritors* is something more than an allegorical fable, a mode he regards as being 'an invented thing on the surface.' It aspires to the condition of myth, 'something which comes out from the roots of things in the ancient sense of being the key to existence, the whole meaning of life, and experience as a whole'. The first manu- script version of *The Inheritors* differs significantly from the published book; it contains no last chapter, closes on what is now the archaeological cum anthropological transition, has very little exploration of the divided consciousness and, most significantly, no waterfall. Like *Lord of the Flies* it started as a simple argument with the smug nineteenth-century doctrine of progress—and proceeded to show, through the tragedy of the People alone, the genesis of the mythological monster in the human skull. After finishing the first draft Golding made an inspired discovery; he began to see what the tale was really about and started from scratch again. Within a month he completed the present and final version.

Two different but metaphorically associated strains brought about the rewriting. Feeling that the Second Law of Thermo- dynamics—which claims that when change, such as the transfer of heat energy, occurs in a physical body the succession of changes results in the return of a substance to its original condition—had a peculiar inverted relevance to the psycho- logical climate of the twentieth century, he brooded on its great example, water, the energy of which moves from a state of high organization to a state of low organization. Concomitant with this was what he said to me, that the certainty that man is 'the local contradiction of this rule'; in him 'the cosmos is organizing energy back to sunlight level.'

In a consideration of Yeats in *Holiday Magazine* (1963) he developed the same argument:

> The Satan of our cosmology is the second Law of Thermodynamics which implies that everything is running down and will finally stop like an unwound clock. Life is in some sense a local contradiction of this law . . . we should be cheered when life refuses to submit to a general levelling down of energy and simply winds itself up again.

Such fusing of physical sciences and anthropological and archaeological data with poetic truths typefies Golding's method. In *The Pyramid*, for example, chemistry jostles with music for the attention of Oliver and we see the autobiographical boy in 'The Ladder and the Tree' caught between the solicitude of a scientific father and the lures of mediaeval romances. Here in *The Inheritors* Golding's imaginative recasting of the scientific Law gradually fused with another element—Heraclitus' philosophical dictum that multiplicity and unity, the existence of opposites in eternal flux, depends on the balancing of the motion of 'the way downwards' while harmony and peace lead back to unity by 'the way upwards'. From these mulchings it became imaginatively clear, Golding explained, that the downward path of the innocent was essentially related to the surmounting path of the guilty: for nature is constantly dividing and uniting herself. An ultimate and, by extension, constant dynamic exists between phenomena and epochs so that death is never a final defeat.

All this brooding settled down, he explained, into 'the perfect image' of the Law: 'a river with a fall', a log going over the fall and men with huge ganglia and enlarged skulls travelling up the river over the fall, pushed by some new

intensity, some vision. Thus in *The Inheritors*, Lok, the pre-
lapsarian, amazedly discovers that, 'They did not look up at
the earth but straight ahead' (143) when he sees the post-
adamite New People swaying upright, 'It was as though
something that Lok could not see were supporting them,
holding up their heads, thrusting them slowly and irresistibly
forward' (144).

Then the island imaginatively placed itself in the landscape,
reared against the fall because, Golding explained to me, it was
technically necessary for the New People to leave this
'impenetrable dark' (127) shelter; they had to retreat up the
slope 'as though [instead of falling] the river itself were flowing
uphill' towards the plains and the mountains. Thus at the
beginning, the bulk of the island, which is shielded by loathsome falling water, seems to Lok as remote as the skies.
'Only some creature more agile and frightened' (41) than the
People could reach it. Some larger creature with larger
intelligence would explore its strangeness, a creature whose
daring power is inconceivable to innocence. And, the island
becomes a macrocosmic image of man's nature, divorced by
his enlarged skull from brute nature: isolated at the foot of the
Fall divided by two falls from the mainland and forest, a
'seated giant' (40) which 'interrupts the sill of the waterfall'
(40). It is a symbolic image of the 'People of the Fall' who will
go against the Fall.

The final extermination of the People by *Homo sapiens* would
occur at the waterfall. Thus in a river of blood,[12] Fa drops
over the fall, as indifferently as the logs that repeatedly drop
over, sitting limply among the branches of a 'whole tree from
some forest over the horizon . . . a colony of budding twigs
and branches, a vast half-hidden trunk, and roots that spread
above the water and held enough earth between them to
make a hearth for all the people in the world' (212).

Golding takes this woman of the 'hearth' to the edge of the
fall; she can never pass beyond it because her nature cannot
comprehend those weapons of destruction and tools of survival

that *Homo sapiens* possesses. Thus her innocence seen against the ritual killing, the religious sacrifice, destructive river, the murderous Fall-nature, is caught in a Dead Tree whose relentless power she cannot avoid; drowned she is carried back below the fall. But the evolutionary life force drives the New People upwards—the word that always attends their description in the book—and forward, at a higher level of energy than that which the People possessed. Something thrusts the New People up the river, some pained need to widen the world, as well as manipulate it.

Our last view of Fa is of her rolling over and over in the river while the fall's current thrusts her back and down to the sea. The whole 'dreamlike' motion and direction superbly repeats that of the old woman's frightening log-like descent to the sea in the deep waters of the river. In contrast to both, the New People's dugout canoes, the '*logs*' which Lok first sees on the river pointing '*up towards the fall*' (115, italics added), can remain stationary, fighting and victorious over the current that urges them downstream. And the navigators move steadily upwards, away from the sea, up beyond the fall, meeting as they ascend towards the plain, thunder like an angry god, which heralds the end of the Ice Age. The fear-driven Tuami feels:

> . . . as though the portage of the boats . . . from that forest to the top of the fall had taken them on to a new level not only of land but of experience and emotion. The world with the boat moving slowly at the centre was dark amid the light. . . . (225)

The New People have moved to yet a new level, then. The water now conquered, a new complexity, a new violence, and perhaps a more refined civility are set afloat.

VI

It is possible to abstract from *The Inheritors* Golding's own conviction that where man is godlike is precisely where he can fall. The old community possesses love and reverence, not hatred, and they are irrevocably drawn by dread and joy to the New People in the latter's capacity as blazing fire and terrible water: the honey 'repelled and attracted' like the People. Lok, because his nature is innocent and loving, cannot obey Fa and ignore Liku; even when Fa has worked out a plan of strategy, Lok has to ask Tanakil where Liku is. He keeps being drawn to his destruction, as he knows the old woman, Ha, and Nil were. Both 'outside-and inside-Lok yearned with a terrified love as creatures who would kill him if they could' (191). The New People have ochre and hunting spears and a potent honey drink, but the artistic images can be used for savagery, the weapons can be thrust into men's flesh, and the drink can intoxicate. Their complex power, like the rationality of Pincher on his island, is both creative and destructive.

The sources and means of power and active creation are also the sources and means of destruction. This is for Golding man's tragic tension: man's primary nature is given and where it seems most formidable it may also be most vulnerable. It is a relatively simple conviction. But the process whereby Golding arrived at its expression in *The Inheritors* is a much more complex matter. Certain 'pictures' and, significantly, clusters of 'pictures', emerged after Golding's thinking coalesced around the waterfall as the image of the Law of Thermodynamics. Thus the People's first displacement occurs because a 'fallen log' has been removed from its habitual place across the river. Their first knowledge of 'a new thing' involves the Tree: Mal makes them run—it is described as '*falling* across' (17) a new log. The description operates both symbolically and realistically, as do many of Golding's descriptions. Running is in a way a falling, since the body is hunched over while pressing against the atmosphere. Similarly the drone of the fall inhabits their ears when they first stop by the Dead Tree. It becomes the place where, the droning in their ears, Fa and Lok watch the antics of the Fallen People.

Now clearly the Tree and the Fall and the Water operate symbolically within the context of the story; they were not 'invented' by Golding so much as 'discovered'. While we can say that the water-world in *The Inheritors* is a destructive world, and the fall's moaning insinuates this destruction, we cannot grasp the actual force these have on the reader when we wrench them out of the continuum of the story. Symbol like myth defies simple classification and analysis—both are in Golding's words 'directions and tendencies, not distinct places'. Indeed, for him the very power that symbol like myth possesses is its power to evade analysis.

Therefore at one level *The Inheritors* seems a network of things, of actions repeated, reintroduced, and expanded. Thus packed into a simple phrase, 'The people are like the river and the fall, they are a people of the Fall; nothing stands against them' .(195), is something like a total recall of the book's mythopœia. Phrases are charged with expressive force because they echo previous passages. The phrases share in turn a kind of micro-macrocosmic intensity but not because they are deliberately denoted that way—this would make them 'signs'—but because like the cell in *Free Fall*, the Castle Rock in *Lord of the Flies*, the cathedral in *The Spire* and the island in *Pincher Martin*, they image man's nature. These congruent, hologram-like symbols compress the theme, yet have concrete and dramatic value, as in a dream or dream-odyssey we are guided through and experience on the way to insight. Lok's first view from the tree of the tribe is a splendid illustration. Here all kinds of resonances from various familiar legends seem to converge and create a moment of sheer terror:

> The blob of darkness seemed to coagulate round the stem like a drop of blood on a stick. It lengthened, thickened again, lengthened. It moved up . . . with sloth-like deliberation, it hung in the air high above the island and the fall. It made no noise and at last hung motionless. (79)

The darkness that spells evil, the blood that causes revulsion, the motion of thickening and lengthening that brings to mind the snake, the picture of it hanging above the island and even the Fall, identified with the two but somehow powerful enough to transcend the two—all reverberate atavistically. Finally, all occurs in silence and from a limited point of view that reports action, step by step, without interpreting it. It seems arrested, stilled. In fact, the passage illustrates the sensuous flexibility of the fable's language: restricted to a relatively narrow range of symbols—Tree, Fall, fire, darkness —it moves from the literal to the symbolic to the literal without any sense of strain. It has verbal intensity on every level, but it grows naturally out of the literal base of the tale. Language is condensed so that a great variety of meanings are implicit in the same phrases. And Golding's conscious myth-striving achieves specificity precisely because of this tight condensation.

The Inheritors, I think, finally arrives at a mythopœic perspective in which a fable of the fall approaches a 'myth of total explanation'. The abstract motion upwards of the New People and the motion downwards of the Neanderthals mirror another cosmic rhythm, that of birth and death. One episode beautifully realizes this; it functions as a kind of epiphany of the mythopœic perspective. At the death of Mal we see, in the burial ground, the evidence of all ages. Digging, the group comes across skulls and bones which have faded beyond their emotional interest. Liku plays with skulls at the side of the grave; Mal's body is folded in a foetal position and he returns to his home. Oa takes him into her belly. The new one, playing at the side of the grave, extracts 'itself arse backwards from the hole' (88). The skull is as much a plaything as the root-shaped toy which resembles Oa—life and death are brought to the point at which each outstares infinity. Appropriately, at the end, Lok draws himself quietly back into Oa's belly. 'It [Lok] made no noise, but seemed to be growing into the earth, drawing the soft flesh of its body into a contact so close that the movements of pulse and breathing were inhibited' (221). Such promise of wholeness is held out to the New People too. As they move to the 'new level' of 'experience and emotion', Tuami and the tribe laugh with a kind of fear as the new one extracts itself from Vivani's hood (surely this recalls Ha's fur where the new one earlier hid) 'arse upwards his little rump pushing against the nape of her neck' (233).

The solution that fear-haunted Tuami gropes towards shaping in ivory, at the fable's close, is in a sense manifested already in the reader's own experience throughout the story. For if structure is ideographic, so too is point of view. Judgment is kept at bay so that the reader can grasp with his whole imaginative self an unanalytical mystery—the drone of the Fall, the stink of honey, the ultimate cannibalism that even Fa turns dead eyes on. This reconciliation of opposites is often difficult to grasp, but clearly the difficulty is deliberate and instructive. Two sets of action are set before the reader without authorial interpretation. Events take place in the landscape and within the protagonist Lok's mind. We alternate between one and the other. Using Lok's eyes we see what he sees and more. Later events take place in the landscape and within the protagonist Tuami's mind. The real matter, then, is that which lies between Lok's perception and Tuami's perception: we can share the tidal waves of terror and pain, the two tidal waves that enter the two protagonists. As Golding told Kermode, 'we are like them [the Neanderthals] and as I am a propagandist for Neanderthal man it is—it can only work so far as *Homo sapiens* has a certain amount in common with Neanderthal Man.'

Egoistic communication and communal life are two of the alternatives which are dramatized here in *The Inheritors* as the tension between two different stages of human growth. In *Pincher Martin* and *Free Fall*, the opposition will become a fragmentation within a single human being. It is the tension of *Lord of the Flies* between those who think and talk yet fail, and those who act yet hunt, between Piggy and Jack. But in *The Inheritors* the tension is sustained in the structure of the fable. Its ideographic structure pictures both man's guilt-consciousness and his innocence. We share Lok's disconnected 'pictures' for most of the time and then see him from the outside as a grotesque red creature. The focus shifts to the newer tribe and the final objectification of Lok is meant to distance him from us at the same time as winning enormous sympathy for his dying. Later our sense of Tuami is similarly modified. The effect is to deliberately complicate the possibility of us choosing between the two communities: the sensuous innocence of the subhuman and the intellectual guilt of the human one so that the reader experiences the sense of loss and the sense of gain—both. By means of the ideographic structure, as well as point of view and symbolic episodes such as the confrontation scene the reader encounters dark and light, moving beyond simple experience/guilt or simple innocence/love to an idea of the possibility of reconciliation of good and evil.

THE INHERITORS—NOTES

1 'Anyone who has read *The Inheritors* and wants to play literary detective', write Oldsey and Weintraub in their summary of parallels, 'can find plenty of clues in the drawings and figures reproduced on pages . . . of *The Outline*. Items: ivory and bone knife points—of the sort Tuami makes at the novel's close; a large horned animal—of the kind Tuami draws on the ground; an antlered stag head done on ivory—like the totemic device of Marlan's tribe; and a small rotund female figure ripened as though in pregnancy—resembling the Oa figure of Lok's tribe.' Oldsey and Weintraub, p. 50.

2 Golding in J. I. Biles, *Talk: Conversations with William Golding* (New York, 1970), p. 105.

3 M. R. A. Chance, 'The Nature and Special Features of the Instinctive Bond of Primates', *The Social Life of Early Man*, ed. S. L. Washburn (Chicago, 1961), pp. 29–32.

4 In addition, Golding's Other People would appear to have many of the

attributes which Henri V. Vallois describes the upper Paeleolithic
tribal society as possessing: sharp division of labour, articulated hunting
patterns, warfare, ceremonial and hunting rites, body ornamentation,
developed language, control of fire and water, ritual self-mutilation,
extensive use of bow and arrow and cave art with ochre. Vallois, 'The
Social Life of Early Man: The Evidence of Skeletons', in Washburn,
The Social Life of Early Man, p. 229.

5 Golding, *The Inheritors* (London: Faber and Faber, 1961), p. 43. All
subsequent quotations will be taken from this edition and be indicated
in textual parentheses.

6 James Gindin, 'Gimmick and Metaphor in the Novels of William
Golding', *Postwar British Fiction* (Berkeley, 1962), p. 199.

7 Gregor and Kinkead-Weekes, p. 67.

8 Marlan and Vivani have their literary origin in Tennyson's *Idylls*. Marlan,
the witchdoctor of the totemic cult of the Stag, brings to mind the
twelfth century Arthurian enchanter Merlin. Golding's enchanter is
forced to take a perilous journey to a devil-infested forest, Tuami tells
us at the end, because he is fleeing the wrath of another tribe from whom
he kidnapped Vivani. Like the wily Vivien in the *Idyll* who wins magic
from the ageing enchanter Merlin and uses the charm to leave him spell-
bound in a tangled tree, Vivani accompanies Marlan to the island.
Against his better judgment—for by now Marlan is losing credence
among the starved tribe—Marlan is beguiled by Vivani into capturing
two forest devils: Liku and the new one. The results are disastrous for
both species. At the novel's close Marlan lies stupified in the hollow hull
of an oak canoe, smaller and much weaker. Other names have special
significance. While the invaders bear names like Tanakil, Vakiti, and
Tuami that correspond to the species' linguistic complexity, the others—
Fa, Ha, Nil, and Mal—possess names whose simplicity accentuates the
People's intellectual primitiveness. Onomatopoeic shading also operates:
Liku, the small Neanderthal, is indeed 'like-you' and Tuami is one
'you-love'; it is the burden of the narrative to make these puns morally
pertinent.

9 *The Inheritors* dramatizes the evolution of totemic demonology, but
unlike *Lord of the Flies* where Simon's recognition of the 'beast' is technically contrived, in *The Inheritors* the ironic juxtaposition of similar
images viewed from the novel's two points of view makes the point
without authorial interruption. The textual passage describes Lok's
bewildered staring at Tuami's drawing: it is a totemic image of the
Neanderthals as *homo sapiens* sees them. Lok does not, of course,
recognize himself in the fierce red figure; it is merely 'some kind of
man'. In a later passage the novel's real 'beast' is portrayed. Tuami (for
point of view has now switched to that of the New People) stares
fixedly at Marlan who lies sprawled asleep in the canoe. 'The sun was
blazing on the red sail and Marlan was red. His arms and legs were
contracted, his hair stood out and his beard, his teeth were wolf's teeth
and his eyes like blind stones' (229). The figure is a mirror image of the

totemic beast Tuami has drawn. Thus when Tuami attributes devilish qualities to the Neanderthals he is really, like the boys' creation of the 'beast', commenting on his own moral evasion.

10 This term is significant; at one point Lok says 'People understand each other' (72) indicating, in Golding's view, the essential understanding between men, necessary for moral life. *Free Fall*, for example, concludes with the riddle 'the Herr Doctor does not understand Peoples.'

11 The total submission here to Lok-other, a subjection of selfhood—if the term indeed can be employed when discussing such a prerational mentality—is strongly reminiscent of Simon's faint before the Head where the 'darkness' or the knowledge of the destructive principle is simultaneously a losing of personality and a capturing of the Other. Simon becomes the Head, as later in *Free Fall* Sammy, by encountering the darkness of the cell, becomes Sammy-Other, thus breaking open the prison of self-hood. In several of the essays a similar fierce brooding on the unknown—Leonides before the pass, a phantom Roman family crouched over their murdered grandmother—results in an imaginative, but no less true, assimilation into personal awareness of the unknown. Thus Golding reports himself penetrating the temporal and historical and phenomenal boundaries to identify himself with a prehistoric corpse in the Wiltshire downs: 'There is a sense in which I share the guilt buried beneath the runway, a sense in which my imagination has locked me to them.' 'Digging for Pictures', p. 70.

12 An alternate but highly articulate system of metaphors introduce a new phase in the evolution of species. Water begins to be described as 'flaming' as the fire of the hearth disappears. The old woman's bright eyes connect no more with the numinous. The last scene shows a water, bloody with the sun's reflection and the combined murders, and a glaring red totemic devil; glittering mountains are welcoming the sun, a sun that ends this ice age, a second fire that eats up the Neanderthal landscape.

PINCHER MARTIN

I

. . . the sea appeals to the English on at least two levels. It attracts the adventurous practical men who make a career out of it until the sea becomes known and ordinary. But it also attracts the other pole of our character, the visionaries, the rebels, the misfits who are seldom conscious of their own nature. It is these . . . who have a grudge or an ideal.

—Golding, 'Our Way of Life'
(unpublished BBC talk)

Much more markedly than *The Inheritors*, *Pincher Martin* reveals Golding's personal conception of contemporary man's consciousness and the condition of his Being. In this fable, Golding treats a more explicitly theological subject than in *Lord of the Flies*. Unlike *Free Fall* where religious claims are secularized so that the reader can choose between spiritual and material explanations, *Pincher Martin* offers a detailed programme of the necessity for religious belief. Unlike *The Spire*'s this religious truth is stated by a calculated distortion since some sorts of truths have to be stated by negation or distortion. As Golding himself commented to me: '*Pincher Martin is based on not merely a psychological impossibility but a theological one too.*' It is about a dead body and an indestructible consciousness; yet the protagonist's particular history of guilt and greed is intended to stand as a fable for contemporary man.

Nevertheless, the line from this fable to Golding's other works, even minor ones like a short story, 'The Anglo Saxon'[1] is a direct and important one. His own familiarity with the

sea, his own intimations of dread at sea, even his own childhood nightmares, have been transmuted and transmitted into a
contemporary Promethean fable about the nature of man.
Ironic universality is achieved by identifying the protagonist
with figures from literature and myth: thus Pincher is associated
with Lear and Hamlet; Scandinavian culture enters through
Thor's lightning; Greek through allusion to Ajax; and Roman
through allusions to the Claudian well. The fable can also be
seen as a grim parody of *Prometheus Bound*, as well as a parody of
Robinson Crusoe. Possibly even an evolutionary context is
involved in Pincher's evolution from the sea; his emergence
on the rock is like the emergence from the birth canal. But the
fable's focus is a bleak and radically delimited one, for it
studies a man alone on a rock in mid-Atlantic.

The tale is much slighter in terms of dramatic action than
even *The Inheritors*. It concerns a naval officer, Christopher
Hadley Martin, who is blown off the bridge of a destroyer
during World War II and his struggle with the Zeus of his own
universe: the natural stupidity of water, the indifference of
rock and sky and sun and rain. Thus for the first time Golding
fashions a protagonist who is an individual character, his stamp
and identity economically suggested by his nickname: Pincher.
It is a clever emblematic invention as all Martins in the British
Navy are called Pincher, just as all Clarks are nicknamed
Nobby. And the course of the novel consists in the illumination
of this Pincher's thieving and cosmic greed.

We first encounter the protagonist flaying about in a black
sea. Our primary imaginative experience is of the physical
stuff as experienced by a man immersed in water; he struggles
to inflate a lifebelt, trying to keep the salt sea from his screaming mouth and stay afloat. Almost immediately he is dashed
against a barren rock:[2] 'A single point of rock, peak of a
mountain range, one tooth set in the ancient jaw of a sunken
world, projecting through the inconceivable vastness of the
whole [Atlantic] ocean.'[3] At enormous pain and with enormous
difficulty he crawls up this rock using limpets as climbing

pegs; the water beats against him washing him back mercilessly but with a final titanic thrust he pulls his body into a rocky trench:

> The man was inside two crevices. There was first the rock, closed and not warm but at least not cold with the coldness of sea or air . . . his body was a second and interior crevice which he inhabited. Under each knee, then, there was a little fire. . . . But the man was intelligent. He endured these fires although they gave not heat but pain (48).

For seven consecutive days Pincher struggles to survive; struggles to maintain his sanity and health; struggles to tame the barren rock. He reasons to himself: 'I am busy surviving. I am netting down this rock with names. . . . If this rock tries to adapt me to its ways I will refuse and adapt it to mine. I will impose my routine on it' (86–87). First, he raises a pillar of stone in hopes that this will be seen by possible rescue flights; this he calls Dwarf. He proceeds to civilize the landscape; a prominent ledge he calls Lookout, a lower ledge, Safety Rock; where he finds mussels to eat he calls Food Cliff; other points in the map he names Piccadilly, Leicester Square, and Oxford Circus. A good British sailor, he even provides himself a pub, the Red Lion.

But panic and fatigue overcome him intermittently. Interrupting his effort at survival, memories from the past torment him and invade his consciousness, pestering him with some message that he cannot or will not grasp. 'But the centre of the globe was moving and flinching from isolated outcrops of knowledge. It averted attention from one only to discover another' (173). As the narrative proceeds what appears to be the heroic aspect of Pincher's endurance becomes increasingly modified by what we learn about his past life. Memory flashbacks reveal episodes in the life of what could only be an arrogant and profoundly greedy man. Pincher is a pincher, a robber, a thief for he eats everything he can lay his hands on; he was 'born with his mouth and his flies open and both hands out to grab' (120), as a rival actor says of him.

In fact, the memory flashbacks depict him as just such a grasping devourer: he maims a friend to avoid losing a motor cycle race; he steals another man's woman and invites the former to watch her in his own bed; he tries unsuccessfully to seduce a woman called Mary whom, incidently, he loves despite himself. As an actor in civilian life, Chris Martin also manoeuvred for success and this willed domination and greedy assertion is what all his adult life has expressed. The only value in the world is his own personality; that which does not serve him, he tries to dominate. Moments before his submersion in the sea his true criminality appeared. Aboard the *Wildebeeste*, he decides to effect the drowning of a generous friend whom he has not earlier been able to control by having the ship turn suddenly. The irony of the matter is that the order, 'Hard a-starboard' (186) is the right order, for at exactly that moment *Wildebeeste* is torpedoed; the suggestion is that Pincher is perhaps the only victim of the sea, for the rest of the crew may have survived.

On the rock Pincher can gradually solidify his identity. He reassures himself of his own precise existence with a faded identity disc, using the photograph to give back his own image as in civilian life he uses mirrors. When he cries triumphantly, 'Christopher Hadley Martin. Martin. Chris I am what I always was!' (76), the rock diminishes from an island to a thing, a simple, meaningless mechanism. But as strong as Martin's conscious determination is, he cannot maintain life alone on the island; his own ego is not sufficient to overwhelm the rock, and the globe begins to be invaded by imagined horrors. Memory and hallucination merge.

The narrative, then, shows Pincher gradually dissolving again into fragments: a rational mind, itself divorced from its knowing centre, and around all a pain-wracked body. The 'pictures' or memory flashbacks become more insistent. At a crucial moment he relives a childhood experience where he dared or imagined he dared to descend steps into a cellar at night, there to encounter the feet and knees of some appalling god-like effigy. This childhood terror fuses with a more awesome hallucination. The Dwarf becomes the cellar-god. A confrontation scene occurs, then, between the seemingly mad Pincher and some kind of godhead with 'immovable, black feet' (196). Just as Simon hears the Head speak to him, Pincher hears this god say, 'Have you had enough, Christopher?'—they are, by the way, the first true lines of direct speech in the narrative so far. But Pincher resists what he takes to be a nightmare or an hallucination, yelling demonically, 'I shit on your heaven' (200). A storm begins to overwhelm the sailor who still resists. At the end of the tale, Chapter XI, we still do not know whether he is alive or dead.

But though the story of survival on the rock has finished, the narrative is not yet complete, for like *The Inheritors*, *Pincher Martin* has an ideographic structure. The last Chapter, XII, offers a coda ending to *Pincher Martin* and as in *The Inheritors*, there is a change in perspective. We find ourselves on a remote island in the Hebrides where two men are talking; a body has been washed ashore. Having lived beside the rotting corpse for a week while awaiting the official who will record its identity, Campbell, a crofter, sadly asks: 'Would you say there was any—surviving? Or is that all?' (208). Davidson instantly replies that Martin (for the corpse bears Pincher's identity disc) could not have suffered, if that is what Campbell is wondering, since 'he [Martin] didn't even have time to kick off his seaboots' (208). The central point is that this story is about a dead man. In the first chapter, Pincher kicks off his seaboots to avoid drowning and later tears apart his already inflated lifebelt to give himself a Wagnerian enema; on the last page it is made clear that Pincher was drowned after he had inflated the lifebelt[4] but before he had time to kick off his boots. The fable then is the report of some after-death hallucination; its events are taking place in the mind of a dead man.

Clearly, *Pincher Martin* is the most vigorously experimental of all Golding's fables. A number of critics think it formally and intellectually the most impressive as well; over the last few years the novel has become the newest ground for critical crossfire as the title of a 1968 *Commonweal* article, 'The Return of *Pincher Martin*', certainly indicates. However, its initial reception was a good deal less happy. While it was often called a *tour de force*, reviewers were generally unspecific and cautious in their comments. The familiar source-hunting occurred again. Thus the technical device in the novel of having memories sweep through a drowning man was thought to have its origins in Ambrose Bierce's *An Occurrence at Owl Creek*. Oldsey and Weintraub examine the possible parallels, chief of which is that both protagonists sustain their illusory life when drowning. But Golding has declared emphatically that it was not his intention to explore the legend about seeing one's whole past in the moment of death—Pincher was drowned on page two of the tale. Other sources have been suggested, among them R. M. Ballantyne's *Coral Island* and Ernest Hemingway's *The Snows of Kilimanjaro*, but one critic has rather cleverly worked out the scenario of the possible inversion of another early popular novel. Ian Blake claims that *Pincher Martin* is a reworking of Taffrail's 1916 survival tale, *Pincher Martin, OD*.[5] Taffrail's Pincher is torpedoed as is Golding's character; flung into the sea he remembers his seaboots and as he removes one, death comes. Not only is he obedient to his fate—one he automatically assumes is predetermined by his 'Maker'—but Taffrail's Martin experiences 'a feeling of relief' that 'the struggle' in the sea is 'hopeless'. Taffrail writes: 'Pincher Martin committed his soul to his Maker . . . [as] the most trivial events and the most important happenings of his short life crowded before him onto his overwrought brain. . . .' The situation is identical, then, but the responses of the two

Pinchers are directly contrary. There is a similar inversion at
the end. In Taffrail's story, Martin is rescued by a fisherman;
in the hackneyed phrase of Taffrail—'from the very jaws of
death Pincher Martin stepped ashore.' In Golding's version,
another sort of Fisherman tries to bring about another sort of
survival, but there is none. For a while a teacup controversy
was waged in the *TLS* regarding the credibility and veracity of
this source, but while the textual evidence would seem rather
strong that some deliberate inversion occurred Golding himself has insisted that he 'got nothing from it but the name.'
He does admit—in the published transcription of conversations
taped in 1965—to having at least read the novel, though neither
he nor his interviewer, Jack Biles, appear to know its author.

Over the years, the most persistent dissatisfaction has been,
of course, with the abruptness and astonishing revelation that
the coda imparts. Generally readers considered it a gratuitous
puzzle which trivialized a triumphant work. Recently, however, commentators have started to consider the coda's
contribution to the theme of death which the novel explores.
Howard Babb's book, for example, makes the interesting
point that symbolically Davidson could represent Death;
Campbell then is left in the position of all of us, confronted
with the profound question of survival. Gregor and Kinkead-
Weekes's analysis, on the other hand, converts Campbell's
question about suffering into the larger question about
eternity itself: 'How do we tell the truth about death? No
matter what any of us believes officially about surviving, in
our minds there obstinately lurks the opposite spectre.'[6]
Noting that the first American title for *Pincher Martin* was *The
Two Deaths of Christopher Martin*, Samuel Hynes' pamphlet
declares that 'the physical death is passed over; there are
kinds of dying that are more important than that instant of
merely physiological change.' For him it is 'the paradoxes of
living death and dying into life that [ultimately] inform the
novel.' But he agrees with most critics that *Pincher Martin* is a
most difficult fable,[7] a view I share.

It seems to me obvious that the struggle on the rock is meant to be a physically dead man's hallucination. What I have difficulty in accepting is this point: that the struggle is hallucinatory makes it no less real, in Golding's view, but rather more real. Martin's hallucination—his 'present' struggle—is intended, first, as a recapitulation of his 'past' career on earth. Secondly, the 'present' resistance to death is intended as an eschatalogical prognosis about Pincher's future career in eternity. Golding himself has said: 'Just to be Pincher is Purgatory; to be Pincher for eternity is Hell.' Thus, in *Pincher Martin* Golding is exploring imaginatively the moment of Purgatory—a moment which contains the present, the past, and the future—in order to make a simple fabulist's point about the 'ordinary universe which on the whole I believe likely to be the right one.' And Golding adds, to this end 'I went out of my way to damn Pincher as much as I could.'

Pincher Martin, then, is a fable which allocates Golding's perennial religious theme—the necessity of vision as a preliminary step to salvation—in a purgatorial moment. The story is intended as only an analogue for the real world because in itself it is both a 'psychological impossibility' and a 'theological one'.[8] Pincher's inability to achieve salvation, therefore, is to be read as an excessive warning on contemporary man's inability to achieve any kind of spiritual vision. As was the case in *The Inheritors*, *Pincher Martin* uses an ideographic structure to make its religious comment; contradictory perspectives are turned on the one circumstance of the shipwrecked sailor. First, we have Martin's view of his own horrendous plight; then, in the coda, we have Davidson's and Campbell's view of it. In their implications, these differ. We are moved from the fevered world of Pincher's mind to the apparently objective and sane conversation about the 'lean-to' (208). Here, the naval officer interprets survival as a question about physical suffering while the crofter's bewilderment suggests that, in his view at least, there might be some spiritual dimension to it. He makes the point, significantly, that Davidson does not know about his 'official beliefs' (208).

The perspectives of the rock-narrative and the coda are not intended to contradict each other. By evidence of the seaboots, the sailor is certainly not 'physically' alive on Rockall during seven days of diminishing strength. Most certainly he is not just a corpse either. He most certainly suffered and—according to the fable's theology—this suffering will now continue eternally. It is continuing in some dimension as the crofter and officer brood over the corpse. The reader builds the bridge between the contradictory views and discovers, by imaginative extension, that man is both more than Davidson's literalism would decide yet less than Pincher's monumental endurance would seem to indicate. This process of understanding takes place outside the fable proper when we snap the several 'official' views across each other, assembling all the views, to arrive at something approaching an eschatologically inclusive perspective in which the 'sad harvest' Mr. Campbell alludes to sadly, gently, and brokenly becomes significant.

II

The stars spin ever in the sky
The moon leaps up again and again
And ceaselessly the seasons fall
Over the rock like steady rain.

The winds fight by the clouds and turn
And turn about, the Night and Day
Are tiny blows of the hammer of time
Wearing the ancient rock away.

Only once in a thousand years,
From hanging cliffs and desolate streams
A crag falls into the moving sea
And a sea-bird screams.

—Golding, 'The Lonely Isle'

Pincher Martin is a report of a soul in Purgatory, not the tale of
a shipwrecked sailor on a solitary rock. Golding told me he
intends it as a vast illustration of one complex law: 'where
there is no vision the people perish.' In the after-death
hallucination, Pincher himself creates the rock out of the
memory of an aching and now missing tooth, and gropes to
control what is in fact an illusion of his mind. As the children
in terror of themselves formulate the Beast, as the New People
make the Neanderthals into hairy demons, so Pincher out of
fear of death creates a demonic Adversary: the sea, the rock,
the sky, even a dreadful Theophany. The 'real', viz., natural-
istic story is effectively recounted in Chapter I: the protagonist's immersion, the few flickering impressions he has as
the gun's tracer explodes and 'green sparks flew out from the
centre' (7), the water thrusting in '*without* mercy' (7, italics
added), and the moment of his death. 'The green tracer that
flew from the centre began to spin into a disc. The throat at
such a distance from the snarling man vomited water . . . [but]
the hard lumps of water no longer hurt. There was no face but
there was a snarl' (8).[9] The last chapter confirms the death: a
body is picked up, two men discuss the 'sad harvest' (208),
and Davidson, the literalist, says there was little pain because
Pincher's seaboots were still on. Now, on the rock Pincher
keeps imagining his feet hurt and are cold because he has got
rid of these boots, yet he is also continually haunted by the
enormous black-booted feet of the gods.[10]

The whole experience on the rock is Pincher's post-mortem
experience of himself; the survival tale is concerned with his
life in Purgatory and his reluctance to surrender to his destiny.
Because the reader, even before the coda's reversal, has a
peculiar access to Pincher's consciousness while on the rock,
he can work with the hints that Pincher keeps turning away
from. Thus, every time Pincher comes close to realizing his
death he turns away—at one point he leaves a sentence
unfinished: 'Strange that bristles go on growing even when
the rest of you is—' (125), and the reader supplies the

conclusion 'dead'. Similarly, he repeatedly flinches from calling the trailing rocks, 'the Teeth' (91) since again 'to lie on a row of teeth in the middle of the sea—' (91) is to be 'dead'. On another occasion he mutters 'the process is so slow it has no relevance to—' (78). Again the reader supplies 'death'. Indeed, evidence for his death is unmistakably present in certain repeated motifs, particularly those involving guano, his lobster/hands, the rock/teeth, as well as certain reiterated symbols including a maggot-box and a curious experimental tool.

The technique is similar to that deliberate obscuration in *The Inheritors*. In that fable the reader had to make intelligible Neanderthal perceptions; here the reader is even further limited, in this case through distortion. Within the tormented hero, consciousness shrinks and expands; his senses report and distort, his memory intermittently corrupts. Until the coda we are never fully outside of him; we stare through the windows of his eyes, 'curtains of hair and flesh' (161). Towards the end of the survival narrative delirium invades Pincher's consciousness and crushes his identity; the reader suffers the distortion. But at a special vantage point.

As was the case in *The Inheritors* when the reader peered down with Lok at the Bacchanals but recognized himself in the figures in the clearing, so in *Pincher Martin* we are both inside and outside the consciousness of the protagonist. We experience the classic battle of man against the elements and acknowledge Promethean nobility while we simultaneously know at another level that the Promethean energy is cosmically irrelevant. Like the structure, point of view is so handled in this novel that the reader discovers—first with growing dismay during the survival tale and then with conviction in the coda—that Pincher's predicament is illusory and self-induced.

It is not Pincher's ability to survive that is being tested but his belief that will and intelligence by themselves define the value of the human species. After all the elementary achievements of building a shelter, designing a watertrough, and using his one weapon, a knife, to get his food and drink, after all that these represent of the expenditure of will and the strenuous assertion of mind, there is not enough evidence to support Martin's conviction of the uniqueness and superiority of his individuality which, given his lack of faith in any other value, he is compelled to assert throughout.

The tale on the rock, this story within a story, is a 'religious' one; this fable is a good deal more theological than the other works. It is a 'fairly objective exercise in finding out what happens to Greed when all things that surround it and give it its food are taken away and it has nothing to prey on but itself.'[11]

> . . . to achieve salvation, the *persona* must be destroyed. But suppose the man is nothing but greed? His original spirit, God-given the *Scintillans Dei*, is hopelessly obscured by his thirst for separate individual life. What can he do but refuse to be destroyed.[12]

The ultimate perspective, however, is apocalyptic, for the 'exact programme' which Golding mentions to Kermode is one that involves all-time. Pincher's experience on the rock, his ostensible 'present' exactly parallels the pattern of his past life: memory flashbacks keep cutting across the 'present' and at certain points the 'past' is gripped in the 'present'. Similarly his 'future' pricks at his consciousness. Nathaniel Walterson is a creature of the past, but his spiritual lectures when recalled insinuate the very future that possesses Pincher/ Christopher, his 'dying into heaven' (71). The hands which Pincher mistakes for red (therefore illusory) lobsters are the fists that grabbed 'the penny and someone else's bun' (120); they are also the claws that the black lightning of the storm pries and picks and plays with infinitely. Thus they are emblematic of Pincher's nature, in the past, in the present, in the future. They represent symbolically the rapacious nature which the black lightning plays over, pricks at, 'prying for a weakness, wearing them away in a compassion that was *timeless* and *without mercy*' (201, italics added).[13] In the past, in the present, in the future, for all time, Pincher has been greedy. All the paths of the fable lead back to his 'centre', the *ding en sich*, the irreducible Being that constitutes this man's nature. And as Lok is reduced to perception, the 'inside-Lok'; as Jack is reduced to savagery, the 'furtive thing'; as Sammy Mountjoy is reduced to irrational terror, the 'frantic thing'; so Martin is reduced to the abstraction Greed, the two claws. Yet at this point, there is still some option, a terrible one: 'The terrible option is up to him', Golding insisted, 'choice between Purgatory and Hell.'

The survival narrative of the rock begins and ends the moment of physical death. Past, present, and future all are tied into an image of all-time (or no-time). Golding intends to show, here, that time is not a sequence but a simultaneity with past, present, and future existing at the same instant, and it is this paradoxical invention that gives the fable its subject and its form. In the remainder of this chapter I will look at the 'action' on the rock in terms of three distinct temporal strands or time-modes. Then I can examine the techniques by which these modes are created: the first, time-present in Section III; the second, time-past, in Section IV; the third, time-future, in Section V. Finally, I will argue in Section VI that all three strands are visible in individual episodes where the supposedly real situation on the rock is mixed with memories of the past and fears of the future. Christopher Hadley Martin's life can be viewed in other words from three distinct temporal angles; each angle possesses an appropriate narrative technique and operates from a separate temporal perspective. In the 'present', the tale of Pincher's survival and extinction on the rock is an image of Promethean man patterning into civilized shapes a hostile Nature. Here an identity gradually evolves and is destroyed by brute Nature as a storm overcomes the fever-ridden body. The novel presents here one possible definition of Man, based on his wholly physical solitude: he is a creature caught between the two forces of consciousness and of a mute unconscious environment. As Pincher mutters, man 'is a freak, an ejected foetus robbed of his natural development, thrown out in the world with a naked covering of parchment, with too little room for his teeth and a soft bulging skull like a bubble. But nature stirs a pudding there . . .' (190). We experience Pincher's 'present' as an accumulation of these physical details, giving the predicament of a man alone on an island. There is the expectation that his situation will change.

Running beside the survival tale is the 'morality play'; Pincher, says Golding, 'isn't [just] a man, really; he is Greed. That's why he's called Pincher. It's a straightforward morality play.' From the second temporal perspective we have another view of Chris Hadley Martin, a particular man, from his past actions. As Pincher lapses in and out of consciousness, 'pictures' in the form of flashbacks disturb and impinge upon him. The pattern of their impingement appears to be random and Pincher can no more connect them than he can note the intellectual discrepancies in his fantastical world. As he had to do in the first part of The Inheritors the reader must himself connect the stills and the quality of the reader's attention will decide the density of his conception of Chris Hadley Martin as a twentieth-century actor. Pincher is what he was; just as he crawled up the rock-face using the limpets, so he crawled over people's face to get where he wanted to go. This point, for example, is nicely made in one of Pincher's hallucinatory flashbacks where he relives a childhood dream/escape from a dark monster by rushing up some stairs. The stairs metamorphose into trodden faces: 'They appeared to be made of some chalky material for when he put his weight on them they would break away so that only by constant movement upward was he able to keep up at all' (145). As (he imagines) he ascends, he screams: 'I am! I am! I am!'

There is a third temporal perspective in which the eschatological reality of Christopher subsists in a 'future' that is

Purgatory or Hell. The rock is a remembered missing tooth, the black lightning the bolts of the godhead, the witch he later imagines the Fisherman King that Christopher-turned-Pincher has made into an image of himself. The technique here is perhaps the most complex of the three. Flashback and stream-of-consciousness merge. Once again the reader sews together significance, detecting that the 'window' (163) through which Pincher gazes at his world is not so much an impaired eye as it might be in the 'present' as a telescope into a different world 'where the invisible is visible'. At this level, it seems to me, much that the author intended to be rendered by narrative details has remained obscure; one must depend on the author's numerous explanatory 'lifelines'.

III

'PRESENT'

We experience the Purgatorial moment at first as an accumulation of physical details, but detail as experienced by a man in a state of fragmentation. From the perspective of the 'present' a man in a state of physical exhaustion lies squinting through a damaged eye at an alien shape, inches from his eyeball. 'He came upon the mouldering bones of fish and a dead gull, its upturned breast-bone like the keel of a derelict boat. He found patches of grey and yellow lichen, traces even of earth, a button of moss' (59). The landscape seems profoundly dislocated and unfamiliar; further, we are intended to grope through general words like 'window', 'wall', and 'centre' to the confusion that Pincher himself feels; thus, it is 'the centre' which knows that 'Christopher and Hadley and Martin were fragments far off' (162) while 'a curtain of hair and flesh' obscures the rock and the sea. Several passages in *Pincher Martin*, in fact, seem condensed statements of Golding's theory of human consciousness which I examined in the 'Introduction'; its relevance will be explored here. Golding's

view involves the radical dislocation of body and soul, matter
and spirit, sensation and perception since Pincher appears, in
the 'present', to be a private individual shut inside his
cranium and beaten by sensations from outside. Consequently,
he is depicted as suffering overt reality as a physical event, an
event either seriously dislocated from the pattern-making
consciousness or hopelessly twisted and jumbled, glimpsed in
detail only through the inward weather of the inner-skull.
On the rock, Pincher sustains a triple alienation, first between
his own consciousness and the world; then between his
consciousness and thought. Thoughts form like pieces of
'sculpture' behind his eyes but 'in front of the unexamined
centre' (162). Finally, there is the separation between thought
and language. Pincher's gropings towards some mode of
rational perception imply, then, something more severely
disturbed than Lok's stumblings through 'pictures'.

After his ascent up the rock it is first physical pain, 'a deep
communion with the solidity' (25) of the crevice which
brings Pincher back to a single unit. Pain organizes into
physical unity, but not conscious awareness. Then like an
animal, consciousness must poke around meaningless impressions; at an enormous effort which approximates physical
action, it must dispense with some fragments to discover the
few significant ones: 'among the shape-sounds and disregarded
feeling . . . *it* was looking for a thought. . . . *It* found the
thought, separated it from the junk, lifted it and used the
apparatus of the body to give it force and importance' (32,
italics added). 'A valuable thought' for Pincher is one that
'gives him back his personality' (27); when Pincher can say,
'I am what I always was' (76), he stops being isolated 'inside
of the globe of his head' and extends normally through his
limbs. He begins to live 'on the surface of his eyes' (76), not
behind windows and shades. The rock becomes a coherent
object: it diminishes, in his phrase, from 'an island to a thing'
(77). Thus Pincher makes the island rationally coherent and,
in his terms, civilized: 'I am busy surviving,' he intones, 'I am

netting down this rock with names and taming it. . . . What is given a name is given a seal, a chain. If this rock tries to adapt me to its ways I will refuse and adapt it to mine . . .' (86). And the ultimate truth of things is physical rock: wetness, hardness, and movement, 'with no mercy but no intelligence either' (115). Pincher believes like the New People in *The Inheritors* that he can survive by his linguistic appropriation of the world. Reduced to a thing, this island is no threat to his carefully 'hoarded and enjoyed personality' (91).

Central, then, to Martin's situation is the dislocation of mind and body, a dislocation which he admits exists—'I was always two things, mind and body. Nothing has altered' (176)—while at the same time resisting the implications of such a division, for to acknowledge those would be to admit some truth about his own body's state. A 'silent indisputable creature' sits at the innermost centre of Pincher, looking out from his 'dark skull' into the 'inscrutable darkness' of the rock landscape. It stares through the window. At other times, his consciousness is described in metaphors appropriate to a creature immersed in water; the irony is intentional, of course: Golding writes, 'it floated in the middle of this globe like a waterlogged body.' The consciousness is balanced between two pressures in the manner of the ingenious doll of the memory flashback, a symbol which I will examine later in the chapter. It is sufficient here to see that the ineradicable 'isness' of Pincher is suspended in his physical body and the suggestion one draws from comments about Nat is that every man contains such an observational point. Nat's centre is disconnected from his body as well; we learn that at the binnacle of the ship Nat rests inside 'attached by accident to life with all its touches, tastes, sights and sounds . . . at a distance from him' (51). Pincher decides that Nat's mind inside 'prayed and waited to meet his aeons' (51).

When in pain, Pincher strives for 'some particular mode of *inactive* being' (49, italics added), the kind of interior balance (ironically like Nat's) that will allow him to 'float' inside 'the bone globe of the world' (48) and his own 'globe' or cranium. He strives for just that suspension between pain and passivity, consciousness and nothingness, that will neither eject him back into the world of the fever-fire nor thrust him away from his 'hoarded personality'. Of course, it is the 'interior balance' or inactive mode that a waterlogged body would possess. We can easily note the deliberate micro- and macro-cosmic correspondences in the following passage which describes Pincher's effort as he tries to sleep:

> He became small, and the globe larger until the burning extensions were interplanetary. But this universe was subject to convulsions that began in deep space and came like a wave. Then he was large again, filling every corner . . . and the needle jabbed through the corner of his right eye straight into the darkness of his head. Dimly he would see one white hand while the pain stabbed. Then slowly he would sink back into the centre of the globe, shrink and float in the middle of a dark world. This became a rhythm that had obtained from all ages and would endure so. (49–50)

This describes the delirium of bruised fever-ridden flesh which trembles involuntarily; the sense of the delirium is conveyed by the inanimate metaphors of 'globe'; limbs which extend and then contract; a body so engaged in its pain that it seems a universe subject to arbitrary motions of nature. At the same time as rendering a feverish state, the passage is a fine description of a waterlogged body; the convulsions which begin in deep space wash through the globe with a rhythm 'that had obtained from all ages and would endure' like the relentless 'minute rise and fall of the sea' which Ralph in *Lord of the Flies* stares at numbly. As in other passages, for example those involving the Dwarf, the reader can operate in the simply physical world as Pincher tries to or detect that this physical world is no more than the mind's extension of its own spirit.

Of course, Pincher cannot admit this. Yet his centre is restless and active, seldom passive. Like Sammy's point of awareness in the dark cell, the activity of Pincher's centre necessarily leads him to one sort of horror or another. This is the essential point Golding makes about human intelligence. Gradually the centre by itself forces itself to encounter its knowledge of death. The mouth 'quacks' on meaning and lectures ease but the 'centre was moving and flinching from isolated outcrops of knowledge' (173). Pincher dodges the knowledge but then is forced back again, haunted by something he makes into a Hag, haunted in fact, by all the rational answers the intelligence provides. Each step towards intelligent acquisition on the rock makes him remember his true state. For example, while he is cutting seaweed for an SOS signal he comes to see the island/thing is somehow evasively familiar: 'He looked solemnly at the line of rocks and found himself thinking of them as teeth . . . they were emerging gradually from the jaw—but that was not the truth. They were sinking; or rather they were being worn away in infinite slow motion. . . . A lifetime of the world had blunted them, was reducing them as they ground what food rocks eat' (78). At other times, through his memory float nagging elusive pictures of eating, Chinese boxes, death again as he associates the maggot-box with a coffin. When he decides he will call the Rocks, the Teeth, he is suddenly terrified and must run from the incipient knowledge that 'to lie on a row of teeth in the middle of the sea' (91) is to be dead. Understanding makes Pincher confront himself and that is to confront the fact of his death. At every stage, even in the sanctuary of madness, an intelligent action brings him back to reality.

Nor can he sleep; he realizes with horror that he is afraid to sleep, for sleep is a 'consenting to die' in which the centre may slip into unconscious bleakness. At one point towards the end Pincher (recalling Ralph and Simon in different circumstances) 'falls into a gap of darkness' (67). 'It was a gap of not-being, a well opening out of the world' (168). Coming back

to consciousness the centre knows that 'something' (169) has
started to emerge, a pattern that he does not want to obey, 'a
pattern now crossed by the gritted mark of teeth' (169), a
pattern of another sort than he can control, over which his
intelligence cannot dominate. Suddenly Pincher recalls a
childhood dream of something coming out of a cellar corner
and 'squeezing tormenting darkness, smoke thick' (138) into
which he descends 'three stories defenceless, down the dark
stairs . . . down the terrible steps to where the coffin ends
were crushed in walls of the cellar—and I'd be held helpless
on the stone floor, trying to run back, run away, climb up'
(138). In the 'night world' there are gods sitting behind the
'terrible knees and feet of black stone' (145). As in the autobiographical essay, 'The Ladder and the Tree', this is the
cellar of boyhood memory whose wall touched a spooky
graveyard and the stairs are the tree to which the same boy
escaped. But though it is a 'night world' where terror might
mysteriously heal and renew, for Pincher it is just terror
without joy.

> Out of bed on the carpet with no shoes. Creep through
> the dark room not because you want to but because
> you've got to. . . . No safety behind me. Round the
> corner now to the stairs. Down pad. Down pad. The hall,
> but grown. Darkness sitting in every corner . . . every-
> thing different, a pattern emerging, forced to go down to
> meet the thing I turned my back on. . . . Past the kitchen
> door. Drawn back the bolt of the vault. Well of darkness.
> Down pad, down. Coffin ends crushed in the wall.
> Under the churchyard back through the death door to
> meet *the master*. (178, italics added.)

'The master' from whom the child tries to escape is 'an
unknown looming' (178), 'the heart and being of all imagin-
able terror'. More than any other passage in the fable, this one
depends for its meaning on the very impact it produces

since here the reader has no point of view outside of the protagonist. The ambiguous 'night world' is created by, first, unspecific terms such as 'pattern', 'the thing', and then the apparently specific house where the descent occurs. Then there is the rhythmic repetition of 'down pad' as the reluctant child/man, victimized by an urgency he does not understand, creeps down past the paraphernalia of ghost tales—coffins, vaults, churchyards. Like Lok's view of the other in *The Inheritors*, the encounter here operates in silence so that the unlocking of the bolt seems to resound in the black emptiness before the death door and 'the master'. The atavistic encounter is, Golding suggests tentatively, 'a pattern repeated from the beginning of time' (179), the approach of an 'unknown thing' from which the dark centre turns away. The pattern is the thing that created it and from which it struggled to escape. Golding sees this 'unknown thing' as a god though he does not employ the term in *Pincher Martin*. As he explains warily: 'The cellar in *Pincher Martin* represents more than childhood terrors; a whole philosophy in fact—suggesting that God is the thing we turn away from into life, and therefore we hate and fear him and make a darkness there.'[14] In *Free Fall* the archetype is much less explicit than in *Pincher Martin* though no less central to the narrative. But the conflict between the remembered cellar and the centre is in miniature the conflict of the entire book. And the cellar with its opaque centre, then, is a microcosmic image of Pincher's own moral life.

IV

'PAST'

To fully understand the meaning of the cellar we must turn to Pincher's past. The Purgatorial 'present' contains 'the past' for as he is busy netting down the rock, the past strikes across Pincher's efforts with intermittent clarity; increasingly 'the past' becomes associated and intermingled with 'the present'.

In the moments when he is conscious, Pincher's centre is plagued not only with the truth of his condition but also with memories: fragmentary snapshots, inclusive pictures of a woman's body, a boy's body, a box office, the bridge of a ship, 'an order picked out across a far sky in neon lightning' (26), and, most important, 'a man hanging in the sea like a glass sailor in a jam jar' (26). Out of these few memory-fragments Golding constructs not only a kind of delirium state wholly appropriate for a man so isolated (where the past bombards, but the impressions appear as sets of stills) but also a past history that goes some way to explaining the particular nature of Christopher Hadley Martin.

This introduction of the past through the characteristic device of the 'picture' is dramatically justified as well as technically rather skilled. At the fable's opening Pincher is flung into the sea; turbines scream and the '*green* sparks' (7, italics added)[15] of a bomb tracer puncture the blackness of the seascape. The only lights cutting the night's darkness, then, are those from the tracer; as he dies the brain/centre 'lit a neon track' (8) and the green sparks merge with 'luminous pictures' (8) that shuffle before him like a bundle of snapshots, 'drenched in light' (8). The green tracer continues to flicker and spin and Pincher's centre, terrified of nothingness, clings to these tracers as, when thrust against the imagined pebbled island before him, it clings to the 'pattern in front of him that occupied all the space under the arches' (23). Inside his head pebbles shake, outside at the right side of his face pebbles nag like 'an aching tooth' (24). As we have seen, Pincher then proceeds to construct an illusory 'present' out of the memory of this missing tooth.[16] From the tracer lights, he constructs an illusory past.

Gradually there emerges a truncated narration of Chris Martin's past life that bears strong connection to his predicament on the rock. An actor in civilian life, he took things —including women as things—not as ideals to be reached but as items to be achieved. 'You're not a person, my sweet,' he

remembers muttering, 'you're an instrument of pleasure' (95).
Embodied in several symbols, the Chinese maggot-box in
particular, is Pincher's particular sin of gluttony. A producer
of a morality play first makes the identification as he introduces
Pincher to the masks of the seven deadly sins and the one he
will wear. 'Chris—Greed. Greed—Chris. Know each other'
(119). Rather in the manner of a case history the identification
is extensively documented throughout the memory-flashbacks
in one episode after another. An actor friend says of him, for
example:

> This painted bastard here takes anything he can lay his
> hands on. Not food, Chris, that's far too simple. He
> takes the best part, the best seat, the most money, the
> best notice, the best woman. He was born with his
> mouth and his flies open and both hands out to grab.
> He's a cosmic case of the bugger who gets his penny and
> someone else's bun. (120)

Significantly the 'random trailers' pointing to this identification
are disconnected snapshots. Until the moment of delirium they
remain so just as the Chinese box and the suspended doll
remain unexplained. But at that moment, the reader is able to
forge a meaningful and coherent pattern, first about Martin's
nature, his determined Being, and by extension about the
nature of the Golding universe. Point of view again is managed
such that the reader attends to and reconstructs what the
protagonist is deliberately made to ignore.

Internal evidence indicates that Pincher—despite his
hardened criminality—has been attracted to goodness; had he
on any of these occasions when grace-abounded acted from
charity not greed he might well have been granted the con-
solation of companionship, perhaps love. Several of the memory
flashbacks focus on two important characters from Martin's
past: his spiritualist friend, Nathaniel Walterson, and the
woman Nat marries, Mary Lovell. Mary is a magnificent but

contradictory figure to Pincher; as her emblematic name suggests onomatopœically she is both sensual and virginal, like her successor, Beatrice Ifor in *Free Fall*. Yet Pincher could never possess her and her unconquered mystery obsesses and eats away at him just as Beatrice's mystery torments Sammy. Pincher associates Mary with 'summer lightning' (151)—Golding's rather too neat inversion of the black lightning which plays such an important part in the fable's outcome—her eyes and impregnable silences make her 'a madness, not so much in the loins as in the pride, the need to assert and break' (148). He cannot understand why she should occupy his centre when the only real feeling he has for her is hate. Occupying his cherished centre she challenges his whole egoistic view of life.

So too does Nat, to whom other 'pictures' revert. Walterson with his lectures on 'the technique of dying into heaven' (70) is the saint figure; like Simon in *Lord of the Flies* he carries the fable's 'ideas'. We see him both on the *Wildebeeste* and in Martin's digs at Oxford, and it is clear that Martin loves him 'unwillingly . . . for the face that was always rearranged from within, for the serious attention, for love given without thought'; at the same time Martin hates him 'quiveringly . . . as though he were the . . . enemy' (103). Since contemporary man lacks vision, Nat argues, since he is unable at the moment to image his *Scintillans Dei* in a positive mythological context, the sort of heaven he might posit for himself would be construed negatively. It would be without form or void, Nat instructs, 'a sort of black lightning, destroying everything that we call life' (183). Pincher, of course, ignores Nat's sermonizing; yet he is overwhelmed by the generosity of the man: 'evidence of sheer niceness that made the breath come short with maddened liking and rage' (55). At a deep level Pincher is offended by Nat's notion that he has 'an extraordinary capacity to endure' (71) and repelled by Nat's gnomic prediction that soon he will die. Above all Pincher realizes with spite that both Nat and Mary stand 'in the lighted centre of my [his] darkness' (158). Both because his dark centre is lit and because he is drawn to them, they interrupt the consistent pattern of his malice. The autonomy of his greedy ego is challenged by goodness; he must destroy that goodness or be destroyed. As he repeats to himself: 'But what can the last maggot but one do? Lose his identity?' (184).

Despite himself he was drawn to goodness in the past; ironically when he is flung into the water, Pincher starts to swim towards the light, not the darkness. 'The riven rock face with tongues of spray' (22) towards which he swims, then, might be the implacable visage of a compassionate god; the thunderbolts splaying from its hand, might well be the golden bough of Aeneas which could take the wanderer to the earth's belly and bring him back. There would seem to be partial evidence for this bough in the elaborate description of light-ning as a tree, which the 'mad' Pincher pretends is an 'engraving':

> It was like a tree upside down and growing down from the old edge where the leaves were weathered by wind and rain. The trunk was a deep perpendicular groove with flaky edges. Lower down, the trunk divided into three branches and these again into a complication of twigs like the ramifications of bookworm. The trunk and the branches and the twigs were terrible black. Round the twigs was an apple blossom of grey and silver stain. (177)

But Pincher can no more interpret the lightning as a golden bough than he can accept a potential My-godness in himself. Thus at the end of Chapter I, Pincher is described as inter-preting the 'pattern in front of him . . . which meant nothing' (23) to be the merciless Rockall, beaten by seawater and lost in Atlantic waste.

In the past, Pincher has been offered ways of breaking his own pattern of greed; he is offered this in the 'present' as well. Confronted with choice he chooses not to break his pattern. His torture then is self-inflicted; a point of the utmost importance since the island is his own invention. Furthermore the pressure which he feels and the black lightning which descends to extinguish him is the heaven he chooses. Because he is bereft of love, he turns away from love and makes a darkness there; his body decays, but the god-resisting centre survives to tear at its own self, rather than submit.

V

'FUTURE'

Like a tormented corpse foretasting hell
He lay eternities stretched out, and stark
Swore like a mangy parrot 'till he fell
Into the sinking limbo of the dark.

—Golding, 'Baudelaire'

The third temporal perspective of *Pincher Martin* is the projection into an unrealized but nevertheless infinite future. Technically the perspective is realized through memory flashback merging with certain symbolic episodes which themselves have been modified by hallucination and stream of consciousness. Chief among these is the descent into the cellar, the recurrent memory which merges with Pincher's more recent past as an actor and his illusory present—his fever-ridden body sweating in the crevice of an illusory rock. In the following passage, for example, Golding has interlocked the three temporal perspectives that make up, in Golding's view, the Purgatorial moment: memories of childhood, the actual death itself, the rock, the fight of the ego, the fear of the future, the greed of the actor, all are bound together. On the level of the 'present', the passage depicts the hallucinations of a man lying in the real crevice of a rock and being drenched by his own sweat which he translates into tears, being shed—Pincher indulgently imagines—for him.

> They wept tears that turned them to stone faces in a hall, masks hung in rows in a corridor without beginning or end. There were notices that said No Smoking, Gentlemen, Ladies, Exit. . . . Down there was the other room, to be avoided, because there the gods sat behind their terrible knees and feet of black stone, but here the stone faces wept. . . . Their tears made a pool on the stone floor so that his feet were burned to the ankles. He scrabbled to climb up the wall and the scalding stuff welled up his ankles to his calves, his knees. He was struggling, half-swimming, half-climbing. . . . The tears were no longer running down the stone to join the burning sea. They were falling freely, dropping on him. . . . He began to scream. He was inside the ball of water that was burning him to the bone and past. It consumed him utterly. He was dissolved and spread throughout the tear an extension of sheer, disembodied pain. (144–145)

Pincher is reliving the escape from death. From the weeping figures, his memory curves back to his 'past' as an actor, and then farther back—to his recurrent terror of the cellar where black-booted gods haunted his childhood. Simultaneously, he looks forward in 'the feet of black stone' to the insistent black seaboots Pincher will see on a figure with whom he will speak. Abruptly, he is reminded of his actual death, so he proceeds to try to escape it again by climbing up the faces. But as he climbs, the tears/fever-sweat metamorphose into water and again he re-experiences his drowning: 'The tears were no longer running down . . . but dropping on him.' Inside 'the ball of water' he is burned 'to the bone and past.' What identity he has is 'sheer disembodied pain.'

The centre is intent on avoiding what will obliterate it; but it must suffer just this effort of escape from death eternally. Only when the final coda occurs does it become clear that *Pincher Martin* is about the paradox of eternal dying. Antecedent, theologically, to the ideographic structure is Golding's premise that the Augustinian view of the world might possibly be a useful one. Golding put the doctrinal blueprint to me in this way: 'Given a cosmos of physical and spiritual duality, God (love) creates man in his own image—since love needs an object. Man, who is free because he is God-like, can either turn outwards or away from this love.' (He can possess charity or lust). From the evidence of the 'past' Pincher obviously adopts lust; turning towards himself he is, Golding explained, 'Greed which has no spiritual sight'. Thus in his 'present' he creates his own world which 'love tries to destroy. . . . Love appears to Pincher as black lightning for Pincher has perverted his original spirit and what is light is darkness, what is heaven—the black lightning—is hell.'

The black lightning can destroy the island-world but not Pincher: this is the essential point. Man contains a duality with body counterpointing spirit; there is a related antimony between his god-nature, his My-godness, and his self-nature. At one time Pincher Martin's nature might have been so intermingled though the fable itself does not show him as anything but the prototype of Greed, and never investigates as *Free Fall* does the process by which Chris becomes Pincher. Golding has commented to Kermode that Pincher is what he became because of what he did to the people: 'Christopher, Christopolus—he who bears the Christ in him—was what he was at the hands of God.' Thus at the end, he is not addressed as Pincher, but as Christopher: 'Have you had enough, Christopher?' (194), a seabooted figure questions. From this slight and obscure dialogue, the reader is intended to surmise that Pincher is being offered—even at the last moment of his desperate escape-from-death—the choice of operating from his My-godness. But just as he has refused to confront the cellar-god in the past and the dying-into-extinction that Nat teaches, so here he rejects this last mercy. He yells his Satantic dismissal of divine pattern: 'I spit on your compassion!' (199). And the compassion, because doctrinally this god is love, has to attack and destroy.

> The lightning came forward. Some of the lines pointed to the centre . . . waiting for the moment when they could pierce it. Others lay against the claws, playing over them, prying for a weakness, wearing them away in a compassion that was timeless and without mercy. (201)

The 'compassion' of God tries ceaselessly to open him up but it cannot force him open since that would violate the given free will. Having dismissed mercy, Pincher, now reduced to his essential Being, claws and centre, will suffer eternally and never be destroyed. He has left Purgatory and entered Hell.

We may fairly ask whether this theology is rendered in fictionally dramatic terms. Some kind of divine pattern interferes in Pincher's petty designs, though there is no explicit image for this cosmic force. It is called simply 'a pattern' or an 'engraving' which if Pincher admits, amounts to 'a split in the nature of things' (177). Pincher, of course, makes several images, all of them horrendous and malignant. 'She [the old Hag] is loose on the rock. Now she is out of the cellar and in daylight' (192) he screams to himself knowing simultaneously that this hallucination is none other than the Dwarf with the silver head, a pile of stones energized by atavistic dreams of childhood and delirium, an ironic signal for rescue. She is the cellar-master as well, a threat which looms in opening darkness, the Adversary that lies in the cellar, the only sort of god that Pincher is capable of imagining. Pincher's mind cannot create a providential island, only a barren bleak rock; when he tries to encompass something greater than himself, his created world contracts. The god that he makes in his own image, on the sixth day of his parody Creation, is the only kind of god he can invent in his terms; facing his own face he yells: 'On the

sixth day he created God. Therefore I permit you to use
nothing but my own vocabulary. In his own image created he
Him' (196). The confrontation scene which follows is more
dreadful than in the *Flies* because the man here is so cunning
that he can claim the apparition is a projection of his own mind.

Yet it may be more. There is evidence in the description of
the figure that Golding intends it to represent God, but met,
he insists, in 'the accidents of Pincher's own culture.' First of
all, the figure is a sailor:

> The clothing was difficult to pin down . . . there was an
> oilskin—belted, because the buttons had fetched away.
> There was a woollen pullover inside it, with a roll-neck.
> The sou'wester was back a little. The hands were resting
> one on either knee, above the seaboot stockings. Then
> there were the seaboots, good and shiny and wet and
> solid. They made the rock behind them seem like a card-
> board, like a painted flat. (195)

Secondly, this is Pincher's garb as well; the laboured point of
the seaboots and their unmistakeable presence may well be to
indicate that Pincher encounters his real (i.e. dead) self in the
apparition, a point all the stronger since the seaboots make
the rock behind into the 'painted flat' which actually it is.
The encounter, then, re-orchestrates that interview between
Simon and the Head; as Simon before him, Pincher confronts
the truth of his condition. But the description of the seabooted
figure is more elaborate than this; furthermore, there is
Pincher's appalled realization that he could not have 'invented'
the question addressed him when the figure asks, 'Have you
had enough Christopher?' (194). In dismay he stares fixedly
past the boots and the knees to the face:

> The eye nearest the look-out was bloodshot at the outer
> corner. Behind it or beside it a red strip of sunset ran
> down out of sight behind the rock. . . . You could look

at the sunset or the eye but you could not do both. You
could not look at the eye and the mouth together. He
saw the nose was shiny and leathery brown and full of
pores. The left cheek would need a shave soon, for he
could see the individual bristles. But he could not look at
the whole face together. It was a face that perhaps could
be remembered later. It did not move. It merely had
this quality of refusing overall inspection. One feature at
a time. (195)

The features, like the clothing, suggest the apparition is
Pincher: the bloodshot eye refers back to Pincher's own eye
where a needle seemed to be nagging whenever he dipped
into the watertrough; and the figure's left cheek (behind
which would have sat the significant missing tooth) grows the
bristle which Pincher commented upon earlier when he
muttered: 'Strange that bristles go on growing even when
the rest of you is—' (125). Even the leathery brown skin
could well be his own flesh in a decomposed state. In fact,
the three features referred to in the passage recapitulate what
were earlier clues to Pincher's death. The figure, then, is
exactly like the dead Pincher Martin, but with one exception.
The total face is conspicuously absent; the dominant quality
of the face—it seems to Pincher—is that it 'refuses overall
inspection.' Pincher fixes on certain features, the sort, given
his illusory world, he would focus upon. Yet he realizes that
'you could not look at the eye and the mouth together'. Nor
can the sunset and the eye be seen simultaneously; one
removes the other. 'It was a face that perhaps could be
remembered later.' Could it not be that the ineluctable and
hidden face, if seen with other eyes, the eyes of the spirit, is
the face of the Living God, whose place is the setting sun?
Questioned as to this matter Golding has replied: 'My intention
was to make this a visualization of the thesis that God can be
known only in part. Dionysios Areopagitikos says that no
matter how profound contemplation is, or how perfect the

beatific vision is, there remains that secret part of God that
can never be known.[17] In the abstract terms of my argument
there is an unseen world which interpenetrates the visible.
Pincher's vision is partial indeed; perhaps what he does not
see, by choice and nature, the reader is intended to infer.
Perhaps Golding's effort here is to make the reader discover
what Pincher himself refuses to discover: the profound reality
of the spiritual world. Pincher then sees God in the accidents
of his own culture; nevertheless he is being offered the choice
of making Thor's black thunderbolts into the setting sun of
the Fisherman King.[18]

VI

Much more strictly than the other fables, *Pincher Martin*
tries to insist on the spiritual dimension. The coda confirms
what ironic undercurrents during the survival-narrative have
moved towards. The fable is about a dead man. Or, at another
level, the fable is about the nature of man, since the implications of the three temporal perspectives—past, present, and
future—suggest that Pincher-dead is Pincher-alive. As Gregor
and Kinkead-Weekes argue so convincingly in their chapter,
Pincher Martin is, in no sense, concerned with Becoming, but
rather with Being. Its starting point is not the past life of
Christopher Hadley Martin and how he became greedy, but
with the given nature of Pincher, the Maggot, and the demon-
stration of that nature in the past, in the present, and in the
future.

Since in this world the self seems to stand created, the
action of the fable does not consist in the process of the
protagonist's developing awareness, but the reader's recapitulation and recognition of truths which already exist. The
mind depicted re-examines static moments in the past which
themselves are sometimes intimations of the future. The reader
is given access to a perspective that Pincher himself rejects.
Though, of course, rejection is a kind of inverted recognition.

The coda insists on a new interpretation of the survival-narrative but earlier clues as we have seen have been concealed so that the reader unearths the truth gradually.

The fable, then, is built very carefully; at crucial moments the plot's significance resides in internal details of symbolic episodes, not overt dramatic actions. In a given passage several different levels of reality—childhood memory, atavistic submersion, actual physical drowning, hallucinatory imaginings—all interlock as we saw in the passage examined earlier. The fable focuses on things in the way *The Inheritors* does; Golding himself said he started with the picture of a man drowning in the sea and, he added in characteristically pictorial terms, that for him it was a book of colour: 'a pair of red claws locked against black lightning.' The image is informative, for it arrests in a static picture the whole meaning of the fable. In a real sense the fable is about red claws, black lightning, and the sea, just as *The Inheritors* is about the fall, the river, and the island.

The fable, then, is built pictorially though it is designed to demonstrate the relevance of the Augustinian view of the world in order to make the larger fabulist's point about the necessity for vision. At certain points, the narrative works through a series of static images which, by juxtaposition and association, and above all compression, inform the three temporal perspectives simultaneously. Thus the evasive Chinese box which comes from a story applied to Martin by one of his friends—it contains one huge maggot that has fed on all the others but will itself be eaten—symbolizes not only Pincher's view of the universe but Chris's demeanour on stage in the 'past.' It reveals him in the 'present' as Pincher-like he nets down the island, and in the 'future' as he grasps his own claws, refusing the mercy of extinction. In madness, Martin fuses the box with a coffin as he hears the spade/lightning knocking against it: Martin cries out in terror at one point: 'I am alone on a rock in the middle of a tin box' (144). Through such symbolic images, the three orders of time

collapse over one another, revealing, like the Chinese boxes
that fit into each other, one chemically pure state of Being:
the cosmic maggot.

Density of suggestion is here achieved not by a rich embroid-
ery of image upon image, but as was the case in *The Inheritors*
by a tight condensation where one symbolic image can operate
successfully at different levels. Take for example the first
'picture' which Pincher sees of an ingenious toy, the Cartesian-
Diver,[19] while he struggles for breath in the sea:

> The jam jar was standing on a table . . . one could see
> into a little world there which was quite separate but
> which one could control. The jar was nearly full of clear
> water and a tiny glass figure floated upright in it. The top
> of the jar was covered with a thin membrane. . . . The
> pleasure of the jar lay in the fact that the little glass
> figure was so delicately balanced between opposing
> forces. Lay a finger on the membrane and you would
> compress the air below it which in turn would press
> more strongly on the water . . . and it would begin to
> sink. By varying the pressure . . . you could do anything
> you liked with the glass figure which was wholly in your
> power. (9)

It is now possible to see that the jam jar is symbolic of the
whole fable's meaning. It focuses evasively and importantly on
Being and Pincher must come to understand that the Cartesian-
Diver's predicament represents his own reality. As the figure
floats, sinks and rises 'in the little world that was quite
separate' Pincher's consciousness floats in the globe of his
skull; his waterlogged body floats in the sea: 'down it would
go, down, down' (9). He is forced to descend atavistically,
down, down to some cellarage in his own mind and then
struggle towards the surface. One can also see in the jam jar's
peculiar isolation Pincher's physical experience on the island
where he feels pressed down upon by the atmosphere (the

membrane of the jar) and pressed into and up by the riven, harsh, hard rock (the water of the jar). And ultimately, the delicate balance of the floating figure represents the condition of man, *sub specie aeternitatis.*

Man floats between two forces—the pressure of some divine cosmic power and the pressure of the merely selfish. Man is controlled inasmuch as he operates within 'a little world'. 'You could let it struggle towards the surface, give it almost a bit of air, then send it steadily, slowly, remorselessly down and down' (9). After the fable, the reader discovers that all the memory flashbacks, all the symbolic images—even the cosmic symbol of man alone on a rock surrounded by sea—are pictorial definitions of a creation whose essence is to be 'delicately balanced between two opposing forces'. Indeed, the reader discovers what Pincher, as well as Davidson and Campbell, cannot know. The Antagonist's 'pressure' is not simply a 'remorseless' cruelty; it might easily be a merciful compassion. And the 'sad harvest' (208) would then be harvest indeed.

PINCHER MARTIN—NOTES

1 Golding, 'The Anglo Saxon', London *Queen Magazine* (December 22, 1959), pp. 12–14. This uncollected short story, 'The Anglo Saxon', is a kind of minor *Inheritors* where innocent, 'animal', non-conceptualizing man—and his country by extension—is superseded by machines of destruction that a new world invents. The story concerns a rural cattle driver whose habits of forty-odd years are rudely interrupted by soldiers from the American Army as armaments are installed in the English countryside. Like Lok, George sees noises as shapes, 'like a drumroll, like a circular saw' (to Pincher words 'and sounds were sometimes visible as shapes', like pebbles hard and enduring); in the pub, noises come out of his mouth: 'the words jumped out from the background and jerked him as they passed through his mouth'. George blinks out of his own 'warped window' like Pincher who must peer at the world through 'arches' of eyebrows and 'fringes' of eyelash. Again like Pincher, George sifts for a thought among 'the six hundred and fifty words'

hanging 'on hooks in George's dark cupboard'; 'blunt words broken and worn, clung to out of custom like a chipped cup.' His mouth 'quacks' on meaning as it tries to shape thought.

2   Philip Drew assumes that this rock is Rockall, a rock off the Hebrides. Kermode explains that 'Martin calls his rock Rockall not only because that is a real rock but because he remembers a poor joke turning on a word that is a bad rhyme for Rockall and which is the obscene word for "nothing." ' Kermode, 'The Novels of William Golding', *International Library Annual*, III (1961), p. 23.

3   William Golding, *Pincher Martin* (London: Faber and Faber, 1960), p. 30. All subsequent quotations will be taken from this edition and be indicated in textual parentheses.

4   Golding intends a double irony to be implicit in the word lifebelt. Thus Campbell looks at the corpse on the stretcher at the end and says, 'they are wicked things those lifebelts. They give a man hope when there is no longer any call for it' (207). Furthermore a corpse does not need a lifebelt to keep it afloat, after a few days.

5   Ian Blake, ' "Pincher Martin", William Golding, and "Taffrail" '. *Notes and Queries* (August 1962), pp. 309–310. (Taffrail was the pseudonym for Henry Taprell Dorling.)

6   Gregor and Kinkead-Weekes, p. 155.

7   Samuel Hynes, *William Golding, Columbia Essays on Modern Writers* (New York, 1964), p. 27.

8   Golding, Personal communication, letter, July 8, 1970 (unpublished).

9   This distinction between death as a 'face' and Purgatory as a 'snarl' informs the rest of the book. Pincher is hidden somewhere behind the snarl, just as his consciousness is floating somewhere beyond his body, in his skull. The notion of someone's 'face' as, on the one hand, the disguise that can be rearranged whatever the treachery behind, and, on the other, as the very seat of truth is used often in *The Pyramid*.

10   This association has biographical origins. Golding remarked that the feet of some British Museum stone statues appeared to his child's eye, when he peered up at them, like seaboots.

11   Golding to Webster, 'The Cosmic Outlook of an Original Novelist', *John O'London's* (January 28, 1960), p. 71.

12   Golding, quoted in Archie Campbell, 'William Golding: *Pincher Martin*', *From the Fifties* (BBC Sound Radio Drama, 1962) p. 35.

13   This is just one example of the density of cross-references and juxtapositions of similar motifs that comprise *Pincher Martin's* verbal surface. When the sailor falls into the sea, as Pincher is suspended 'between life and death', the water pushes in 'without mercy', the exact phrase that will close the survival tale.

14   Golding in letter quoted in Peter, 'Postscript', p. 34. Further remarks of Golding—brought to my attention following my own study, are useful here. Asked to comment on the cellar, Golding replied that it was an effort to represent a theological concept; if man were given free will, he would obviously have the choice either to turn to God or away

from Him. 'When you turn away from God, He becomes a darkness; when you turn towards him, He becomes a light, in cliché terms.' *Talk: Conversations with William Golding*, p. 74.

15 Golding admitted that the green tracer seen in water was associated with his own sensation on fainting when green lights seem to split. The image is often used in the fables: see Sammy as he falls unconscious in the cell, and the boys on the mountain top as they glimpse the parachutist.

16 Thus the importance of the island-Teeth; when Pincher's tongue feels along the barrier of his own teeth—the pinchers in his eating mouth—he feels a gap. 'His tongue was remembering. It pried into the gap between the teeth and recreated the old, aching shape. It touched the rough edge of the cliff, traced the slope down . . . towards the smooth surface where the Red Lion was . . . understood what was so hauntingly familiar and painful about an isolated and decaying rock in the middle of the sea' (174). Rockall's entire topography is an imaginary tooth in the mouth of the ravenous Pincher. An interesting gloss here is Golding's comment in his review of *Treasure Island*: 'An island must be built, and have an organic structure, like a tooth.' 'Islands', *The Hot Gates*, p. 109.

17 Golding, Personal communication, letter, July 8, 1970 (unpublished). Saint Dionysios the Areopagite was an Athenian Christian in first century A.D. St. Paul converted him (Acts 17:34). Tradition has it that he was a martyr and first bishop of Rome; in the Middle Ages he was erroneously revered as the author of Neoplatonic treatises which influenced mediaeval Scholasticism, particularly through St. Thomas Aquinas.

18 Golding intends the figure in the seaboots to be associated with several transcultural accounts of gods. Pincher sees the figure as a sailor, viz., 'in the accidents of his own culture', but he might have been seen as the Fisherman King. Golding writes (letter, August 24, 1970, unpublished) 'the Fisher King is a type of sacrifice occurring in the *Rigeveda*', one of the sacred Hindu books which praises different gods. 'He is also tied up with the Rock at Scylla and Charybdis-fig tree' and thus would reflect details of Sir James Frazer's account of gods figuring as sacrificial victims in *The Golden Bough*. In the legends of the Holy Grail, furthermore, the Fisherman King is the uncle of Percival, and dweller in the Castle of the Grail, where the holy vessel is enshrined. The figure then is deliberately ambiguous, representing simultaneously the godhead as it has appeared in the 'accidents' of Hindu, Greek and Christian myth, and the wise old man who asks questions for the purpose of inducing self-reflection.

19 The ingenious toy doll between two pressures is very possibly an experimental tool, the 'Cartesian Diver': a small hollow glass figure placed in a vessel of water that has an elastic cover so arranged that by an increase of pressure the water can be forced into the figure producing the effects of suspension, sinking and floating as the pressure varies. Golding's imaginative extension of a scientific postulate parallels his use of 'free fall' in *Free Fall* and the Law of Thermodynamics in *The Inheritors*. *Pincher Martin*, then, would represent an ironic sublation of the Descartes dictum: *cogito ergo sum*.

FREE FALL

I

When I make my black pictures, when I inspect chaos, I
must remember that such [merciful] places are as real as
Belsen. They, too, exist, they are part of this enigma,
this living. They are brick walls like any others. . . .
But remembered, they shine.

—Golding, *Free Fall*[1]

The Inheritors and *Pincher Martin* show Golding as a patternmaker for whom pattern is inadequate; structural pattern is
used to invalidate thematic pattern. Structurally, the fables
create an ideogram for the truth by setting up a tension between
two contradictory and inadequate patterns, one of which is
represented in the first narrative movement, while the other
is represented in the coda's reversal. While, after *Lord of the
Flies*, the novels forbid any simple or 'right' interpretation the
emphasis in all three is on the criminality of man. With *Free
Fall*'s appearance in 1959 definitive thematic changes occur.
The work's neat progression from mankind's collective evil
which *The Inheritors* dramatized to the perdition of Being in
Pincher Martin narrows further in *Free Fall* to the exploration
of one guilty person, enigmatic and individual. Unlike the
others this novel concerns itself with the rehabilitation of a
damned soul. Yet *Free Fall* must be declared a dramatic failure;
it is *The Spire* which brings its thematic preoccupations to
structural fruition.

Pincher Martin, we have seen, implies and seeks to demonstrate the presence of a spiritual reality, an unseen world
which interpenetrates the visible one. But it is the nature of
the protagonist's cosmos that we have to infer its presence

negatively. With *Free Fall* changes in technique, focus, and authorial tone—for here Golding approaches a more traditional reader/author relationship by narrating the tale from the first person point of view—all combine to allow a narrative rendering of the moments of vision in religious ecstasy. Thus *Free Fall* offers one vision of sanctity, not merely the 'heaven of sheer negation' which can be construed from the blackness of Pincher's hell. To achieve this 'heaven' Pincher has to surrender his own personality to God's love and pity: the purgatory he occupies is a specifically theological, one albeit unorthodox. *Free Fall*, on the other hand, posits the possibility of another mode of existence, a world of magic and terror, spirit and miracle: suggests a place to which Sammy Mountjoy, the protagonist, can direct what he describes as his 'need to worship' (109). And furthermore the novel tries to liberate this imaginative mode in the reader.

Indeed the whole book's effort is not to define, reduce, or recast mystery but to discover it. *Free Fall* affirms a magically potent force in the world and a scene of transfiguration balances the confrontation scene, that familiar extreme situation in which character is tested by destruction. A dynamism and vibrancy exists in the world within which the child, the innocent, and the saint live by nature. Except at certain moments when the sensuous immediacy of the past comes flooding back and fuses with the present, the guilty adult (he who, in the novel's theology, has lost by his own free choice his freedom) has no access to this celestial mode. Yet his paradox is to be troubled by its beauty and simultaneously tormented by his own defilement. 'I am a burning amateur torn by the irrational and incoherent, violently searching and self-condemned' (5) remarks Sammy as he explores his condition of 'free fall'. For 'we are neither the innocent nor the wicked. We are the guilty. We fall down' (251).

The theme is, of course, unmistakable: the nature of fallen man, Adam unparadised, the loss of innocence. Yet the novel counterpoints at least two explications of man, the scientific

and the religious, its title alluding not simply to Milton's
Paradise Lost ('Sufficient to have stood/But free to fall') but to
the physical condition of free fall, a condition of unrestrained
motion in a gravitational field.[2] Furthermore the novel
breaks away from the remote settings and narrow focus of the
earlier fables, taking as its subject the circuitous reflection by a
twentieth-century painter upon the events of his past, events
which involve a detail of social texture that was new in
Golding's fiction to that date.

II

And who are you anyway? Are you on the inside, have
you a proof-copy? Am I a job to do? Do I exasperate
you by translating incoherence into incoherence?
                                    —Golding, *Free Fall* (8)

Critical response to *Free Fall* has, for the most part, been
antagonistic; in 1959 its immediate reception was extremely
negative. Most reviewers ignored or neglected to apply Golding's
barbed admonition in the passage quoted above. Commenting
on the chronological irregularities, reviewers interpreted
these distortions as proof of Golding's penchant for obscurity
and fortuitous cleverness. Gaps in the narrative were judged
wilful, the style meretricious, and the story pretentious.
Generally, people felt the novel tumbled from the blows of its
philosophical quest, unable to bear the weight of its theme.
Although *Pincher Martin*'s verbal texture with its multiple
shifting meanings had been admired in the past, stylistic
innovations in *Free Fall* were read as blunders and evidence of
failing imaginative power, especially in the mock-heroic
parody of courtly love language in the Sammy/Beatrice
sequences. Nowhere was it suggested that the novel's mixtures
of style—colloquialisms are often poised between scientific
jargon, sensuous images and lyrical cadences—were intended

as verbal counterparts to the thematic distinction drawn between the world of flesh and the world of spirit.

My feeling is that *Free Fall* is a difficult work, yet rewarding and enigmatic in new ways. In a real sense it amounts to what Golding himself remarked to an interviewer was, 'a confession of growth or a confession of failure.' In fact, Golding has insisted that with *Free Fall* he was 'moving much more towards novels where I don't understand what everything is about', a declaration in keeping with his distrust of conceptual categories and his romantic affirmation of metaphor and myth as vehicles which find but do not impose order and coherence in the world. Thus Sammy Mountjoy seeks desperately to find pattern, not to impose it. And Golding's problem is to avoid imposing pattern while creating a metaphor which implies the order of mystery. For 'to name is to destroy, to suggest is to create' as Arthur Symons instructs us. Thus Golding explained that he was trying to incorporate into his work 'the immediacy of inexplicable living.' Its intention was 'to give a picture of the patternlessness of man's existence in the west at the moment' when no system of reference, no spiritual gravity, no creeds or codes operate to sustain the individual.

Consequently the novel takes as its protagonist an artist who has 'hung all systems on the wall like a row of useless hats' (6) having worn a Marxist cap, a Christian beret, a rationalist bowler and 'a school cap' (6) and then thrown them all down. Yet despite this indifference, on his crucial encounter with the German psychologist (a demonic/angelic Interrogator) he is driven, by his own nature, that 'mystery' that Halde believes 'opaque' (145), to find 'some indications of a pattern that will include me, even if the outer edges tail off into ignorance' (9).

From the quest for a pattern, a quest which determines the novel's spiritual outline, and the experience of a patternless world, the story emerges. Once again Golding's strategy is one of indirection, for as Kermode remarks, against Sammy's 'assertion of uniqueness and discontinuity we have to set the patterns, the elaborate echoes, the profoundly organized plotting of the novel itself. Between what the hero says and what the book says there is a relation which you might call contrapuntal.'³ Sammy is brought back to the point where he can choose freedom, a freedom he has lost in youth when he chose freely, but because of his given nature, to commit a sin. I shall examine this apparently contradictory view of behaviour later in the chapter. The consequences of his new found freedom is to discover a pattern emerging from the events of his past, a pattern whose shape the fable's structure follows. And the pattern is one of guilt.

III

Essentially *Free Fall* remains ambiguous in its vision. Like *Pincher Martin* it aims at bridging two sorts of explanations of existence, the religious and the materialist, and fusing the two. To this end it employs the ideographic structure and the confrontation scene where ego atavistically encounters its psychic darkness. Furthermore, *Free Fall* employs another feature common to the fables: the inversion of a literary model, in this case, Dante's *Vita Nuova*. Here the model is taken as the right explanation while its reallocation is intended to be wrong; in the cases of the inversions which precede *Free Fall* the literary model is corrected by Golding's recasting of the story.

The formal narrative consists of seven sequences, each involving pictures from the past. Chapters I to III deal with early childhood—when Sammy has freedom. Chapters IV to VI involve his youth and manhood—when he has lost his freedom. The conclusion of both presents the same dilemma: once there was freedom; once it was lost. Chapters VII to IX involve the central confrontation of the book and of Sammy's life; it is itself subdivided into three panels with the outer two concerning Sammy's interrogation in the prison camp and his terror-stricken experience in a dark cell. The middle panel reverts back to his childhood and deals in preparation for the following chapter with the question (one that evidently holds Golding's imagination in a vice), 'How did I come to be so frightened of the dark?' (154). Chapters X to XII give the climax of the narrative proper, moving from a transitional episode in the prison yard back to Sammy's early tutelage under Nick and Rowena. Chapter XII outlines the act which cost 'everything' (236) and the choice of physicality. The fifth section, Chapters XIII and XIV, elaborates the 'everything' that his choice had sacrificed and in the coda gives the reversal that gathers the whole fable together. Throughout, Sammy returns intermittently to the present. One system of rhetorical leitmotifs—'Here? Not Here'—makes the transition and marks the climax of the narrative quest for that point at which Sammy physically crossed the bridge to East London and lost his freedom, a loss of the bridge between the flesh and the spirit. Various running images bind the fragments as well, chief among which are those associated with Sammy's coveted fag-cards, the Kings of Egypt. As in 'Egypt from My Inside', the heroic aspect of man is conveyed by the traditional metaphor of royalty so 'abashed before the kingship of the human face' (150), Sammy captures the transfigured prison camp in his 'smuggled sketches of the haggard, unshaven kings of Egypt' (188).

In *Free Fall* time shifts, chronological discontinuities, and these elaborate verbal echoes are designed to show the religious significance of a man's life while at the same time accounting dramatically for his loss of the world of miracle. However, the result is flawed. Two independent quests operate throughout the fable: the quest for Being *qua* Being, and the quest for the bridge between the worlds of the flesh and the spirit. Put another way, one can see that the resolution implied by the confrontation scene and the coda's reversal relates thematically but not dramatically to the fable's religious core. Consequently the fable's vision never coalesces, and in the end becomes merely notes towards a problem, not the solution of one. The major quest involves Sammy's search for spiritual freedom in twentieth-century social chaos: this is particularized as an effort to discover that bridge between the world represented by the indestructible burning bush and that world represented by the bell-jar candle where matter is neither destroyed nor created. Thematically the quest has affinities with other religious patterns of transformation like the Dantean analogue which it relates to ironically and contrapuntally. It is overtly theological (though again not orthodox in nature) and in a sense the impasse to which this journey finally comes is a rational one. The suggestion, and this is at a thematical level only, is that since freedom is experienced as well as guilt, there may be some place where the two worlds intersect, a place 'sometimes open and sometimes shut, the business of the universe proceeding there in its own mode, different, indescribable' (187). This place is closed to the eye of logic. The riddle posed in the coda is intended to resurrect this dead eye of logic in order to make Sammy and the reader cast the new eye of the spirit back over all that has occurred before the riddle is posed. It fails to accomplish this difficult task.

There are other flaws in the fable; it aims at merging two methods of narration by grounding the inexplicability of felt life in some search for cosmic value. Thus Sammy Mountjoy is given a strong and specific social context; we see him at school with Philip fighting for his fag-cards of the Kings of Egypt, we see him playing bombers on the gray chalk hills of Kent with another friend Johnny, we watch him swagger histrionically before Beatrice Ifor as she leaves a training college in East London. And yet Golding would have Mountjoy's particular repudiation of the spiritual in his desecration of Beatrice identified with both its historical implications and its cosmic one as well. Thus the episode between Sammy and Halde in the prison camp recalls the interrogations Beatrice suffers under Sammy's fervent questionings: 'Don't you feel anything?' Certain motifs reverberate: answering

Halde's crucial probings as Beatrice answered his, Sammy mutters 'Maybe'. 'Do you feel nothing then?' Halde questions, and Sammy replies 'Maybe' (142). And the implication is that Sammy's failure to accept responsibility and his inability to live within a coherent world is that of contemporary man. 'For maybe was sign of all our times. We were certain of nothing' (108).

> I welcomed the destruction that war entails, the deaths and terror. . . . There was anarchy in the mind where I lived and anarchy in the world at large, two states so similar that one might have produced the other. The shattered houses, the refugees, the deaths and torture— accept them as a pattern of the world and one's behaviour is little enough disease. (131–132)

Throughout the fable, however, psychological motivation wars with the formal demands that Sammy's pursuit imposes upon the structure. Several times he appears to be engaged in moral dilemmas whose outcome is in the balance; his fortune appears to be affected by recognizable social gradations (removal from Rotten Row to the rectory brings physical comfort but a loss of creature comfort); and yet he seems to be influenced by forces beyond his immediate understanding. Still, social matters are diminished often by symbolical explanations; this is especially true at the important juncture when Sammy chooses Nick's rational universe. The world of symbols, especially the metaphor of the door, formulates Sammy's predicament rather than any social or cultural matter:

> This was a moment of such importance to me that I must examine it completely. For an instant of time, the two worlds existed side by side. The one I inhabited by nature, the world of miracle drew me strongly. To give up the burning bush, the water from the rock, the spittle on the eyes was to give up a portion of myself, a

dark and inward and fruitful portion. Yet looking at me from the bush was the fat and freckled face of Miss Pringle. . . . I hung for an instant between two pictures of the universe; then the ripple passed over the burning bush and I ran towards my friend [Nick]. In that moment a door closed behind me. I slammed it shut on Moses and Jehovah. I was not to knock on that door again, until in a Nazi prison camp I lay huddled against it half crazed with terror and despair. (217)

The conventions of actuality are twice violated by a deliberate blurring of action. In fact, narrative method shifts between autobiographical meditation where character encounters event and dramatically atavistic episodes where ego confronts psychic darkness. If *Pincher Martin* in alternating 'past' and 'present' places greatest emphasis on the latter by striking fragments of memories across Pincher's efforts, then *Free Fall* almost exactly inverts the method: Sammy's past predominates though its presentation as a set of expanded 'pictures' is no more than a development of the montage effect of *Pincher Martin*.

Again in *Free Fall* as in *Pincher Martin* the revelation of character in retrospect is a manifestation of character not as process but as state. Sammy is no more self-creating, viz., capable of moulding his own consciousness, than Pincher was seen to be. The change in Sammy after his 'sin' is not an alteration of what previously existed but merely the fulfilment of a latent possibility. 'Now I have been back in these pages to find out why I am frightened of the dark and I cannot tell. Once upon a time I was not frightened of the dark and later on I was' (165). Reality in *Free Fall* is a closed and static system: man carries his destiny within him; it confronts him from without only because his acts externalize his nature. Yet Sammy is looking beyond those closed walls, seeking the freedom that is experienced and known as acutely as 'the taste of potatoes'.

What men believe is a function of what they are; and what they are is in part what has happened to them. And yet here and there in all that riot of compulsion comes the clear taste of potatoes, element so rare the isotope of uranium is abundant by comparison. (212)

IV

I have walked by stalls in the market place where books, dog-eared and faded from their purple, have burst with a white hosanna. I have seen people crowned with a double crown, holding in either hand the crook and flail, the power and the glory. I have understood how the scar becomes a star, I have felt the flake of fire fall, miraculous and pentecostal. My yesterdays walk with me. They keep step, they are grey faces that peer over my shoulder. I live on Paradise Hill, ten minutes from the station, thirty seconds from the shops and local. Yet I am a burning amateur, torn by the irrational and incoherent, violently searching and self-condemned.

—Golding, *Free Fall* (5)

Free Fall's opening paragraph sounds the thematic dichotomy between the world of flesh and the world of spirit that the book will explore. 'To get the point of this paragraph', as one notable article remarks, 'is to get the point of the whole book.'[4] The world of empirical observation and the world of imaginative vision, both exist and both are real. Sammy has perceived hosannas and pentecostal fire; he has witnessed the miraculous transmutation of scar into star; yet he lives 'ten minutes from the station, thirty seconds from the shops and local'. And the stylistic counterpointing of this secular colloquialism with those biblical echoes and rhythms of alliterative phrases such as 'I have felt the flake of fire fall' presents the separation of the two worlds. In childhood the two worlds interlocked but, for the adult Sammy, the past follows to condemn like grey faces forever unreconciled. There is no bridge. There is no forgiveness; the world of the spirit is experienced only as a condemnation of guilt, not as holiness or wholeness.

The fable opens with a prologue, reminiscent in many ways of a dramatic monologue in which the listener is directly confronted by the narrator as a participant in the unfolding confession, invoked, cajoled, and then asked to sit in judgment on actions. Sammy comments: 'My darkness reaches out and fumbles at a typewriter with its tongs. Your darkness reaches out with your tongs and grasps a book' (8). The metaphor of darkness here represents the internal landscape of psyche as it does in Pincher Martin's case, and the chapter is a logical development from the filmic technique of *Pincher Martin* where Pincher while drowning sees the essential factors of his life as neon lights and expands them. Sammy, in fact, is a kind of compassionate Pincher with whom he has several traits in common, especially egotistic sensuality. At one point, there is a verbal echo: elucidating the conservation of energy to the young Sammy, Nick says it holds both mentally as well as physically. 'You can't have your penny and your bun' (216). However, in conversation Golding remarked to me that Sammy took off from the point where Tuami sat, brooding over his ivory dagger. Unlike Pincher who imposes a pattern on the Rock, naming things Piccadilly Circus and Regent Street in order to bring them within his control, Mountjoy is seeking desperately to discover a pattern. He organizes and reorganizes past events not as they occurred but in the order of their affective significance.

> For time is not to be laid out endlessly like a row of bricks. That straight line from the first hiccup to the last gasp is a dead thing. Time is two modes. The one is an effortless perception. . . . The other is memory, a sense of shuffle, fold and coil, of that day nearer than that because more important, of that event mirroring this, or

those three set apart, exceptional and out of the straight
line altogether. (6)

The distinction—well within the Romantic tradition involving
as it does the affective memory—gives *Free Fall* its principle
of composition and, not unexpectedly, its metaphor for truth.
Thus chronology is distorted deliberately. Unscrambled, the
story involves the childhood of Sammy Mountjoy, born of a
woman of easy virtue in a Kent slum, Rotten Row; his
schooling and friends; his adoption by a homosexual rector,
Father Watts Watt; his seduction of the beautiful Beatrice
Ifor; his betrayal of her and marriage to a Communist comrade,
Taffy; his experience in a German prison camp; and finally
his postwar experience when he returns home to encounter the
mad Beatrice and revisit his 'spiritual' (194) parents, the
school teachers Nick and Miss Pringle. In temporal chronology
the final 'event' is the narration of the story as Sammy's
'darkness' 'fumbles at a typewriter' (8). But the novel closes
with a flashback to the prison and the German Commandant's
ambiguous 'Sphinx's riddle' (253) and reference to Dr. Halde
who in the words of the novel's very last sentence 'Does not
know about peoples' (253).

The narrative proper then is all retrospect. Instead of submerging character in development—presenting Sammy
Mountjoy progressively—various snapshots of character at
various ages are displayed. In one sense, the reader, in juxta-
posing the motionless images, experiences the effect of the
passage of time as the narrator has experienced it. Take for
example the sequence at the end of the fable when Sammy
faces the insane Beatrice, and he surveys the consequences of
his desecration. The asylum stands at the peak of Paradise Hill,
yet it has around it the sense of institution like the '*greyness* of
a prison camp' (238, italics added).[5] Originally it was the
General's 'magic house' (45) whose apocalyptic cedar tree,
fairy lights, and dark Gardens of Persephone had bathed the
young interlopers, Johnny and Sammy, in wonder as they

'wander in paradise' (45). Now it is merely 'the grey house
of factual succession' (237) unredeemed by spirit because
denied of spirit, where a wholly physical Beatrice pisses on
the floor. Just as the consequences of denying a cosmic spiritual
dimension had robbed the mansion of its beauty, so the consequences of choosing physical lust with Beatrice—then, 'I
could not paint her face; but her body I painted' (123)—is to
reinforce the reality of physical life and further to make it
contemptible. He sees her sagging face shadowed by her body;
only 'a little light was reflected from the institutional wall and
showed some of the moulding' (242). The parallel between the
past and the present is neatly drawn by the analogy between
the architecture of a building and that of physiognomy here;
it is a technique Golding often uses in *The Spire* and *Pincher
Martin*.

Since the narrator himself is commenting and assembling
episodes, however, time itself is arrested in another sense and
the major character can be viewed as a continuous being.
'Pictures' of the past are not altogether random, Mountjoy
concludes, as he surveys himself:

> They are important simply because they emerge. I am
> the sum of them. I carry round with me this load of
> memories. Man is not an instantaneous creature, nothing
> but a physical body and the reaction of the moment. He
> is an incredible bundle of miscellaneous memories and
> feelings, of fossils and coral growths. (46)

Presumably Golding constructs several episodes with formal
echoes of earlier episodes to make just this point, that man
(Mountjoy specifically) is not so much a creature of the
moment as a continent of 'miscellaneous memories'.

For this reason, the narrative method is retrospective
meditation. It consists in brooding on some time spot which
will bring about a total recall of a certain epoch, not as a faint
memory but as a vividly relived experience containing its

own significance. Thus Sammy, as he gropes to capture the essential nature of Ma whom he experienced as 'warm darkness' (15) and a blocking of 'the tunnel' (15), remarks to the reader: 'And now something happens in my head. Let me catch the picture before the perception vanishes' (15). He proceeds then to reconstruct the Epic Bog Brawl when Ma defends her 'throne' (21), her voice bouncing 'off the sky in brazen thunder' (19). And he concludes, 'I have no memory of majesty to match that one from Rotten Row' (21). If he sets aside theoretical categories acquired by the guilty man, Sammy can see in this static image some rounded aspect of a whole truth, unfragmented and unabstracted. Or he can try to. Thus the comic yet awesome death of the lodger is seen through the 'mind's eye' (29) when the adult Sammy stoops to knee height and becomes the small child, 'the empty bubble' (29), who confuses the cessation of a clock ticking with the lodger's death. The lodger too is an agent of imagination and hence a bridge to the world of miracle; thus Sammy is suddenly haunted by a 'moustache of white swan's feather' (176) when he is cringing in the cell but he cannot be armoured against death any more than he could be in Rotten Row. 'And the shape of life loomed [in Rotten Row] that I was insufficient for our lodger's thatch, for that swan-white seal of ultimate knowing' (29). He is, as Golding puts it many times in *Free Fall* as well as *The Pyramid*, 'on the pavement'; he believes testimonies of miracles, he sustains a 'worried faith in the Kings of Egypt' (149) but he himself is insufficient to inhabit that world.

On the other hand, Mountjoy has the capacity to live in a divided and double world. He is, as he himself realizes before Halde, 'not an ordinary man. I was at once more than most and less' (150). The lesson the '*mind's eye*' (29, italics added) seeks to discover is the point at which his inadequate being opted for one of those two worlds.[6] Golding seems to be suggesting that Mountjoy might always have kept his double vision but that he was also free to decide for egocentric and sensual reasons that it was unimportant. As his headmaster advises: 'If you want something enough, you can always get it provided you are willing to make the appropriate sacrifice. . . . But what you get is never quite what you thought; and sooner or later the sacrifice is always regretted' (235). Sammy makes the appropriate sacrifice; wanting Beatrice Ifor's white body he turns his back on the world of spirit and loses his freedom and ability to enjoy both worlds.

V

> . . . again this is trying to move on a level of revealed religion, a rather sordid kind of twentieth-century beginning which might lead to a pilgrim's progress. But the pilgrim has got his feet in the mud. There are no trumpets sounding for him on the other side: the trumpets are a long way off.
>
> —Golding

Though he justifies it as the logical outcome of his adopted materialism, Samuel Mountjoy's worship of the sensual is a manifestation of his inherent spiritualism: 'At the moment I was deciding that right and wrong were nominal and relative, I felt [and] I saw the beauty of holiness and tasted evil in my mouth like the taste of vomit' (226). Though he purposely disregards the spirit in seducing Beatrice he is trembling to contact her beyond the 'shoddy temple' (108) of sex: 'a sadness reached out of me that did not know what it wanted; for it is part of my nature that I should need to worship, and this was not in the textbooks, not in the behaviour of those I had chosen and so without knowing I had thrown it away' (109). Ironically, he denies the spirit by means of the spirit, a point illustrated neatly by his Tate painting celebrating Beatrice's body imaginatively in a way he never touches her physically. Indeed, he captures her nature despite himself and despite his negation of it: 'I added the electric light-shades of

Guernica to catch the terror, but there was no terror to catch. . . . The electric light that ought to sear like a public prostitution seems an irrelevance. There is gold, rather, scattered from the window' (124). In the very first instance of repudiation he adopts materialism as an expression of his heart's affection for the kindly Nick. Indeed it is Nick's kindness not his materialist system which makes Sammy forsake the world of the symbol made intolerable by Miss Pringle's obsessive cruelty. In the final instance, when his physical eye cannot function in the cell's darkness and the world of the senses—the world he declares real—is no longer available, his mind's eye creates monster after monster. His own darkness is not still; it forces him to explore the centre both of the cell and his own internal darkness and ultimately his cry for mercy is an affirmation of Spirit.

His very name suggests this paradox, for it has essentially religious connotations. In the first phase of his career, fragments of biblical patterns are relevant. The Old Testament prophet, Samuel, is conceived by Hannah through the ministerings of a priest; Sammy's parentage is associated with a church since Ma's favourite fiction (and the one Sammy finds most attractive) is that his father was a parson. Like the Old Testament prophet who was brought to the altar to do service, Sammy too is drawn to the altar though by the bad influence of Philip who urges him to defile not honour it. If these biblical allusions are, in part, ironic, Sammy like his namesake does at least become a judge over himself and a proclaimer of kings. Yet Sammy's nature is predominately hedonistic, a point made obvious by the pun associated with his second name. Here one kind of mount-into-joy is replaced by another and if the infant Samuel is banished from Paradise Hill, then the post-pubescent Mountjoy conquers (as Peter Green has happily phrased it) the Mons Veneris.

In the second phase of Sammy's career—'the whole time of the other school' (192)—another literary allusion is ironically inverted. It is Beatrice whose name hints at the Dantean

pattern underlying this quest for the bridge between the
world of the flesh and the world of the spirit. She is seen first
before a drawing class, 'a palladian bridge' (221) behind her
transparent and illuminated face. Issuing from the girl's brow
Sammy perceives 'a metaphorical light that none the less
seemed to me to be an objective phenomenon, a real thing'
(222). Living in freedom (a state defined as unconscious
undifferentiated perception) he looks upon Beatrice and
experiences two worlds simultaneously; they interlock and
since he does not appropriate them he experiences the bridge.
The light is of course the light of Paradise, for Golding intends
Beatrice to refer back to the exalted Beatrice of Dante's *Vita
Nuova*. Further, Golding intends his own fable as an ironic
inversion of Dante's sublime sequence, a collection of thirty-
one lyrical poems celebrating the beloved woman, interspersed
with a prose narrative which comments upon the course of
the developing devotion. Aside from the heroine's emblematic
name and the representation of Sammy's sensual desire as a
parody of all the torments, intolerable ecstasies, and anguished
mortifications attendant upon a courtly lover's unrequited
love, there are numerous scenes in *Free Fall* which correspond
to ones described in the prose chapters of the *Vita Nuova*.
Dante unexpectedly sees Beatrice for the second time since
her girlhood as she walks down a street in Florence accompanied by two women (III); Sammy, in turn, manipulates
events so that he can happen upon Beatrice as she leaves the
training college in South London accompanied by two girl
friends. Dante, soon after, writes a *ballata* to justify his love
in Beatrice's eyes (XII); Sammy sends a heady letter declaring
his ensnarement. The crucial moment in the transformation of
Dante's despair to active praise—which issues in the famous
canzone, 'Ladies who know by insight what Love is'—occurs
as Dante walks in the country beside a stream of very clear
water (XIX). Similarly, Sammy's devotion undergoes a crucial
transformation as he wades through cathedral-like woods;
passing through a stream of 'providential waters' (235), he

feels his manhood strong and decides to sacrifice everything for 'the white unseen body of Beatrice Ifor' (235).

Beatrice is to Sammy, then, what Beatrice is to Dante, a creature wholly superior to himself, wholly Other. But whereas to Dante Beatrice becomes an instrument of contemplation, exaltation, and finally salvation (in the *Paradiso* she leads him through Heaven), to Sammy she is merely an instrument of lust. He confuses her mysterious, baffling beauty with simple salt sex—'I love you, I want to be you!' (105), he intones. By a deliberate act of the will he makes that foreignness a servant of his passion and egoism : sex becomes his 'shoddy temple' (108) of worship. By a positive act of the will he damns himself and rejects in that damnation the possibility of living by vision.

In conversation with Peter Green, Golding put the ironic inversion this way :

> But where Dante, presented with a coherent cosmos, was able to fit her into it, Sammy's confused cosmos ended by putting her through the whole mill of seduction —a scientific, rationalistic approach so to speak, so that Beatrice who took Dante up to the vision of God becomes a clog to Sammy and a skeleton in his cupboard.

This Dantean analogue operates only in one phase of the protagonist's journey, specifically Chapter XII, where Beatrice is introduced in the context of the art class. It is not employed as a literary inversion consistently through the entire fable as, for example, is *Coral Island* in *Lord of the Flies* where not only do the characters represent ironic inversions of Ballantyne's boys but the officer himself, in the coda, refers to its title in his admonition of the savages before him. Golding obviously intends us to look back at the Sammy of the Van Gogh seduction room and re-evaluate Beatrice's 'opaqueness' (113) not as the 'avoidance of the deep and muddy pool where others lived' (112), but as the clear presence of generosity. The

Dantean inversion, however, is not grounded in the total shape of the fable structure; it has no significance in the coda's reversal of Sammy's destiny nor does it have any relevance to Sammy's purgation which occurs in the confrontation scene. Golding is forced to resort to explanatory comments, in fact, because the symbolic aspect of Beatrice is not really grounded in dramatic feasibility and particularization. Beatrice (unlike Taffy) is never a character in her own right but rather a focus on Sammy.

Nevertheless, this Dantean inversion is posited as the answer to the book's question: 'where did I lose my freedom?' Further, it is given as the explanation for error. Sammy might have taken Beatrice as the ideal and been led presumably to the twentieth-century mystic Rose. But he takes her, Golding has mentioned, as the opposite, 'the very concrete present to be achieved, conquered, and beaten.' He confuses her miraculous Being—what he experiences as 'metaphorical light'—with his own lust; his greed tries to appropriate her mystery and possess it by a physical act.

> What had been love on my part, passionate and reverent, what was to be a triumphant sharing, a fusion, the penetration of a secret, raising of my life to the enigmatic and holy level of hers became a desperately shoddy and cruel attempt to force a response from her somehow. Step by step we descended the path of sexual exploitation until the projected sharing had become an infliction. (123)

Whereas Dante places Beatrice in heaven in his last vision of her, Sammy, in words recasting Milton's Satan—'Musk, shameful and heady, be thou my good' (232)—decides his heaven will be sex; and since, of course, Beatrice is frigid, she becomes Sammy's hell, not his heaven at all.

Mountjoy, unlike Johnny Spragg and Nick, is no innocent. Nor is he, like Rowena Pringle and Philip, one of the wicked. 'The innocent and wicked live in one world' (251); each operates in mutually exclusive but existentially inclusive spheres. Mountjoy belongs to a third category; he is one of the guilty and his sentence is to live in both worlds, suffering 'the mode which we call the spirit' (253) as self-condemnation.

> Cause and effect. The law of succession. Statistical probability. The moral order. Sin and remorse. They are all true. Both worlds exist side by side. They meet in me. We have to satisfy the examiners in both worlds at once. (244)

There is no bridge.

VI

What we know is not what we see or learn but what we realize.

—Golding, *Free Fall* (149)

Yet the sources and means of evil are also the sources and means of power and active creation; Sammy's shabby victory over Beatrice nevertheless and paradoxically complements his mysterious victory over the bleakness of the cell and the darkness of his centre. Each manifests his special power, that reverence for beauty, that intense sensitivity, that 'nightmare knowledge' (28) that lets him 'see unusually far through a brick wall' (133). In earlier chapters, I argued that both *The Inheritors* and *Pincher Martin* conclude that the point at which man becomes godlike is precisely the point at which he can fall. What ultimately makes a specific action 'good' or 'bad' is what one Being affirms or denies; what in fact one Being does with the ideal. The Neanderthals can do nothing but love; Pincher can do nothing but desecrate; yet both are drawn by an ideal—one in the figure of the People of the Fall, the other in the person of the (fragmentary) Nathaniel. The implication is that there is a certain crucial occasion where the test occurs and what a man has carried within him confronts him in the lineaments of choice. And Golding seems to be saying that at this point there is evidence—he would take it literally—that freedom exists. At this point one is not determined by one's predetermined nature. Thus Fa, unlike Lok, can understand that the Other People are dangerous: she remains awake and witnessing their transgressions. Furthermore, she possesses in her being something of Oa (since she is woman) which Lok does not possess. At the crucial point when he might have obeyed Fa's instructions to ignore Liku's absence and recapture only the new one, he reverts to, or, more precisely, remains with his original nature. He tries desperately to find Liku, simply because he is unable to imagine that the New People are evil enough to sacrifice her. His innocent nature contributes to Fa's death, his own death, and by extension that of the Neanderthal species. Similarly Christopher Martin's particular power is his ability to survive; and it is precisely this endurance (Christopher under the aspect of Christopolus, the Christ bearer) that Martin under the aspect of Pincher corrupts. Earlier I suggested that both *The Inheritors* and *Pincher Martin* offer this mythopœia in structural terms. But whereas the structure of those fables allows an initial interpretation to be revised by the reader, *Free Fall* modifies this ideographic device. We can see this technique and intent in the coda as well as the confrontation scene, the nightmarish experience in the cell; however, the technique of reversal plays no consistent part. For example, it plays no part in revising the reader's conception of Sammy's early childhood. The important question why he grew frightened of the dark, a question Sammy poses to himself in the cell, is not answered. Golding may regard darkness as the spiritual dimension of which contemporary man is incapable of conceiving except in terms of guilt and malignancy. But *Free Fall* does not locate the reason why darkness should suddenly be something that terrifies; why darkness should be imagined as malignant. It just *is*.

Sammy typifies his confused historical time because he is

unable to experience spirit except as guilt. Why then does
Golding let him escape from 'the forcing chamber of the cell'
(190) into a kind of merciful freedom? I put the question to
Mr. Golding and he remarked that the flashback at the novel's
close was like the 'handprint on the canvas that changes the
whole thing', bringing it all into a true focus. The 'key to it
was that the door of the cell opened. I suddenly saw that, and
it became [for me] the first genuine passion I felt about the
book.'[7]

Another theme can then be detected in Free Fall; this second
pursuit seems to be the one which most vividly engages
Golding's imagination, for it grows from a radically anti-
historical view of man as does Pincher Martin. As the ironic
Dante, Sammy represents a twentieth-century figure living in
society, but here at the heart of the fable, 'the forcing chamber
of the cell', he is a moral being facing some kind of god, that
inevitable thrust or bar of steel, what The Pyramid terms that
'god without mercy' which operates in and on him. In the
prison camp, Sammy is deprived of institutions, society, even
memories, and is reduced under Halde's interrogation to his
elements: fear and conjecture. As Halde puts it to Sammy:
'For you and me, reality is this room' (140), a comment
which Sammy enlarges on symbolically when he mutters in the
cell:

> I? I? Too many I's, but what else was there in this thick,
> impenetrable cosmos? What else? A wooden door and
> how many shapes of walls? (169–170)

And given Sammy's adolescent choice of a material world, all
that the cosmos is can be imagined as an impenetrable dark
prison with a wooden door and no exit. Thus, in this novel's
confrontation scene action flows inward as Sammy retreats
into himself to explore his fear.

It is a quest in search of Being qua Being then that occupies
Free Fall's centre, not the quest for a philosophical bridge

between two worlds. Its terms are inexplicit though they
recall imagistically Pincher's purgatorial surrender; its end,
like Sammy's definition of art, is 'partly communication but
only partly. The rest is discovery' (102). The experience
proceeds out of what Sammy calls his 'painful obsession with
discovery and identification' (103), for he is portrayed
throughout the fable as wanting to make what is outside
himself inside himself. Finally, the journey bears similarities
to archetypal journeys underground and the imagery of door,
wall, darkness, and encirclement all are metamorphic: they
suggest that a total change of being follows when the separating
medium between consciousness and the Other is broken
through. The process involves stripping the protagonist down
to that very last thing which cannot be destroyed. This
Golding takes as a definition of the human: an impenetrable
target that will not buckle under pressure.

In the dark, Sammy first finds some comfort in the wooden
door that his back rests against since it is a still and familiar
point in the maze of imagined walls. But once he discovers
that the shape of the confining room is a cell, he realizes that
the door, though wooden, only allows him to suffer in a
recognized corner. For the cell is an objective counterpart of
the material cosmos that exists outside it; even if the door is
breakable no escape follows its collapse since outside of the
cell waits Halde, the avenging judge, and 'prison inside prison'
(171). To unlock the door is not to escape as Christian and
Faithful did from Giant Despair's dungeon, for in a century of
disbelief, it is matter, not a supreme and merciful principle,
which supports the world. To get outside the door is simply
to return where one has started. And with vistas turning back
on each other Sammy admits 'total defeat' knowing that this
view of life both blights man's 'will and [is] self-perpetuating'
(171).

Yet this is only the first step in Sammy's torture, a torture
he rapidly realizes is self-inflicted. Though he cautions himself
not to move, some interior thrust compels him to leave the

6

door and investigate the cell's centre: 'The centre was the secret' (173). He understands another prison now encircles him—and this one is wholly of the spirit: 'One way you take the next step and suffer for it. The other way, you do not take it but suffer on your own rack trying not to think what the next step is' (177). He begins to populate the centre with imagined demons. He cannot just stay by the door; he must deduce that something exists in the centre: he forces himself to guess, wonder, invent. It boils with shapes. Then 'compelled, helplessly deprived of will, sterile, wounded, diseased, sick of his nature, pierced' (173–174), he stretches out his hand. He touches something wet, imagines: snake, acid, coffin, dead slug, gnarled body then, sum of all terror, a dismembered phallus.

Sammy Mountjoy screams. He screams, expecting nothing beyond the threshold of his own consciousness but pain and perhaps its cessation, accepting 'a shut door, darkness and a shut sky' (184). The wholly physical organ in the centre makes him scream in terror. It is the instinctive unconscious scream of a rat or captive animal but it becomes a human plea (Golding claims) because directed towards some place for 'the very act of crying changed the thing that cried' (184). Instinctively 'the thing' or point of consciousness that is Sammy searches for a place where help may be found, and that pursuit Golding posits as a unique characteristic of the human. Since the external and substantial present offers only a twitching body and the concrete of the cell, it (the point of consciousness) looks with 'not physical eyes' (184) into an interior world. But the internal and insubstantial world offers no comfort either; if the present is only 'the physical world . . . and no escape' (185), then the past, against which the thing pitches, holds 'some forgotten thing' under layers of concrete[8] which cannot be unearthed in the urgency of terror. A thing against 'an absolute helplessness' (184), screaming for mercy, it can only pitch towards the future, hurling itself along a purgatorial furnace, experienced as a flight of steps from horror to horror. Flesh, language, thought, present perceptions, and past memories, rind by rind, the identifying skins of Mountjoy's person are pared away; finally even the refuge of madness, which for Pincher was the last proof of singular identity, is destroyed. Then and at this point the thing comes up against something which does not capitulate, an 'entry where death is close as darkness against the eyeballs' (185). And breaks through that veil: 'And burst that door' (185).

Golding is deliberately ambiguous about the cell door's opening, leaving it to the reader to decide, depending on his religious sensibility. The Commandant comes 'late' and opens it physically, but in one sense Sammy has opened it by his spirit since the physical fact that it is closed is no longer relevant to the transformed Sammy. From blackness, then, 'it' appears to escape through the veil into a world transformed by spiritual freedom, but this thing, what the dead Samuel sees as 'the human nature inhabiting the centre of my awareness' (190), has not been destroyed.

> To die is easy enough in the forcing chamber of a cell. . . .
> But when the eyes of Sammy were turned in on myself . . .
> what they saw was not beautiful but fearsome. Dying,
> after all, then was not one tenth complete—for must not
> complete death be to get out of the way of that shining,
> singing cosmos and let it shine and sing? And here was a
> point, a single point which was my own interior identity,
> without shape or size but only position. (190)

With innocent eyes, he perceives the prisoners as burning bushes and the dust and camp as brilliant and fantastic jewels; Sammy accepts its spirit whose source is 'a place . . . I did not know existed but which I had forgotten merely' (187). It is a Traherne-like cosmos whose door is 'sometimes open and sometimes shut' (187) but always there. Yet he must also accept living with his own 'unendurable' (190) identity. For though the door has been burst open—a spiritual and physical door—and opens back on to the world of mystery, the inadequate Being that is Sammy's centre still persists.

The cell then with its opaque centre is a microcosmic image of Sammy's own moral life as the Rock was Pincher's interior landscape. The Nazis, Sammy conjectures, are psychologists of suffering and appropriate to each man the terror that is 'most helpful and necessary to his case' (173) and for such a hedonist as Sammy it seems appropriate that a phallus occupies the dark middle. Thus in this horror, central to the cell, Sammy recognizes his own interior identity: it is an objective counterpart for his own centre, an odious and mutilated organ. Later in the coda we learn that, as the Commandant was releasing him from the cell, Sammy turned backwards and noticed a wet rag in the cell's centre, not a mutilated penis.

The method used here is the characteristic one of the ideo-graphic structure—a delayed disclosure for in this, the coda's flashback, the reader discovers the odious fragment is nothing more or less than a damp floorcloth. While conscribed in the cell Sammy's imagination invested the fragment with shape and infection—he decides it is a penis when he imagines that Halde will choose the appropriate punishment for such a hedonistic man as he. We now judge, as Sammy himself has not by the story's close, that what Sammy perceived as his unendurable identity (when he turned the eyes of the spirit inwards) may be similarly innocuous. Furthermore, depending on how Sammy (and, by extension, man) judges himself, he may discover some release from guilt, from darkness, some opening door. Were he not blinded by his own guilt—his conviction of his unendurable identity—he might see the Redeemer in the Judge.

Thus the Sphinx's riddle which closes the fable—'The Herr Doctor does not know about peoples' (253) we might translate as a shorthand negation of mechanistic assumptions about morality which ignore the fact that even creatures as guilty as Sammy can experience moments of freedom, still are offered

release from the cosmic prison by creatures apparently as
guilty as Halde. Golding intends this reversal of perspective
and the puzzle to operate back through the entire fable; in
reality it primarily touches only on the atavistic journey. It
hardly answers the question of the bridge.

Of course, the bridge between the grey world of flesh and
the golden world of spirit might have been the darkened cell
with its reductive process, a kind of whipping which releases
moral energies from their paralysis. For like the nightmare
fragmentations of Pincher's illusory 'present', this atavistic
exploration concerns itself with the darkness that spells
magic, terror and awe. The darkness, then, is a kind of
preternatural world that Sammy the younger (like the boy in
'The Ladder and the Tree') 'inhabits by nature' (217). It is the
source of his real creativity: 'Sometimes I would feel myself
connected to *the well inside me*. . . . There would come into my
whole body a feeling of passionate certainty. . . . Then I
would stand the world of appearance on its head, would
reach in and down, would destroy savagely and recreate' (102,
italics added). Decidedly this darkness and its mysterious
connection with creation and destruction bears little relation
to 'the world of miracle' (189), the Traherne-like singing
universe. Nor is it the detached, understandable, and usable
universe of cause and effect. It simply *is*: 'it reveals though we
cannot explain what it reveals.'[9] And Golding would leave the
discovery there. In my mind *Free Fall* does not achieve the
'miracle of implication' which Sammy/Golding cites as the
aesthetic end of any portrait where 'the viewer's eye' and not
the artist's pen creates a completed line and brings itself 'slap
up against another view of the world' (102). On the other
hand I find it no mean example of 'laborious portraiture', a
confession of failure and a confession of growth.

FREE FALL—NOTES

1 William Golding, *Free Fall* (London: Faber and Faber, 1961), p. 77. All subsequent citations will be taken from this edition and be indicated in textual parentheses.

2 Golding's remark in a review of Jules Verne's *Round the Moon* is relevant here: 'It is a, or rather *the*, moment of free fall—not the modern sort which can be endless, but the nineteenth-century sort, the point where earth and moon gravity is equal.' William Golding, 'Astronaut by Gaslight', *The Hot Gates*, p. 115.

3 Kermode, 'Adam's Image', *The Spectator* (October 23, 1959), p. 564.

4 Gregor and Kinkead-Weekes, p. 118. The sense of this passage in relation to *Free Fall* is discussed at some length by Gregor and Kinkead-Weekes though their contention that 'the first paragraph presents 252 of *Free Fall's* 253 pages in miniature' is perhaps too sweeping, since in fact many minor motifs—notably the darkness conception—do not enter the paragraph.

5 The elaborate echoes deliberately recall many motifs established earlier in the story; Beatrice's nittering recapitulates the lodger's bird-like breathing ('She was jerking round like the figure in a cathedral *clock*' [243; italics added]), as well as Sammy's dream of a dying cat where 'marsh-birds' are crying. Of course, the central recapitulation is the madness itself, for Sammy had pretended madness in order to seduce Beatrice. Thus he remembers her saying, 'You musn't ever say such a thing, Sammy' (240) as he watches her in the asylum.

6 Nick is an innocent even though he lives in the world of matter; in other words, his nature remains complete even though his vision is confined to one mode. Sammy alone extends the materialism to its moral field.

7 Compare the genesis of *Free Fall*, where Golding discovered significance at the novel's conclusion, with a similar discovery in the genesis of *The Inheritors*. In the case of *Free Fall* there was, Golding maintains, no rewriting. He admits it being so close to him still that he has not reread it—the many technical errors in the text attest to this.

8 Cf. *Pincher Martin*: 'Pattern repeated from the beginning of time, approach of the unknown thing, a dark centre that turned its back on the thing that created it and struggled to escape' (179). This is the pattern that Sammy, again like Pincher, deliberately turns away from and is to be understood as the presence (*in absentia*) of God.

9 Gregor and Kinkead-Weekes's comment on the 'meaning' of the spire, p. 255.

THE SPIRE

I

To begin with there is a deep desire in the minds of people to break out of the globe of their own skulls, and find the significance in the cosmos that mere measurement misses. Any man who claims to have found a bridge between the world of the physical sciences and the world of the spirit is sure of a hearing. Is this not because most of us have an unexpressed faith that the bridge exists?

—Golding, 'All or Nothing'

Free Fall's final page challenges the limitations of pattern. Though ultimately the novel remains bifocal in its vision, ambiguity rather than prescription informs the divided world which Sammy Mountjoy inhabits. The coda indicates that Mountjoy's certitudes about moral guilt and the undiscovered bridge collapse internally simply because such a pattern is too blunt to express (or reveal) the complexities of truth. Abstractly then, and at the expense of its own unity, *Free Fall* comes to essentially the same point as do the other fables of insisting that any scheme is self-contradictory because in some sense it is a metaphor. None the less, there is the urgent search to find a link between separate phenomena. *The Spire* takes precisely this paradox as its subject: the world it invokes is pluralistic, intermingling, complex, yet it places a wilful and unrelenting patternmaker as its central intelligence. Out of the confrontation and inevitably intense collision of the two emerges what *The Critical Quarterly* has described as 'the greatest of Golding's novels so far, but [also] one of the most ambitious and fascinating novels of the century'.[1]

The Spire represents, it seems to me, the completion of one phase in Golding's development as a fabulist. It recapitulates many of the features of the preceding fables. Again Golding has written a fable in which character is presented not only in torment but through torment. A crisis brings about the meeting of two worlds, a meeting which is represented in the confrontation scene. Here conscience and circumstances fuse in judgment of crime, and a painful purgation eliminates all but the essential *ding an sich* of the major character, that bar of identity that does not buckle. The protagonist seeks explanations and justification for his action in one pattern after another, one at each stage of the building; he is left staring out of a window at the physical spire whose one symbolic focus reveals its mysterious centre.

The plot line is simple enough, and like the narrative that extends chronologically over a two-year period, moderately straightforward. To this extent the novel represents a return to the manner of *Lord of the Flies*, but it resembles *Pincher Martin* and *Free Fall* in that the action is steeped in the inner consciousness of its leading character—though presented from the third person point of view rather than the first. Again structure is bare, severe, and formalized, taking its shape from the gradual erection and evolution of a cathedral spire. What excess there is exists at the level of language not of action which is economic throughout.

The fable is isolated temporally and spatially; its action takes place in a setting as delimited as that of the island in *Lord of the Flies*, for it is confined within the cathedral walls, particularly the expanding stone flesh of the rising structure. Events move out into the close and village only after the spire has been constructed and then sparingly in the coda of the narrative. Psychologically, action is even more intensely confined within the increasingly unreliable consciousness of the protagonist, Jocelin. Here *The Spire* recalls *Pincher Martin*. As events that comprise the plot line become blurred, the physical boards, levers, nails and ropes of the tower are fiercely rendered.

Minor characters—and there are a number masterfully sketched, including a dumb sculptor, a jabbering, clacking wife, a flippant courtesan—exist as they pass in and out of Jocelin's obsession. If the huddled roofs of the city are viewed solely from the spire's high vantage point, shrugging their shapes into it, then the spire and its builders are looked at almost completely from Jocelin's perspective. Social context in the manner of *Free Fall* has been abandoned and when the reader sees Jocelin from the outside, as he does at several important junctures, it is with the sense of jolted strangeness that recalls the transition to Tuami's view of Lok in *The Inheritors*. As the narrative continues these jolts become more and more powerful since the reader occupies Jocelin's mind which is itself increasingly, obsessively closed.

The fable is built on two movements: Chapters I-X and Chapters X-XII: the building of the spire is followed by an examination of motive. On the completion of the spire's construction a dramatic reversal occurs which shatters the protagonist's illusions; Jocelin is forced to review his own motives and acknowledge his own deceptions. This inspection comprises the fable's second movement and here Jocelin comes up against the cellarage of his own mind, those things which he has deliberately repressed. In terms of *The Spire's* ideographic structure this movement is an extension of the characteristic concluding coda that in all other fables hinted at a mythic integration to be accomplished by the reader when various clues were assembled. Peculiar to *The Spire* is the protagonist's own realization of the full import of his actions; Jocelin accomplishes the fusion of alternate explanations. In his last cryptic cry, 'It's like the appletree', the fragmentations of pagan and Christian, cellarage and sky, panic-shot darkness and bluebird-over-water and all that these elements represent are brought into essential relationship.

The story concerns a Dean of a fourteenth-century English

6*

cathedral who is convinced in a vision that he is chosen by
God to cap the magnificence of his cathedral with a four-
hundred-foot spire. One morning lying at the church's crossways, he feels himself initiated into a 'newfound humility and
newfound knowledge' which he senses physically as a fountain
bursting up with 'flame and light, up through a notspace,
filling with ultimate urgency and not to be denied . . . an
implacable, unstoppable glorious fountain of the spirit, a
wild burning of me for Thee—' (193). At the novel's opening
a physical spire, what Jocelin calls his ultimate 'diagram of
prayer' (120), is in the first stages of construction: the nave is
filled with dust, a hole has been torn through the church's
side to bring through wood and stone, and Jocelin is laughing
in 'holy mirth' (8) while the sunlight throws the coloured
refraction of the Abraham and Isaac window on his shining face.

Jocelin now meets opposition to his plan from both his
friend and confessor, Sacrist Anselm, and from the master
builder, Roger Mason, who finds that the foundations are
scarcely adequate for the cathedral's existing structure. By
force of Jocelin's will the spire continues to be constructed,
though now against the judgment of the clergy, the teams of
masons who risk their lives at each level, and above all Roger
who counsels the folly of the enterprise. Jocelin is reflective
in his remark: 'The net isn't mine, Roger, and the folly isn't
mine. It's God's Folly' (121).

> The building is a diagram of prayer; and our spire will be
> a diagram of the highest prayer of all. God revealed it to
> me in a vision, his unprofitable servant. He chose me.
> He chooses you, to fill the diagram with glass and iron
> and stone, since the children of men require a thing to
> look at. (120)

Faith overrules advice; Jocelin trusts his vision, is reassured
by a warmth at his spine that he calls his guardian angel, and
finds encouragement in the promise of a Holy Nail from Rome.

Then it becomes clear that foundations do not exist. A break-down in Christian faith coincides with the threatened destruction of the cathedral. Pagan riots ensue and the Verger, Pangall, vanishes.

Jocelin's fanaticism is now so intense that he deliberately exploits the masterbuilder's desertion of his wife and illegal attachment to the Verger's wife, Goody Pangall. As in *Free Fall*, the decision to use adultery to further one's own end becomes the moment when freedom is lost. Jocelin thinks to himself:

> . . . Goody and Roger, both in the tent that would expand with them wherever they might go. And so distinct that it might have been written . . . there was the thought. It was so terrible that it went beyond feeling, and left him inspecting it with a kind of stark detachment, while the edge of the spire burned into his cheek. . . . 'She will keep him here.' (64)

Her horrible death in childbirth, the master builder's drunken-ness and attempted suicide, even the changed countryside whose landscape is altered by the tower 'laying a hand' (107) and enforcing a new pattern of streets, roads, migrations—'The countryside was shrugging itself obediently into a new shape' (108)—all are the costs and the sacrifices, and the lessons of the holy exploit.

This pattern ends with the arrival of ecclesiastical authorities from Rome to hear the complaints against the Dean. A Visitor brings the Holy Nail. Seeing Jocelin deranged, his skirt tied high for climbing, his services abandoned, his hair disarrayed and full of wood shavings, the Commission indicts him, and relieves him of his Deanship. Jocelin's only concern is that the spire should be nailed securely to the heavens. In the midst of a raging storm he ascends the tower and performs the last act of faith by hammering in the Holy Nail at the spire's apex.

It is the conclusion of the first and major movement. The

spire stands. In the extended coda, Chapters X-XII, menacing facts begin to emerge: Jocelin finds his appointment was due to a debased aunt, the mistress of the King; he discovers his clergy loathe him for his arrogance and pomposity; Father Adam denounces the record of his original vision of the spire as spiritually naive. Even the mighty pillars are hollow; they were filled with rubble by 'the giants who had been on the earth in those days' (188). The world seems corrupt, a whirligig of grinning, noseless men. In despair Jocelin flings himself down on the crossways, his place of vision and 'his place of sacrifice' (189), and there like a broken snake he is scourged: 'Then his angel put away the two wings from the cloven hoof and struck him from arse to the head with a whitehot flail' (188).

But his angel may be a delusion too—spinal tuberculosis (possibly syphilis) has wasted away his body. During the six months left him to live, Jocelin inspects the falsity of all that has gone before. The two sorts of cellars, his hidden nature and the pit at the spire's base, each is surveyed. Slowly he acknowledges his repressed lust for Goody that made him marry his daughter-in-god to the impotent, aging Verger; he acknowledges Pangall's murder, for the pagan workmen had used the Verger as a ritual scapegoat for their fears, burying him in the pit at the crossways. Jocelin then knows himself responsible for four ruined lives. And all that remains is the spire, 'an ungainly, crumbling thing' (193), a monument to his error, once an act of devotion, then the repression of sexual energy and the crude expression of lust, now a cruel hammer of vengeance pressing down on the world. Crawling back from Roger's den the townsfolk attack him, just as earlier Pangall had been reviled by the workmen.

Moments before his death and the giving of the Last Host, however, Jocelin suffers another vision. Through the window he glimpses a thing surpassing in beauty any other vision: 'It was slim as a girl, translucent. It had grown from some seed of rose-coloured substance that glittered like a waterfall, an upward waterfall. The substance was one thing, that broke all the way to infinity in cascades of exultation that nothing could trammel' (223). It is the spire, still standing, and the fable takes this as the moment of truth as Jocelin dying whispers his beatitude: '*It's like the appletree.*'

II

Few reviewers committed themselves solidly to the support of *The Spire* when it appeared in 1964. For several reasons the book's appearance amounted to a literary watershed for Golding's reputation, a verification of the earlier accomplishments, a kind of test case for the 'white hope' of the English novel. Several years had intervened between its publication and that of *Free Fall* and while Golding had written a substantial number of reviews and articles for British and American journals, with the increasing popularity of *Lord of the Flies* he sought personal isolation, refusing interviews by the media, and generally avoiding the kind of literary conviviality expected of him. *The Spire* received, then, the kind of attention that placed it immediately in an area between notoriety and critical recognition: a best seller, grudgingly credited but often discredited. Thus a critic no less perceptive than V. S. Pritchett could write in his *New Statesman* review that Golding had succumbed to the 'underworld of fashionable paranoia' and the consequences were 'obscurity, monotony and strain'. Others also argued that allegory and ambitious design overwhelmed concrete novelistic features.

Style was assailed much in the manner *Free Fall*'s verbal texture had been attacked as rhetorical, obscure, and needlessly constricted. In fact strain and obscurity were the key critical terms and few articles suggested that Gothic excess operated as an ironic and descriptive analogue of character, event, and theme. Nor was there much analysis of style, though it shows some interesting innovations appropriate to its mediaeval spirit.

On the whole most criticism misapprehended the increasing egoism of the obsessive Jocelin and interpreted his isolation and in turn the fable's theme as necessitated by Golding's weakness in presenting human relationships. A related point was that the fable lacked humanity, that both the integrity and inviolability of the individual consciousness were sacrificed to the interests of moral and metaphysical ideas. Golding is consistently charged with being inhibited from handling any but adolescent or pre-adolescent relationships, a point more irrelevant than accurate to *The Spire* since it appears that Golding abandoned whole sections of narrative devoted to the early relationships between Jocelin and Anselm, and Jocelin and Alison, in a strict paring down of the fable's structure so that both relationships could become the instruments of ironic reversals in the protagonist's fortune. Thus in the fable's final version Jocelin discovers that the origins of his funds and Deanship are soiled by human corruption only after the spire's construction is completed.

An inordinate amount of discussion of *The Spire* has focused on the historical/literary source for the tower and its tale; it has been assumed that since the earlier novels used simple-minded literary ancestors as their starting point, then *The Spire* too must be a reversal of some other writer's version of hubris attendant on cathedral construction; and if not this, then a popular tale, some church record or legend. Thus Kermode wonders where Golding boned up on facts about the mason's craft, and assumes some 'useful' point of departure might exist there. As a matter of fact Golding told me he briefly consulted an architectural book on tower building in the Harvard University Library, but then abandoned it, preferring his own considerable knowledge of seamanship: 'I did the whole thing in sailor's terms.' He continued: 'Seamanship has been defined as the art of moving heavy weights—with the implication that you only use the most primitive means: blocks, tackles, levers. I know about that.' This accounts for one system of images where the cathedral is a 'stone ship' fitted with a mast; its pillars 'float' and its foundations are a 'raft' on which the 'ark' rests.

In their speculations on the origins of The Spire, critics have been rather presumptuous; two commentators, for example, suggest Carlyle's Past and Present gave Golding both detail and attitude for his version of Carlyle's Abbot Samson. On the crudest of parallels, Oldsey and Weintraub—along with several others—adopted Ibsen's The Masterbuilder as the primary source for The Spire. The argument here is that since Solness, the master builder of the play's title, falls to death in an attempt to scale the spire of his own house, he is a prototype for Jocelin who does not fall to death, and who is not the master builder of the cathedral's spire. Similar whimsy construes the following sources as well: Ibsen's Brand (both protagonists are obsessive zealots who build spires); T. S. Eliot's The Rock (vulgar workmen construct foundations in churches); Robert Browning's 'The Bishop Orders His Tomb at St. Praxed's' (both works have priests named Anselm); in this last case, perhaps Golding had an ironic echo in mind when he chose, as the name for his scrupulously correct Anselm, the name of a twelfth-century Archbishop of Canterbury who was attacked as a hypocrite. Anyway, Golding adamantly denies any literary predecessor: 'no work comes out of another unless it is stillborn.'

Perhaps such debates about The Spire's derivativeness are significant more in what they reveal about the state of reviewing than in any accurate judgment on the fable's originality or value. Some opposition is legitimate, of course, particularly those critical appraisals which see any radical modification of novelistic techniques as fundamentally a violation of the genuine business of the novel. However, a substantial number of The Spire's critiques now seem ill-advised, if not hastily considered, where literary reviewing functions as a kind of trend-spotting. Many of the reviewers worked solely in terms of the standing clichés about Golding's fiction. This, of course, does disservice to authors since it makes them victims not

forgers of their own reputations, forever feeding the doctrin-
aire orthodoxy of critical expectations. This is very much the
case in the matter of the influences on Golding's fiction where a
sharp distinction must be drawn between source, allusion and
association. Golding remarked to me, for example, that
Trollope's Barchester series was used or 'sewn in negatively'
to the extent that precisely that which Trollope's secular age
avoided, Jocelin has foremost before him. 'Trollope included
everything but the church', viz., everything but the spirit and
its corruption. Presumably, then, Golding would agree with
David Lodge's point in *The Spectator* that, instead of Trollope's
concern with secularized religion and ecclesiastical careerism,
'we have the age of faith, just as disedifying, when Christianity
was still in rivalry with pagan devil-worship and when
worldly desires sublimated into religious zeal could have
terrifying consequences.'[2] Of course, *The Spire* suggests the
great century of mediaeval corruption by reference not only to
Alison whose money builds the spire but also by reference to a
minor character, Ivo, who is made Chancellor simply because
his father owned the forests from which the cathedral beams
were constructed. Golding alludes to this corruption by
having Ivo's installation occur ironically in the qualified
sunlight cast through the St. Aldhelm window. (St. Aldhelm
was a seventh-century Bishop who was celebrated for insisting
that faith was only granted in the tradition and that the duty of
accepting derives solely from Peter and the tradition of the
Roman church.)

III

The truth is, we have a primitive belief that virtue,
force, power—what the anthropologists might call
mana—lie in the original stones and nowhere else. . . .
Our old churches are full of this power. I do not refer
to their specifically religious function or influence.
There is a whole range of other feelings that . . .

coagulated around them. . . . The historians of
religion might mutter about the stones that they were
'relics by contact'. But contact with what? It was mana,
indescribable, unaccountable, indefinable, impossible
mana.

—Golding—'An Affection for Cathedrals'

No simple source or scenario underpins *The Spire*. Rather,
diverse fragments contributed to its genesis, coalescing
according to the logic of imagination, from whose final soil the
fable has grown organically. 'The Ladder and the Tree', for
example, with its antitheses represented by the ascending
ladder to the tree-house and the dark fearsome graveyard at its
base seems entirely relevant to the symbolic opposition of pit
and tower in *The Spire*. Jocelin climbs away from the crossway's
stirring earth; as he divests himself of its 'confusion' (100) he
feels 'the same appalled delight as a small boy feels when first
he climbs too high in a forbidden tree' (101). Similarly,
The Spire adapts the cellar metaphor which occupies *Pincher
Martin*'s thematic core; there the metaphor invoked that
morbid terror beneath the conscious mind which the conscious
mind itself had substituted for some good (Golding's letter
called it 'god') that formerly rested in the darkness. Jocelin
is described as 'a building about to fall' (222) in the fable's
coda. And as he interrogates the drunken Mason about the
contents of the cathedral's pit, he asks, 'What's a man's
mind, Roger? Is it the whole building, *cellarage* and all?'
(213, italics added).

Several minor works are germane. A BBC play 'Miss
Pulkinhorn' and the short story from which it derives
(published in 1960 by *Encounter*) show Golding preoccupied
with the problem of faith and guilt several years before *The
Spire*'s appearance. Setting a conventionally religious but
perniciously bigoted spinster against a religious eccentric who
prays ecstatically before an illuminated window, the play
explores the inevitable opposition between orthodox belief

and the unaccountable certitude the mystic possesses which
defies reason, reasonableness, and the data of the empirical
world. It is significant that the church within which all the
action occurs is Salisbury Cathedral and the Abraham and
Isaac window has a dramatic and thematic role in the development of the play's eschatology of the sacrificial victim. *The
Spire* elaborates on the notion of the scapegoat and sacrificial
victim—in fact the theme is introduced in the fable's very
first paragraph when a complex image describes the Dean's
face illuminated by the Abraham window: 'He was laughing,
chin up . . . God the Father was exploding in his face with a
glory of sunlight through painted glass, a glory that moved
with his movements to consume and exalt Abraham and Isaac
and God again' (7). Certain motifs from 'Miss Pulkinhorn'
reappear in the fable, including the metaphor of the growing
tree to represent the entanglement of human motives and the
early English hymnal, 'Tomorrow Must be My Dancing Day'
with its enigmatic refrain, 'Sing O my love, O my love, my
love, my love/This have I done for my true love'. In the play
and fable this refrain alternates between the regular church
ritual of Mass, though with less justification in 'Miss
Pulkinhorn' than in *The Spire* where it nicely reveals Jocelin's
confusion of motives and love objects. Perhaps the most
important similarity between the fable and the play is in the
characterization of the man, for though he is in the line of the
Nat/Simon visionary figure he is more complex. He is a
believer yet self-deluded, living on the very fringe of lunacy
yet innocent, nevertheless.

Among Golding's occasional pieces, another relevant
document is a 1960 review of an amateur antiquarian's book.
Quite possibly this book suggested to Golding the dramatic
possibilities of having Jocelin feel physically his vision as the
angel of God at his spine, a delusion which allows the alternate
motives of sexuality and spinal tuberculosis to enter the story
and function as alternate explanations for vision. Golding
shows considerable psychological insight into the innocent,

Jimmy Mason, whose diary the antiquarian had unearthed, but what is interesting is the lyrical tone which pervades the review, and Golding's singular interest in Jimmy's religious conversion. The following passage is the sole portion of Jimmy's diary Golding quotes in his review:

> Went to bed at half past eleven, and not lain many minutes before felt something so strange come down from heaven. It seemed as if come so many times and would never go away. How bad it made me feel I cried and prayed to God. Directly it went I felt no more. It could never be anything evil, but good as one of the angels of God.[3]

The prose rhythms of the dream/vision are unmistakedly sexual as the experience itself might possibly have been since contextually this part of the diary was written at a time when Jimmy Mason was bewilderingly attracted to a woman. Jocelin's first phallic dream has striking similarities to the one recorded in the diary; waking in loathing Jocelin lashes himself 'seven times, hard across the back in his pride of the angel, one time for each devil' (65). If indeed this remote diary suggested certain elements of Jocelin's mysticism and its connection to repressed sexuality, then it combined with another germinal figure, adamant in its energy. Golding has mentioned to me as one of the imaginative seeds for the ravenlike egoism of Jocelin, one of Viollet-Le-Duc's gargoyles which perches on the balustrades of Notre Dame Cathedral in Paris. It is known as the Le Stryge gargoyle and is made famous by Charles Meryon's well known nineteenth-century etching. A grimacing inhuman bird-man with half human face, it seems immensely powerful though its chin rests on folded hands as it stares sternly over the city.

Other historical fragments and their attendant fictitious legends are relevant to *The Spire*'s genesis. In particular, there

are a host of legends surrounding Gothic cathedrals that anyone living in England—the country which experienced the
apotheosis of mediaeval construction could not help but
absorb in part. It is a matter of historical record that in 1322
the tower of Ely Cathedral fell; Canterbury Cathedral's
builder, William of Sens, fell from scaffolding and broke his
back; in 1646 the central spire of Lichfield Cathedral was
demolished by Royalist forces such was its symbolic arrogance;
the spire of Chichester fell in 1861, tumbling in February after
singing during the Christmas services; Peterborough Cathedral
was built on a peat bog and Bath Abbey in the vicinity of
ruins of successive Roman baths; Carlisle has two streams
flowing beneath its tower; Wells ascends from a ring of pools;
and Salisbury Cathedral, the country's tallest and most extraordinary spire surmounting its top, rises from marshland.
Golding's essay, 'An Affection for Cathedrals', on Salisbury
and Winchester, shows his delicate familiarity with many of
their chronicles. He seems attracted imaginatively by the
element of irrationality which overrides practical confirmation
and sanctions. Thus writing here on Salisbury Cathedral's
legendary origin he celebrates the victory of faith over
technological commonsense.

> Round about the year 1200, Bishop Poore was standing
> on a hill overlooking the confluence of the local rivers,
> according to legend, when the mother of Jesus appeared
> to him, told him to shoot an arrow and build her a
> church where the arrow fell. The arrow flew more than a
> mile and fell in the middle of a swamp. There with
> complete indifference to such things as health, founda-
> tions, access and general practicability, the cathedral
> was built. Eighty years later with a technological gamble
> which makes space travel seem child's play, the builders
> erected the highest spire in the country on top of it,
> thousands of tons of lead and iron and wood and stone.
> Yet the whole building still stands.

So it is likely these legends or known fragments of them have—
to use his own figure—rotted to compost; have 'mulched
down' in the fertile soul of his imagination.

There is the added and absolutely essential matter that
Golding has passed much of his life under the twin towers of
Salisbury Cathedral and Stonehenge, teaching beneath one and
living very close to the other. For him the high chalk Downs of
Wessex that surround the two monuments are alight with
legends, even artifacts, from four thousand years of historical
activity. As he remarked to his interviewer: 'Wiltshire is not a
place so much as a kind of palimpsest of various generations
and centuries.'[4] The area is thick with the bones of ancient
peoples: Roman, Norman, Saxon, and Celt.

Salisbury Cathedral, then, is the historical original for
Dean Jocelin's 'bible in stone'. Some of its features, such as
the number of transepts, have been altered so the fable can
have a general relevance but it is clear that the story is based
on the construction of the spire in Salisbury Cathedral;
several of its elements are similar.[5] Begun in 1220, a 404-foot
spire (Jocelin's stretches 400 feet) was added a century later,
its apex topped by a capstone all of which rests on four pillars
whose diminishing thickness thrusts appalling weight into a
marshy bog on which the whole edifice is supported. As in the
fable, one of the pillars slipped out of perpendicular, despite
thick iron bands which had been used to strengthen the spire's
structure: 'It leans. It totters. It bends. But it still stands',
writes Golding in 'An Affection for Cathedrals'. Until
recently the whole structure was a source of considerable
anxiety but now we know that this watery meadow conceals
one of the strongest weight-bearing geological formations in
the world. However, the builders' faith (or foolhardiness)
and their astonishing engineering feat still amount to little less
than a miracle, since they could not possibly have suspected
such a stratum. 'It is a miracle of faith', Golding has declared,
'A definite act of faith.'

Not far from Salisbury Cathedral itself lies Old Sarum. A

rather formidable symbol of continuity, it is the site successively of a British and possibly Roman camp, of a Saxon and
Norman town. Its cathedral was the bishopric of two twelfth-
century bishops, Jocelin and Roger, and at the end of the
fourteenth century its stones were raised to provide materials
for the building of Salisbury Cathedral close. Earlier, stern,
straight roads crossed Salisbury Plain and converged at what
used to be a prehistoric metropolis whose 'cathedral'
(Golding's word) was Stonehenge. The landscape—which is
re-christened Barchester in *The Pyramid* and *The Spire*—seems
as much a mythic landscape to Golding as Wessex to Hardy.
And no more simple in its imaginative influence. He writes in
the essay, 'Digging for Pictures':

> For me there is a glossy darkness under the turf, and
> against that background the people of the past play out
> their actions . . . I have only to twitch aside the green
> coverlet of grass to find them there. Might I not come
> face to face with that most primitive of Europe's men—
> Neanderthal Man—who once loped along the track where
> I used to take my Sunday walk?

The monuments, their ruins and annals and legends, the soil
itself represent a rather complicated metaphor for human
effort it would seem, for they confirm mutely an ancient
repetition of creation and destruction in historical as well as
geological times. Their presence speaks both of the anonymity
of human enterprise and its essential autocratic origin so
much so that: 'The very stones cry out'. They possess *mana*.

IV

*It was so simple at first. On the purely human level of
course, it's a story of shame and folly—Jocelin's Folly,
they call it. I had a vision you see, a clear and
explicit vision. It was so simple! It was to be my work.*

I was chosen for it. But then the complications began.
A single green shoot at first, then clinging tendrils,
then branches, then at last a riotous confusion . . .

— *The Spire* (168)

The Spire represents a major development in Golding's technical strategy. First it does not invert a conventional or
popular model to arrive at its theme. I have argued that no
simple scenario underpins the fable though several associative
strands are relevant to the book's imaginative growth.
Second, though the structural shape of *The Spire* functions
ideographically, reversal occurs at a dramatic level not just by
the juxtaposition of two structural frames. The fable is
divided into two movements, the second of which corresponds
to the slighter codas of the earlier fables since it consists in
several important disclosures that throw into suspicion all
that has preceded it. It differs from the earlier codas in that the
new perspective is not a new point of view but rather the
enlightened viewpoint of the protagonist himself as he looks
back upon events with different eyes. Consequently the
resolution of those alternate patterns the fable has set in
motion is accomplished by the protagonist, not the reader
alone, as is the case in the earlier fables. Inasmuch as there is
no other consciousness which views the events we share Jocelin's perspective throughout the fable.

It is true that point of view is handled so that certain ironic
asides, as well as the symbolic patterns certain metaphors
assume as they are reiterated throughout the text, are intended
to hint at Jocelin's folly, the purity of his dedication, and
complexity of his motives. Among these the tent, the may-
flower, the kingfisher and raven, and above all the burgeoning
tree are relevant, the latter especially so since one of the
major thematic preoccupations of the book is the nature of the
generative process. Thus we interpret the dreams in their
sexual context whereas Jocelin deliberately denies them their
sexual origin, even when the buried creatures haunt him.

Consider, for example, the careful identification of Goody with the dumb sculptor of the story where the red-haired 'devil' (178) of his dream's 'uncountry' hums from an empty mouth. Both figures are, of course, objects of Jocelin's suppressed desire, silent servants to his prurience and prudery but he prefers to interpret them as bewitchments or bad angels thus creating a demon from the stuff of his own mind in the manner of the New People and Pincher. A similar identification between the cathedral and a man's body with the obvious phallic symbolism of the spire is made, on the whole fairly decorously, at several junctures in the fable. In the very first chapter Jocelin surveys the model of the cathedral which resembles, he thinks:

> a man lying on his back. The nave was his legs placed together, the transepts on either side were his arms outspread. The choir was his body; and the Lady Chapel . . . was his head. And now also, springing, projecting, bursting, erupting from the heart of the building, there was his crown and majesty, the new spire. (8)

Asleep the cathedral/body analogue undergoes another modulation as the spire becomes the phallus of Jocelin's loathsome dreams:

> It seemed to Jocelin that he lay on his back in his bed; and then he was lying on his back in the marshes, crucified and his arms were the transepts with Pangall's *kingdom* nestled on his left side. People came to jeer. . . . Only Satan himself, rising out of the west, clad in nothing but blazing hair stood over his nave and worked at the building. . . . (74–75, italics added)

Characteristically the metaphoric referents of the cathedral, like the cellarage and the spire, have personal and public correspondences. Thus Jocelin's sexual crisis corresponds

precisely with that of the building; he speaks of himself as a
'building about to fall' (222) just as the spire seems to be
toppling.

It would be an oversimplification, however, to interpret
the whole of the spire's construction as 'the phallic sublima-
tion of Jocelin's repressed yearning for the red-haired wife'
as *Time Magazine* archly commented. In fact, the construction
lends itself to a wide range of metaphoric treatment: it is
successively the 'mast' of a ship, 'a dunce's cap', a 'stone
hammer' waiting to strike, and the stone diagram of the
highest prayer of all. Kermode's remark, that 'it gives one
some idea of the nature of this writer's gift that he has written
a book about an expressly phallic symbol to which Freudian
glosses seem irrelevant,[6] seems much more to the point.
For the element of phallicism operates as just one aspect of the
primordial, that ritual terror, barbarism and magical awe that
exist within the civilized psyche. The whole ambiguous
continuum is imaged here by the pit/cellarage where again the
metaphor of seething water and darkness conveys the horror
implicit in death, decay, and destruction. To Jocelin it is
'Doomsday coming up . . . the damned stirring or the
noseless men turning over and thrusting up' (80).

It is a dimension of his nature that Jocelin has always denied;
thus like Pincher and the children in *Lord of the Flies* he comes
to regard the dimension as darkness and evil. During the
crucial episode at the pit, the symbolism of the cathedral
model assumes this larger relevance when Jocelin 'in an
apocalyptic glimpse of seeing' catches the impotent Pangall
being mocked by a workman dancing 'the model of the spire
projecting obscenely from between his legs' (90). Jocelin
turns away in disgust. In fact, Jocelin is disgusted by any
relationship between flesh and spirit; in a sense he is the
obverse of Sammy, rejecting the flesh in lieu of the spirit.
'Renewing life' (58) horrifies him—it is like mud overcoming
his body; Rachel is 'a furious womb [that] had acquired a
tongue', woman, or in words of the fable 'Beldame', strips the

sparkling honeybars and phantom light of existence down to where 'horror and Farce' take over. He tries to escape into free air and light away from darkness and marsh, where creation is 'not the burgeoning evil thing, from birth to senility with its complex strength between' (62–63).

He tries to move away from 'all this confusion' but each new level brings a new effect, a new cause, a new lesson. A funnel is built over the crossways, the pit is filled in, yet a new pit emerges on the higher level in the swallow's nest that Goody and Roger occupy. There is a lesson for each height; like 'dark waters in his belly' he feels that he brings 'essential evil' (106) with him all the way to the 'stork's nest' (124), a third kind of pit at the head of the tower. Yet something new is learned, something that could not have been predicted. 'We're mayfly. We can't tell what it'll be like up there from foot to foot; but we must live from morning to evening every minute with a new thing' (117). And though Roger insists that Jocelin should 'Look down . . . look down' (117) the bird in flight dreads the dreary factual pavement. He longs to be the raven 'that knows what the sunrise is like' and have 'some knowledge of yesterday and the day before' (117).

When he can control his thoughts, Jocelin suppresses the images of red hair, mistletoe, wolf-howl, and burning fires. The reader's understanding suffers a similar suspension. Indeed, for the reader these images sustain their ambiguity and threatening power because they are inexplicable to Jocelin—what, at this point in the narrative, for example, is the hideous obscene berry Jocelin scrapes from his foot? Why does the memory of the pit, 'A grave made ready for some notable' (13), erupt in his memory as he scans the shuddering bale fires in the Valley of the Hanging Stones? What 'devils from hell' torment him, swooping with scaly wings past his spine as he mounts the corkscrew stairs? What plant with strange flowers and fruit, complex, twining and caught with red hair does he see? Obviously they are the imaginings of an obsessed mind, but their very insistent repetition and elaborate

interweaving with each other suggest 'a pattern' (187) that
Jocelin is deliberately ignoring. 'There it came again,' Jocelin
ponders, 'the notsong, the absence of remembering, the overriding thing—' (166). Point of view is managed so that the
reader must experience the terror before he understands it:
he is confined within a confining mind. However, the actual
physical sense the fable imparts is more arduous than this
since the reader, at times, has access to the wider angle of the
third person omniscient point of view. Things come marginally
into focus so that we get exactly the same impression of
Alison's face as does Jocelin—to him she appears enormous.
But we also have our own perception. Thus point of view is
managed so that the reader can construe some of the social
and moral implications of Jocelin's obsession as he himself
cannot: Roger is terrified of heights and is being driven by an
unrelenting will; his wife is churlishly dismissed when she
requires sympathy; Alison is no more or less wanton than
the Dean whose position she established by a boudoir giggle;
Anselm's 'stately head' is steeped in petty malice.

On the other hand, the reader identifies with the protagonist
so strongly that when Jocelin's motives are inspected by his
interrogators it is impossible not to find the questions repellent
in their simplicity. During these interrogations and questionings the reader finds himself sharing Jocelin's total conviction
of the inadequacy of words to explain the entangled course of
events: 'That's too simple, like every other explanation.
That gets nowhere near the root' (195). We understand
Jocelin's point that there seems no way of tracing all the
complications back to their root, no way of disentangling the
anguished faces from the concrete construction. The reader is
caught—and this is a frequent metaphor in the book—
between the outside and the inside of things, unable to make a
judgment. We are never allowed to settle into one view.

Everything in the novel seems to glance two ways. The
workmen are 'good men' yet infidels and blasphemous; the
cathedral is rich with the 'Fabric of Constant Praise' (165)

yet seems a 'pagan temple' (10); Jocelin is a brutal self-deluded egoist, nevertheless when exalted by vision—whether God-inspired, flesh-inspired, or disease-inspired—he accomplishes the concrete construction of a spire that 'joins earth to heaven' (69). Its very stones are windows by which men look at the infinite, yet 'they cry out' (223). The allusion here is to Luke 19:40, 'I tell you if these [disciples] were silent the very stones would cry out and rejoice.' This is a motif woven through the fable's verbal texture as part of the complicated metaphor for human effort that is the novel's major preoccupation. In a sense, Jocelin in death becomes himself such a stone monument: he is a 'building about to fall' (222), his ribs are like the stone vaulting which he inspects during delirium; breathing he pulls himself 'down into the stone mouth, [which] would break up the stone, and eject a puff of shaped air' (218). His memory is constantly pricked by 'the cellarage and the rats' that rustle through his mind. And, of course, his death effigy sculpted by Gilbert is a stone skeleton lapped in skin: a *momento mori* and a *momento vivere*.

Everything in the fable is like this: protean, ambiguous. An ostensibly sturdy Christian cathedral rests on the uncertain foundations of 'the living pagan earth' (80). Its four pillars are less majestic saints than human lovers; they dance over slime and stirring grubs. An exultant prayer is supported by the corrupt money of an adulterous aunt and a murdered man, who 'crouched beneath the crossways with a sliver of mistletoe between his ribs' (212). Creation brings with it violence and death. The man of God rejects God: '*How proud their hope of hell is. There in no innocent work. God knows where God may be*' (222), Jocelin cries out on his death-bed, convinced of his own guilt. Moments later we learn that a sexual explanation for sin is as inadequate as that Calvinist-like religious one. Through his burning delirium Jocelin fumbles towards a formula for his folly and decides his spire was nothing but 'a great [phallic] club' lifted towards a tangle of hair blazing in the sky. He mutters aloud, 'Berenice'. But no single con-

ception of corruption suffices either, for it is Golding's point
that the physical and spiritual are perpetually intermingled.
Golding makes this point —very obliquely—by having Father
Adam (who is set upon helping Jocelin into heaven) read the
Berenice of the Catullus poem to whom Jocelin refers as
Berenice, a most obscure early Christian martyr.

Seconds later, at the moment of his death, Jocelin glimpses
the physical spire through the window and this physical sight
leads him into the spiritual vision which will close the fable.
In fact, in this the confrontation scene, the oppositions of the
fable are resolved and in that resolution, Jocelin is released
from his sense of guilt. Like Pincher before the Dwarf and
Sammy before the rag, Jocelin confronts an object, emblematic of his own guilty self: for him it is the 'stone hammer'
that he has 'traded for four lives' (221). Unlike Sammy and
unlike Pincher, Jocelin experiences not just purgative panic
but astonishment and joy which 'split the darkness' (222)
into light. Mystery is experienced not as malignancy but as
terror-and-joy. Before him there is an object which rushes
towards infinity but glitters like a fountain that falls. It is an
'upward waterfall', and that verbal paradox images a multi-
farious dynamic reality where nevertheless pattern can be
perceived. The truth it embodies is one composed not of sets
of opposition—profane/sacred, sexual/ascetic, physical/spiri-
tual, innocent/guilty—but as a suspension of perpetually
interfused antimonies: a bluebird/over/panic-shot darkness.
To extend the vision to moral terms, then, human acts may be
seen to have elements of innocence and guilt, each modifying,
each creating the other. As was the case in Free Fall, pattern
emerges; it cannot be imposed.

Appropriately, then, the Church immediately translates
Jocelin's affirmation of the spire and all that that entails in his
final cry, 'It's like the appletree', into a gesture of Christian
assent when Father Adam reads the whisper and joy on the
dying man's lips as 'God, God, God.' The protagonist, however,
has reconciled the upward unstoppable thrust of the unruly

member to the seething underside, panic-shot darkness to struggling kingfisher, by relating them. Like the Original Tree itself, the 'long, black springing thing' (204), Jocelin had noticed among the scatter of angelbuds is blighting plant, but bursting apple blossom too.[7]

Conclusion seems too strong a word for the notions about terror-and-joy that close this fable. But the sensuous resolution invoked by the ongoing rhetoric—'In the tide, flying like a bluebird struggling, shouting, screaming to leave the words of magic and incomprehension—' (222) is, by the necessity of Golding's craft, oblique and compressed. The rubic's meaning cannot be decoded and put into conceptual terms. As seems the case in most representations of intense illumination, conceptual terms are inadequate to portray the felt experience. Words that seek to embody 'magic and incomprehension' can only be presented through sensuous images, by some linguistic ultimate that will invoke all the earlier associations that have been planted to grow. Since the burden of Jocelin's story is that all things do grow and twine with each other, his ultimate vision of kingfisher/over/deepwater does nevertheless emerge from multiplicity as a unifed focus.

V

> It is not too much to say that man invented war at the very earliest moment possible. It is not too much to say that as soon as he could leave an interpretable sign of anything, he left a sign of his belief in God.
>
> —Golding, 'Before the Beginning'

> The two signs of man are a capacity to kill and a belief in God.
>
> —Golding

All Golding's fables move towards an inclusive vision. *The Spire* differs only in that the inheritor of this integrated vision is the protagonist. We have seen as well that *The Spire* confines

its technique of reversal to the dramatic overturning of
fortune, rather than the kind of thematic inversion the
Beatrice/Dante analogue represented in *Free Fall* or the use of
'The Grisly Folk' in *The Inheritors*. This stronger emphasis on
character and narrative resolution of theme can be detected
in *Free Fall*'s atavistic quest which we saw was the imaginative
centre of that fable; though the reversal was confused in the
coda's shorthand it grew out of Sammy Mountjoy's atavistic
journey through darkness. *The Spire* develops and completes
this new structural element by making the delayed disclosures
that constitute the fable's extended coda spring directly from
Jocelin's self-deception. Specifically, the delayed disclosure of
Pangall's death coincides with Jocelin's revelation about his
own repressed lust. Throughout the spire's building Jocelin
tries to avoid the 'whole train of memories and worries and
associations which were altogether random' (95). Yet there
are urgent memories buried away in his head; he is happy, for
example, when perched at the top of the spire but when he
looks two hundred feet down at the pit 'unlooked for things
come . . . things put aside from the time when the earth
crept' (105). And Jocelin's recognition of the 'cellarage' of
his mind in the coda corresponds to the larger theme of all
human activity.

At a dramatic level the connection between Pangall and
Jocelin is clear enough—Pangall's mismarriage to a young
woman, arranged by Jocelin himself so as to keep his daughter-
in-God pure, is the springboard for one of the book's major
complications, the liaison between Roger and Goody. Furthermore, the counterpointing of a celibate Dean with an
impotent Verger has a certain deft economy in a fable
investigating the varieties and ironies of progeniture. But
Golding stresses Pangall's character rather more strongly than
normally a minor character requires. The fable seems at pains
to locate Pangall's significance in the distant past; he is the
last of a line who has served the Cathedral for four generations
and he is connected through these ancestors to oak out of

which the beams were fashioned, and incidentally the wood on which mistletoe flourishes when the tree is green. Thus Pangall's warning about unseasoned and burning wood has a symbolic as well as dramatic relevance when one recalls the omnipresent metaphor of a plant with 'strange flowers . . . engulfing, destroying, strangling' (194).

Then there is the matter of Pangall's cottage resting against the Cathedral side—this even appears in one of Jocelin's dreams. It is a 'kingdom' and built like a 'monument against the architect's intentions' (17). In fact, some of its fatigued piecemeal construction predates the Cathedral, and the Normans themselves by over 'a thousand years'; presumably, then, sewn into its decaying fabric are fragments of Roman origin. In conversation, Golding elaborates upon this historical point. 'The intention was that the Pangalls picked up what was lying about and also "won" building materials. The Saxon wayfarers, by the way, used Roman ruins as shelter, thus calling them Cold Harbours. Where you get the name, Cold Harbour, you get or had got a ruin, probably Roman. There are, for example, reused Roman tiles in a Mildenhall church near Marlborough. I put a Cold Harbour in *The Spire* to render the whole concept critic-proof.' Recall the proximity of the two 'monuments', Salisbury and Stonehenge, at this point, and the historical density of this landscape. It is this Kingdom that is actually and symbolically invaded by the pagan workmen as they taunt Pangall and insolently pile the rubble of construction around the cottage. It is this Kingdom that is vanquished as the whole town and Cathedral undergo a convulsion of change. So perhaps the *Critical Quarterly* article is correct when it argues that Pangall's kingdom shares something with the Neanderthal kingdom which also was overcome, regrettably and by the nature of change itself. One way of life lost, another grows from its place; Pangall and his line testify to that ancient repetition of rise and fall, growth and decay-and-growth. They witness the cycle figured in the 'upward waterfall' which Jocelin affirms at the fable's close.

From the outset Pangall, dusty brown and 'dung coloured'
(20) with his devil-broom and deformity, is identified with
the earth that Jocelin rejects. As the poor knave sheds tears of
humiliation, sunlight draws the Dean's eye away from the
'sharp tap on the instep of Jocelin's shoe' (20), an incident
adroitly prefiguring the crucial episode at the pit. Here
Jocelin scrapes from his instep the brown obscene berry of
mistletoe and tries to close eyes and ears to the long wolf-
howl and 'hunting noise of the pack that raced after' (90) the
vanishing Pangall. In fact, Pangall has not fled from his per-
secutions but is murdered and buried in the pit's earth. Here,
'Misshapenness and Impotence are ritually murdered. The
sacrificial victim is built into the pit to strengthen the
inadequate foundations.'[8] The whole incident is covertly
handled, for the same reasons as, but rather more skilfully
than, those ritual murders in The Inheritors and Lord of the Flies
of Liku and Simon, both of whom functioned as religious
scapegoats sacrificed to ensure the group's solidarity. Drawing
on the evidence of Pangall's death by mistletoe, and Jocelin's
aside when at Solstice he thinks the pit is 'a grave made ready
for some notable' (13), Crompton in a very stimulating
analysis maintains the Balder myth is as essential to The Spire's
construction as the Grail legend to 'The Wasteland'; he
argues that it underlies Pangall's murder.[9] Balder, the central
figure of many Norse myths, is vulnerable to everything but
mistletoe out of which an arrow is constructed by his rival
Hodhr; during a struggle for possession of the exquisite
Nanna, Balder is slain. It is true Pangall is convinced he will
die as some kind of scapegoat for the vengeance of the workmen and the disrepair of his kingdom.

It seems to me more likely that Golding had in mind
rather more general folklore than one particular myth; he
specifically employs the site of Stonehenge (Stangheist or
'Hanging Stones') where the sun was worshipped, and the oak
tree was venerated, and the mistletoe performed a specific
part of ritual attached to the monument. The sacred oak

could not be felled nor a human proxy slain before a ritual cutting of mistletoe from the tree on Midsummer's eve. Frazer and Graves argue that this ritual cutting and sacrifice symbolized the emasculation of the old king by his successor. In anthropological and mythic terms, then, the death of deformity and sterility constitutes the necessary antecedent to a release of generative powers in the new kingdom. At this level Pangall is both scapegoat and fertility god; the terrors of the cellarage contain their own paradoxical 'joy', for the grave possesses as it does in *The Inheritors* the mystic power to renew.

The pestilence is, of course, not entirely dispelled, only the painful evolution from one religious variant to another occurs, though this transition involves, it would appear, a measure of fortunate advance. Golding appears to place the religious pulse in an evolutionary scheme whereby historically it undergoes refinements. An interesting cross-reference here is Golding's notion that Greek religion is a thing which comes in layers, 'each age superimposing on an obscurer and more savage one.' When I asked Golding about this matter, he remarked:

> The fact is primitive religion is (all, of course, really) contradictory and at the same time conservative. So the religion of my masons would have much in common with what ever went on at Stonehenge—and indeed with what went on in caves and clearings; but its systematization would be partial, shifting. The workmen would kill Pangall . . . because of a generalized feeling that he might make a good guardian of the foundations—and a conservative feeling that the job can only be done really decorously with flint or mistletoe.

Pagan scapegoat is supervened by Christian Fool and while one is murdered the other is merely taunted. High in the 'wooden dunce's cap' (159) the workers adopt Jocelin as their totemic figure. He will ward off their superstitions about

heights: 'no one at the top tried to drive him off, and he could
not think why this was until one day he asked Jehan who
answered him simply: "You bring us luck" ' (151). In some
sense Jocelin already supports the pillars as much as does
Pangall's body, for the first set of his sculpted heads are flung
into the pit to steady the foundations. These heads were to
have been 'built in' to the cathedral. Originally they were
intended to surmount the spire, exhibiting on four corners a
'Nose like an eagle's beak. Mouth open . . .' (23) proclaiming
the Holy Spirit, Jocelin thinks, day and night till doomsday,
spouting their Hosannahs as the gargoyles spout rain. Obviously,
in one sense, their dramatic burial in the earth's seething
bowels has the symbolic value of prefiguring the (necessary)
eradication of Jocelin's wilful pride. But a whole set of
associations cluster around Jocelin's physiognomy, and the
image of the raven jostles that of the eagle as he appears under
the guise of Devouring Will.[10] Though he believes that Gilbert
(who is actually modelling the Dean's head) is sculpting a
stone image of an Eagle—up in the tower he mutters 'as far as
I'm concerned it's an eagle' (107). Ironically, Golding has
Jocelin squatting among the ravens (154), the bird traditionally
associated with the devil. Jocelin is associated also with
another primordial figure of disintegration and decay, for his
physiognomy resembles the 'diseased' (67) gargoyles who
spout rain during plague and flood. With straining mouth
and blank eyes they appear to 'yell soundless blasphemies and
derisions in the wind' (67). Yet against the cathedral they
perform the purgative role, 'some infinite complexity of
punishment' (97), that Jocelin himself adopts:

> . . . with what accuracy and inspiration those giants had
> built the place, because the gargoyles seemed cast out of
> the stone, burst out of the stone like boils or pimples,
> purging the body of sickness, ensuring by their self-
> damnation, the purity of the whole. (67)

Jocelin's attack by the townsfolk at the fable's close is clearly meant to duplicate Pangall's persecution and ritual function: lying in the filth of the gutter, his stinking rotten body stripped of clothes, Jocelin hears 'hound noises', baying and yelpings. The tribal mob 'created their own mouths fanged and slavering' (215) as they pound the beast into the earth. 'What Jocelin hears above everything else is laughter. He has become a re-embodiment of Pangall, re-enacting his death. We are in at the beginning of another hunt to the death as the clown becomes the scapegoat.'[11] He is saved from Simon's fate, however.

It gradually becomes clear that central to Golding's vision is an eschatology of the sacrificial victim, the deity or saint who performs the necessary exorcism of fears. Speaking in *Free Fall* of 'that man who reached out both arms and gathered the spears into his own body', Golding suggests tentatively that 'the nature of our universe is such that the strong and crystalline adult action heals a wound and takes away a scar not out of today but out of the future. The wound that might have gone on bleeding and suppurating becomes healthy flesh,' (75). At each evolutionary stage of religious impulse there is this scapegoat-figure, a 'saint', though Golding would deny the specifically Christian attributes of that word, who performs the necessary exorcism of fears by taking on the attributes of those fears. Of course they then often meet the fate of those who remind society of its guilt; man prefers to destroy the objectification of his fears rather than recognize the dark terrors of his own 'cellarage'. But by performing action that like Jocelin's ultimately goes beyond personal gain such a figure becomes an instrument not of his own egoism but the executor of some implacable cosmic pattern. Golding implies that such behaviour is no less severe at a qualitative level of Being for men like Ralph or Sammy Mountjoy. Golding's point is that it is open to every man to affirm/assent in the mind's dark cellar the god that is both creator and destroyer. This as Nat puts it in *Pincher Martin* is the 'technique of dying into heaven', a phrase Father Adam only slightly modifies when he instructs the dying Jocelin that the priests are 'going to help you into heaven' (222).

The Spire, it has been said, is about 'vision and cost'. Creation involves bloodshed, sacrifice, and murder; the crossways over which the spire grows, for example, is 'a grave for some notable' yet 'a pit to catch a dean' (39). It is the place of sacrifice yet the place of vision too; 'here where the pit stinks, I received what [vision] I received' (58), Jocelin ruminates. Like The Inheritors, The Spire dramatizes a chronicle of one phase in what Golding takes as the ancient repetition of rise and fall—and rise again: one phase in man's 'upward waterfall'. Its first page opens on a substantial manifestation of both triumph and sacrifice as the story of the Abraham and Isaac window fuses with the joy on the Dean's face. Its last page closes on another substantial manifestation of triumph and sacrifice in Jocelin's sight of the rose-coloured spire.[12]

> It was slim as a girl, translucent. It had grown from some seed of rosecoloured substance that glittered like a waterfall, an upward waterfall. The substance was one thing, that broke all the way to infinity in cascades of exultation that nothing could trammel. (223)

Here the extended metaphor combines the physical and the spiritual, the primordial and the divine; like the appletree with 'its long, black springing thing' (204) it records Jocelin's final fusion of those apparent opposites subsumed under the phrase 'vision and cost'.

The fable's closing pages present this theme obliquely. Jocelin's vision of the spire as 'an upward waterfall' is crucial to the book's overriding meaning and especially crucial to the condition which Jocelin finally reaches—just as Free Fall's final focus on the rag at the cell's centre is crucial to the condition which Sammy Mountjoy has been striving to reach.

The comparison is an instructive one for there is a major difference between the two protagonists. At the fable's conclusion, Sammy remains burdened with a profound conviction of his own guilt. In the second narrative movement of *The Spire*, Jocelin also experiences the world of the spirit as self-condemnation. The coda of the ideographic structure consists in a series of disclosures which force Jocelin to accept the 'cellarage' of his own mind and its part in vision; he admits his responsibility for the anguished faces which cannot be disentangled from the riotous confusion of the spire's growth. While he abandons his spiritual arrogance, at the same time, he despairs of his own guilt and thus abandons, for a time, the possibility of merciful miracle. Like Sammy, Jocelin's eyes are turned in upon his own darkness:

> Heaven and hell and purgatory are small and bright as a jewel in someone's pocket only to be taken out and worn on feast days. This is a grey, successive day for dying on. And what is heaven to me unless I go in holding him by one hand and her by the other? (222)

Since, however, Jocelin dies at the fable's conclusion with the Host being lain upon his lips by Father Adam, the reader is put in the position of concluding that Jocelin, unlike Sammy, is granted forgiveness. The confrontation scene on the last page, in fact, dramatizes Jocelin's release from punishment as his primary guilty perception of the spire transforms itself into one of transfigured astonishment. Implicit in Jocelin's initial perception of the spire as two eyes looking at him, 'an eye for an eye' (222) is an allusion to the revengeful, punishing Judge of the Old Testament. It is as though Jocelin is encountering in these eyes his own loathsome vision of himself; the encounter recalls similar ones in *Lord of the Flies* and *Pincher Martin* where Simon and Pincher brood before a face which is both their own and a god's. As Jocelin concentrates, however, the two eyes slide together and become

the figure of the physical spire; we watch the Judge metamorphose into triumphant 'flashes of thought which split the
darkness' (223, italics added). Jocelin's last words which
relate the divine exultation to the apple tree complete his
spiritual regeneration and they may be interpreted, though in
a different context, in the way in which Father Adam interprets
them as evidence of Jocelin's atonement and God's mercy.
Thus just as *The Inheritors* offered the hint of sanctity in the
level of the plain beyond the Fall as the artist Tuami sculpted
the death-weapon into the life-image, so too at *The Spire*'s
conclusion there is suggested, in the fabric of the 'upward
waterfall' connecting earth and heaven, the promise of a new
heaven and a new earth.

THE SPIRE—NOTES

1 An uncompromising claim but the article continues: 'Great claims such
as this demand a careful defence, and what follows is . . . based on the
general proposition that the book's impressiveness resides not only in
the rich complexity of its themes but in the poetic intensity by which
these themes are realised'. D. W. Crompton, 'The Spire', *Critical
Quarterly* (Spring 1967), pp. 64–65.
2 David Lodge, *The Spectator* (April 10, 1964), p. 490.
3 William Golding quoting from the diary recorded in Raleigh Trevelyan,
A Hermit Disclosed (London, 1960), 'In Retreat', *The Spectator* (March 25,
1960), p. 48.
4 Golding, *Talk: Conversations with William Golding*, p. 94.
5 Despite its historical setting, *The Spire* is not a historical novel. Golding
did not intend to recreate a particular historical age; a case like that of
R. C. Sutherland's 'Mediaeval Elements in *The Spire*', *Studies in the
Literary Imagination* (October 1969) that there is nothing strictly
mediaeval about the novel aims correctly, but at the wrong target.
6 Kermode, 'The Case for William Golding', p. 4.
7 The reference here to the apple tree draws together all the other trees
and growing plants of the fable including the oak and the cedar trees
brought by Ivo and by which he secures his position. Another tree is
relevant to the image system. At the book's opening Jocelin stands by a
window and sees sunlight as 'an important dimension' (10). The figure
used to describe the sun blossoming against the workmen and the
dust-filled nave, when inspected closely, is that of a branching tree.

8 Gregor and Kinkead-Weekes, p. 211.

9 Crompton, p. 66. To date, only this discussion treats pagan folklore as a
   structural principle in *The Spire*; though the evidence he gives is inadequate to support structural exposition, my chapter is indebted to
   Crompton's exposition of the relation between the pagan rituals and
   Sir James Frazer's *The Golden Bough*.

10 To Anselm his movement seems 'flying like a great bird' (201); to
    Alison he resembles 'a great bird hunched in the rain' (184). But the
    whole image system is more complex than this since along with the
    raven/eagle antitheses there is the dark/light angel, the devil-birds he
    imagines swooping at him during the storm, and finally the kingfisher
    at the fable's conclusion.

11 Gregor and Kinkead-Weekes, p. 228.

12 Both the colour of the mystic rose and blood sacrifice.

CONCLUSION

I

PENNYFEATHER: *No. You're all so godlike—*
(laughter) *you go on day after day—you know
about boys. I don't. You can call me dedicated if
you like; or, if you like, you can call me a rather
dull middle-aged man with little more than one
interest. . . . But I've never understood a boy yet.
There is always a central opacity.*
BALHAM: *What a muddle-headed lot you religious
chaps are!*
MACPHERSON: *You believe in original sin and free
will but you can't take it when a boy endowed
with the first thinks fit to exercise the second.*

—Golding, 'Break My Heart'

One of our critical commonplaces at present is that contemporary writers can no longer write big books; that no
modern mind can embrace the terror and malignity which the
twentieth-century has wrought and experienced, so fragmented
is society and its mores, so inured to depravity is modern man.
Jumping off from here, current spokesman such as A. Alvarez
in *The Savage God* and R. D. Laing in *Knots* argue that only
maladjusted psychotic personalities can faithfully interpret
the deranged personality of the age in which we live, as though
the truth about ourselves and about the *Zeitgeist* is no longer
available to those who clutch at traditional outmoded notions
of order and normality. In this view, writers like Norman
Mailer, Sylvia Plath, Jerzy Kosinski turn to violence and
perversity since that which overwhelms us comes not from

without but from within. Similarly, formal decorum as a fictional strategy must be rejected as an inadequate vehicle for a valid representation of psychic and social disorder.

Quite possibly Golding encountered such a creative dilemma; he has commented in several places that before World War II he trusted in the efficacy of social and political effort. Afterwards, he profoundly distrusted man's potential for progress. Not that the basic nature of man has changed in the three decades since the bomb, for as he remarked: 'surely the hydrogen bomb is only an efficient way of wiping out the other tribe —a pastime we've always been prone to.'[1] Quite simply the war witnessed again man's inhumanity to man. 'I have observed the world', Golding remarked to a Leningrad conference of European writers. 'I started to write late—and I have reached certain conclusions. I have always been struck by the thing which men do to other men. I know of deeds which took place during the war, about which I still cannot think without feeling physically ill.'[2] A direct consequence of this sort of pessimistic, 'Aesychelean preoccupation with the human tragedy'[3] is a bleak fable like *Lord of the Flies* which portrays the malignity of man's heart.

For our purposes what is significant is that Golding came to tackle the moral wretchedness which he saw the twentieth century had re-ratified by moving away from, as it were insulating himself from, twentieth-century literary influences. He allows that recent discoveries in biology, astronomy, and psychology are a necessary part of any mind's equipment, but that his own fables have very little genesis outside himself. As he explained to Kermode: 'To a large extent I've cut myself off from contemporary literary life, and gained in one sense by it though I may have lost in another.' The sturdiest literary furniture of his imagination dates from the nineteenth century—Wells, Dickens, Thackeray and the robust popular tradition of Henry, Ballantyne, and Burroughs—while the most influential, in atavistic terms, derives from his serious commitment to Greek drama and poetry.

For this reason, to Golding, man appears to be a much more important matter than men; for example, even the titles of the recent publications—*The Pyramid* and *The Scorpion God*—suggest his deep, excited bewilderment with how the species behaves under the interrogator's eye. These novellas and the five fables, therefore, tend to be isolated temporally and spatially while their action is steeped in the inner conscious-ness of the leading personage whose character is closed and determined rather than being open and capable of change. He admits, of course, to thinking in terms of the fabulistic rather than the immediate situation. From the beginning he has written under the influence of dominant ideas rather than dominant people, for he explained that both upbringing and nature kept him from an immediate delight in people. This retirement from the battle of personal and social life has left him—indeed, leaves him—free to explore 'a lifelong pre-occupation with the nature of the universe.'

However, as any accomplished story teller, a Fielding or even a Thackerary, knows, the novelist seldom needs the god's-eye view. It is the novelist's job—Golding insists—'to count the hairs on the individual human head in the human way rather than in the divine way.' In one sense each new book of Golding's represents a trying on of new hats (to borrow *Free Fall*'s happy metaphor); each new book arises from the breakdown of an earlier coherent pattern, a set of expectations which have collapsed under the pressure of that inexplicable life the book has created. Thus Golding's insistence that each new fable should spring from new ground; though it can hardly be true of C. P. Snow or Anthony Powell, for Golding there does not appear to be much point in writing two books which resemble each other.

This is not to claim that the fables themselves are self-sufficient or totally independent of each other; in thematic terms one is struck by the way in which the mythopœia of *The Inheritors*, for example, breeds that of *The Spire*. One easily detects strong structural similarities and symbols, even phrases, which one fable derives from another. Thus in the crucial scene at the circular pit in *The Spire* when 'the earth creeps' (81) there is a chant: 'Fill the pit! Fill the pit! Fill the pit!' which recalls a similar call for a scapegoat in *Lord of the Flies*. There, as 'the centre of the ring yawned emptily' (187), its mouth opens for Simon: 'Kill the beast! Cut his throat! Spill his blood!' the boys chant. A most telling pattern develops in the various escapes from atavistic horror which inform *Lord of the Flies*, *Pincher Martin*, *Free Fall*, and even *The Pyramid*. In this last book, the protagonist's 'running away' from the revulsion of an eccentric's gravestone, 'as though he found himself once more in the long corridor between the empty rooms',[4] reiterates but modifies by muting Pincher's hysterical race through 'the endless corridor' (145) away from some terrible gods.

Golding's achievement represents, in an identifiable way, a continuous progress, indeed continuous development. To judge from one remark to an interviewer, Golding now appears to have the creative conviction that he must move away from morally dogmatic fables which, to his critical eye, reveal a kind of adolescence—'a feeling that one has specific *ideas* that have to be put over.'[5] Wedded to this is his effort to arrive at the sort of story in which the human being is treated in his abundant totality, beyond the threshold of merely moral judgments. His tribute to Tolstoy's sense of character is instructive here: 'We know [Natasha, Prince Bolkonsky and Pierre] and we do not understand them, nor did Tolstoy. Is not the greatness of the book measurable by the number of circumstances in which he implicitly admits his own defeat?'[6]

Like Doris Lessing, Golding does not avoid the vital large questions about man. He chooses, however, far more difficult fictional material—the sea-tossed body of a sailor, the origins of man's guilt, the essentially autocratic nature of vision—and unlike Lessing, he writes 'as though the possibilities of greatness—of wholeness—still existed.'[7] Even so common-place an image of contemporary life as that portrayed in the

unpublished BBC play 'Break My Heart' (1962) involves the
dramatization of fundamentally moral matters. Here, a
schoolboy's delinquencies and dumb pain index ironically his
schoolmasters' weary cynicism, their class prejudices, and
above all the inadequacies of their moral imaginations. The
play, in fact, reorchestrates in an English grammar school
setting the insight of *Lord of the Flies* into the heart's 'central
opacity'; we watch constrained, bored adults try half-
heartedly to bully their charges out of essentially cruel behaviour. Towards the end, we discover that the boys are in no
way different from the adults: all lie, and squabble, and cheat,
and seek powerful positions, and all are silent about their
breaking hearts. The most silent and sullen is the boy, Malcolm
Smith, whose refusal to memorize Hamlet's 'too, too sullied
flesh' soliloquy—its last line is: 'But break my heart, for I
must hold my tongue'—comes not from idle ignorance but
from the terrible fact that his own mother, like Gertrude, is
sleeping with his uncle. The other schoolboys know, of course,
and Smith's nightmares and schooldays are tormented by their
gleeful persecution.

For all its grim comment on human nature, 'Break My
Heart' is surprisingly unsolemn and is, I think, entirely free of
the heavy hand of the moralist. Such is certainly the case in the
zany novella, 'Envoy Extraordinary' (1956), and its stage
dramatization in the play in which Alastair Sim first starred,
The Brass Butterfly (1958). Free floating fantasy creates the late
Roman world displayed here which in mood is akin to science
fiction—what Golding considers the intellectual counterpart
of free association in words. Thus we are made to laugh at the
possibly serious consequences of technological invention when
Phanocles, a Greek inventor, brings three inventions—a
steamboat, the explosive, and a pressure cooker—to the court
of one of the Caesars in Imperial Rome. Though the Emperor
may well be based on Marcus Aurelius (AD 161–180), there
is really no attempt at historical authenticity in the counterpointing of the rational inventor with the superstitious,

urbane Roman. One laughs sedately as technology in the shape of the printing press is neatly banished from at least one Roman court and the spectacle of change is momentarily checked.

II

Pyrrha's Pebbles, Jehovah's Spontaneous Creation or the Red Clay or Thoth: but it has always appeared to me that some god found man on all fours, put a knee in the small of his back and jerked him upright. The sensualist relies on this. The wise man remembers it.

—Golding, *Envoy Extraordinary*

Enlarged skulls on wasp-thin bodies, men with huge ganglia being pushed forward by some intensity, some vision. This is a persistent image which saturates much of Golding's fiction for his preoccupations are widely religious ones—he treats such perennial themes as innocence, guilt, mystery and malignancy quite purposefully in their antique religious sense. I have argued that he consciously tries to construct a religious mythopœia relevant to contemporary man. In Golding's view contemporary man lacks vision; he discounts the spiritual world but it—in Golding's view—does not discount him. Thus contemporary man experiences mystery as a dark thing.

In the first fable, *Lord of the Flies*, we see Golding focusing on the innate brutality of boys lost on a desert island and when Ralph cries, at the end, for 'the darkness of man's heart' (248), he weeps for the forces of violence on the island whose triumph has been averted only by the chance arrival of a ship. Simon, alone among the boys, acts with the intuitive belief that some rescue may be possible. In his encounter with the emblem of violence and fear, the Head on the stick, there is the first appearance of a theme which the later fables elaborate and extend. Man, in fear, abstracts from his own brutality, and projects it as a demon or ogre which will destroy him. *The Inheritors* locates this psychic and moral evasion in prehistoric times and uses it to account for the genesis of guilt in man. In the fable's action can be seen strong outlines of what I have called the notion of darkness. The New People project their terror and uncertainty upon the Neanderthals and in doing so impart to the prelapsarians their own aggressive, rapacious natures. Thus when Tuami broods upon 'the line of darkness' (233) at the end, he is brooding upon his own internal landscape, his own guilty darkness.

Pincher Martin develops this notion of darkness in considerable detail and through the book's saint figure, Nat Walterson, gives it the religious context which *Free Fall* employs in its own investigation of loss of innocence and emergence of guilt. The protagonists of both fables are modern men convinced of their own significance as self-sufficient creatures in a materialistic world. This Golding dramatizes as their rejection of the world of spirit and their curious attendant fear of physical darkness which seems mysteriously to threaten their persons or 'centres' with extinction. At crucial moments, both refuse to investigate this irrational fear of darkness; indeed, each populates his world with spectres from his own malignant imagination, much in the way the New People created ogres in the dark forest before the waterfall. Thus to Martin, heaven —since it extinguishes his centre—can be nothing but 'sheer negation, the black lightning destroying everything that we call life' (70); to Sammy, 'the central not-comprehended dark' is occupied by odious objects. Pincher imagines that he faces a bully and an Executioner while Sammy despairs of the Judge, whom he imagines stands on the other side of the cell's door preparing to punish him for his guilt. In both fables, however, Golding tries to suggest ambiguously that the merciless punishment which each protagonist imagines is the projection of that character's darkness. Mercy is made to operate in the world—though it is hidden to the eye which rejects such goodness. *The Spire* begins in vision—the obsessed vision of the egoist Jocelin—and proceeds by correcting that vision, refracting it through the physical world; thus, the notion of darkness is treated in a new manner. Jocelin, unlike other Golding characters, believes in and trusts only the eye of the spirit; he is brought to the pit of seething darkness where through punishment he comes to contrition and humility. 'Then the angel put away the two wings from the cloven hoof and struck him from arse to head with a whitehot flail' (188). Having all the time before rejected his own physical nature, humility now consists in recognizing the witch who haunts him as a creature of that 'cellarage'. Thus the novel carries him to the place where he can admit the eye of lust. At this point he is granted the momentary sight of two emblems, a kingfisher and an apple tree, which Golding intends to represent the My-godness of man and evidence of mysterious Mercy.

In the light of just this theme, we can detect a steady progression through the five fables away from the insistence on human malignancy. Just as *The Inheritors* offers some bridge between innocence and guilt in the Neanderthal infant with which the inheritors sail away, so in *Free Fall*, Sammy's conviction of his own responsibility for Beatrice's insanity is counterpointed by those moments of joy in the prison camp. I think it is significant that *The Spire* concludes on exultation and love as the dying Jocelin sights the spire, built in stone, in faith, in sin, and presumption, yet knows nevertheless that it is 'an upward waterfall' (223), connecting earth and heaven, a symbol of malignancy-and-holiness: in fact, a symbol of wholeness.

In order to bring about the reader's imaginative participation in the events and insights of his fables, Golding has devised numerous fictional techniques based for the most part on technical compression. He constructs rigorous structures and exclusive forms to illuminate his own inconclusive vision. I have examined two of these strategies of indirection: the deliberate obscuration of point of view and the inversion of literary models. In varying degrees and with increasingly less reliance Golding subverts other writers' view of the same situation. It is Golding's intention that the reader judge the moral distance between Ballantyne's view of small boys in *Coral Island* and his own recasting in *Lord of the Flies*. Important to *The Inheritors*, then, is Wells's *Outline of History* as well as a short story, 'The Grisly Folk'. *Pincher Martin* finds at least its title, if not certain other symbolic details, in a popular survival story, Taffrail's *Pincher Martin, OD*. With *Free Fall* there is a significant variation in the use and ironic abuse of a literary model, for here Dante's *Vita Nuova* is taken as the morally correct pattern while its twentieth-century recasting is intended to represent a corruption of these values. In *The Spire* several works have been important but no single one appears to have been inverted; rather numerous legends and commonplaces about the mediaeval world have, in Golding's phrase, 'mulched down' to an imaginative compost. From this fertile soil *The Spire* has grown.

Deriving from Golding's concern with the spiritual and contemporary man's apparent rejection of this realm is the unorthodox structure of each of the fables. I have suggested that Golding creates an ideographic structure in each of these fables to allow two contradictory perspectives on one circumstance. Following the plot's major movement there is a coda ending in each of the fables which reverses and often contradicts the implications of the first movement. But Golding intends the two perspectives to be linked, not contradictory, thus the coda's surprise is integral to the final theme of each fable. The bridge between the two perspectives is there to be built by the reader who is driven by the paradoxical structure of each fable to accept paradoxes of existence which are to Golding symptoms of the spiritual world.

Thus in *Lord of the Flies* just as the children assume demonic proportions in their regression, there is a coda ending where they are cut down to child-size since they are viewed by an adult. But there is the further paradox that the officer who rescues the children is himself involved in an 'adult' war, a good deal more potentially violent and widespread than that of the children. Therefore, the compassion Ralph achieves represents a hard-won knowledge which the officer himself does not possess. In *The Inheritors* there are two perspectives on the same events, that of the innocent Neanderthals and that of the inheritors themselves, the violent New People who demonstrate in their efficient skill that the meek do not inherit the earth. Yet neither do the violent, for the New People have been irrevocably altered by their fear of the tree-ogres; guilt and introspection have evolved. In *Pincher Martin*, the coda's reversal of the initial survival story consists in the shocking discovery that the tale has concerned a dead man in Purgatory, not a hero struggling through tenacious will power and intelligence to survive on a rock in the middle of the Atlantic. Once again it is the intention of the author to force the reader to fuse the two contradictory patterns and see, for example, that spiritual survival is more than Davidson's literalism would seem to suggest. In *Free Fall* the ideographic structure is only partially employed, for the coda ending with its sphinx riddle is not so much a dramatic shift to another character's point of view as the presentation of a final clue towards the interpretation of the whole fable. Nevertheless the reversal—with its news of the innocuous centre of the cell— is intended to cast into new light all the story which has gone before. In *The Spire*, the coda ending has been extended considerably and now consists in a dramatic disclosure and the protagonist's discovery (as well as the reader's) of the fusion between apparently contradictory explanations for vision.

Throughout these fables, we can detect a progressive evolution in their structural shapes. They evolve from an externally wrested structure where pattern sublates pattern and the reader profits from the imaginative discovery of the bridge to an internally realized structure which grounds its final fusion in the narrative's total movement, allowing its protagonist to suffer the implications of wholeness. We can see, therefore, how *The Spire* may represent the completion of one phase of Golding's technical evolution. Nevertheless, its

themes and ideographic structure still grow from Golding's
belief that 'where there is no vision the people perish'.

III

*There is nothing quite so real as the eyes of a primitive
carving . . . I know that it is necessary to meet that
[Egyptian mummy's] stare, eye to eye. It is a portrait of
the man himself as his friends thought he should be—
purified, secure, wise. It is the face prepared to penetrate mysteries. . . . It is the face prepared to go down
and through in darkness. . . . It dwells with a darkness that is light.*

—Golding, 'Egypt from My Inside'

The passage above dramatizes, in the encounter between a
boy and the Egyptian mummy upon which he broods, one
more example of what I have called the confrontation scene, a
scene which functions in the fables as a single crystallization of
that fable's ideographic structure. To Golding, contemporary
man appears ill at ease with the ambiguous, the obscurely
meaningful, the mysterious, the unspecific, the tentative, the
unexorcised—all that threatens the assumptions of the
materialist who builds his world view on collected facts. He
must be positioned, somehow, to feel on his pulses, not as a
supposition but as an imaginative experience, the unseen world,
that Egyptian amulet which is 'at once alive and dead', which
suggests 'mysteries with no solution', which mixes 'the
strange, the gruesome and the beautiful'—I quote here from
the essay, 'Egypt from My Inside'. At the heart of each fable
Golding constructs a psychic and purgative episode where a
reductive process is enacted to bring the character up against
this world. Here Golding presents character *in extremis* not
only through torment but in torment. In this process the
protagonist is stripped down to that very last thing which
cannot be destroyed; this Golding takes as a definition of the

particular Being. In the confrontation scene which precedes such atavistic reductions the character is forced to accept or reject the darkness that inhabits his internal landscape.

In *Lord of the Flies* and *Pincher Martin* this encounter takes the form of an interview with an ambiguous but obscurely animated object: a pig's Head and a pile of stones, respectively. Following his conversation with the Head, Simon falls inside its vast mouth and the 'blackness within, a blackness that spread' (178). On regaining consciousness, he is able to recognize himself in the Head and having admitted evil is able to act without evil. In contrast, following his fall into 'a gap of darkness' which he experiences as 'a gap of not-being, a well opening out of the world' (168), Pincher composes a horrific god from his own murderous nature. The figure in the seaboots is a figment of his own imagination but when this figure asks, 'Have you had enough Christopher?' (194) Pincher knows in the recesses of his self that he could not have simply invented it. He is still defying his own darkness as the fable closes; yet we know that he is in Hell.

The confrontation scene in *The Inheritors* occurs when a nightmare spectre emerges in the world of water as Lok leans out across the river, suspended from a tree branch. Though it is a reflection of his own face, symbolically the Lok-face represents a formless thing, a terrifying stranger, disengaged and alienated from his own psyche. When the body of the old woman descends the river and drifts past him, the two spectres merge and I believe it becomes clear that what is being dramatized here is the opposition of the two worlds of innocence and guilt. Deep-waters exist in *Free Fall*'s protagonist as well and the confrontation scene occurs in the cell when Sammy imparts shape to the shapeless thing at the centre of the dark cell. He then undergoes an atavistic reduction as he rushes 'awash in a sea' through 'generalized and irrational terror', to the 'entry where death is close as darkness against the eyeballs' (185). Here, darkness represents a preternatural world with its inexplicable relation between the sources of creation and the sources of destruction. In abstract terms the scene dramatizes a flagellation which releases moral energies from their malignant agency so that Sammy can momentarily enter a world transfigured by vision. A similar metamorphic transformation occurs in *The Spire*. After Jocelin has learned to accept the 'rising tide of muck' (58), the unspeakable feelings and seething darkness associated with his cellarage, he confronts the spire and experiences terror and joy. The darkness is described as 'panicshot' but above it struggles a magnificent kingfisher. In this confrontation scene, Jocelin, alone among Golding's fictional heroes, is granted release from the conviction of his own guilt.

I have been viewing Golding's novels in the light of several propositions which are outlined above. However, the two most recent publications, *The Pyramid* (1967) and *The Scorpion God* (1971) presents quite tangled critical problems which I firmly believe cannot be solved at present. In the strictest of definitions neither can be called a novel. Initially, *The Pyramid* was not conceived of as a fable, but arose from two short stories, the 'Bounce' and 'Evie' episodes in the present book which first appeared separately in different publications, one in *The Kenyon Review* and the other in *Esquire Magazine*.[8] To these a third was added and structural binds then introduced. *The Scorpion God*, similarly, consists of three separate stories, one of which is a republication of 'Envoy Extraordinary.' Yet both works are provocative enough to demand a significant place in a survey of the author's development; by way of contrast, this cannot be said of such a minor short story as 'The Anglo Saxon'.

The Scorpion God makes, in one sense, an ideal testing ground for a judgment on Golding's achievement since it is rich in his strengths and particular limitations; nevertheless, such an invigilation rests on the critical assumption that a writer will never move outside of his fixed imaginative world. In the case of a living author, such a speculation is folly, of course. What of *The Pyramid*, then? On its appearance, many of its reviewers argued that it broke away from the earlier novels by treating social rather than cosmic man. Did this then mark the end of one phase in Golding's development and signal a new direction which—on the evidence of *The Scorpion God* tales—he was unable to tap four years later? Here we would have to assume that the works were conceived in the order of their publication. We cannot be sure.

Questions abound. For the purposes of this study is seems best to glance through the two books here in the conclusion. I hasten to add that my decision not to treat them at length is less a remark on their possible significance than the recognition that Golding may write other works—he has mentioned one that is in progress at present—which will set these two in perspective.

V

And it could be, in this great grim universe I portray, that a tiny, little, rather fat man with a beard, in the middle of it laughing, is more like the universe than a gaunt man struggling up a rock.

—Golding, *Talk*

On its publication in the summer of 1967, Golding remarked to me that he had toyed with the idea of subtitling his book, *The Pyramid, Or As You Like It* as an ironic quip to readers. It was designed in part as a jeu to demonstrate that he could write—he said—something 'limpidly' simple, though of course its thematic preoccupation with social class and spiritual entombment implied by the title is fundamentally serious. On first reading, one is struck by the apparent lowering of tone and narrative tension at the same time as one is charmed by the facetious, adroitly mannered, self-mocking fun. Slapstick jostles a rather more bitter irony as the narrative progresses, however. As Leighton Hodson notes, we inhabit, with *The Pyramid*, a world of tragi-comedy, a tone which has existed in

Golding's work as far back as *Free Fall* where the Rector Watts-Watt is portrayed both grotesquely and nostalgically.[9] There is a similar fusion of the grotesque and pathetic in the portrait of the ghastly religious spinster, Miss Pulkinhorn. Like Rowena Pringle of *Free Fall* and Bounce Dawlish of *The Pyramid*, she suffers the miseries of thwarted virginity—a particularly English brand of loveless snobbery and religious egoism eats in acidly on the soul until it erupts to infect everyone outside.

To trace the continuity of this mixed mode in Golding it is useful, finally, to consider the autobiographical essays of his Marlborough childhood. 'The Ladder and the Tree' evokes an inscrutable small child, obsessed by a shadowy churchyard, until the rational, logical, commonsensical adult world dismisses his terrors as unfounded superstitions; he writes: 'Cosmology was driving away the shadows of our ignorance . . . the march of science was irresistible . . . and I should be part of that organization marching irresistibly to a place which I was assured was worth finding' (173).

In *The Pyramid*, Golding adopts the same materialist premise and creates a world conspicuously devoid of ambiguity, mystery, spirituality, and terror. Just as Trollope's Barchester series ignores the real matter of religion so *The Pyramid*, with its several Trollopian placenames, pictures a place where religious possibilities are deliberately blocked out. The world's spiritual dimension becomes simply 'the sky over Stilbourne' (196) and the threat of Darkness becomes simply 'an unnameable thing' that 'blackened the sun' (213) when the narrator broods in grief that 'we were all known, all food for each other, all clothed and ashamed in our clothing' (205). Everything, in fact, is scaled down to the immediately observable. But we should not conclude that this represents a lapse in Golding's imaginative energy or that he has abandoned his preoccupation with the world of the spirit. Events are deliberately made typical. The subject matter is deliberately ordinary, the narrator deliberately imperceptive, the social norms hugely conventional so as to make the reader—when certain ambiguities arise—question the viability of a world so stillborn. In this modified way, Golding once again adopts the ideographic strategy.

Yet the day-to-day life depicted represents no mean achievement. *The Pyramid* wryly observes the warped respect-ability and genteel passions of a very English provincial town, a placid, suffocating town with its square, hiccuping gas lamps, Amateur Operatic Society, and precisely gradated social pyramid. Placed at first in the 1920s and extending through to the 1960s, the plot consists of a first person narration of three interconnected but distinct stories. Golding regards the structure as the literary equivalent of the sonata form in music where the two themes of social class and deficient love are successively set forth, developed, and restated; the *scherzo* or comic interlude, where appropriately enough the deadly serious antics of an amateur Musical Society are spoofed, treats farcically the motif of musical—and, by extension, imaginative—entombment while the first and third episodes treat it more seriously.

In the first episode, eighteen-year-old Oliver, the town dispenser's son, avidly and ineptly, is initiated into the prerogatives of his class position when with considerable social guilt, he manages to seduce Stilbourne's 'local phenomenon', the sexy Evie Babbacombe. Both because she is the daughter of the Town Crier, someone much his social inferior, and because it appears to the mortified Oliver that she has already been possessed by his rival and social superior, Doctor Ewan's son, Oliver drags Evie off to a clump of woods, convinced that the eighteen-year-old beauty is promiscuous and available. They meet a few times—on one occasion, Oliver happens to flick up her skirt and discovers her body covered with welts, a shocking discovery whose emotional import he cannot at all grasp. He imagines—since it is the only kind of perception he possesses—a socially inferior culprit: 'staring at her, and not seeing her but only the revelation, the pieces fell into place with a kind of natural inevitability' (89) and he immediately decides a war wreck, Captain Wilmot, is responsible since Wilmot lives opposite the Babbacombes in the squalor of Chandler's Close. But before anything is actually said, the frightened Evie mutters that 'I was sorry for 'im'; a few moments later she says 'it'—meaning the sex—started when she was fifteen.

What follows from this obscure, and maddeningly ambiguous, interchange amounts to a modified use of the confrontation scene where we watch two worlds in collison. Face to face—with his eyes upon hers—Oliver can only laugh in sheer embarrassment; he then turns away in loathing and refuses to encounter her timid efforts at explanation. Instead, rather in the manner of the New People of *The Inheritors*, he constructs out of his own imagined sadistic explanation for the beating a devilish world of fallen bestiality. Evie is its central 'object'.

> I looked away from her, down at the town made brighter by the shade under the alders, it was full of colour, and placid. . . . and there below were my parents, standing side by side. . . . All at once, I had a tremendous feeling of thereness and hereness, of separate worlds, they . . . clean in that coloured picture; here, this object, on an earth that smelt of decay, with picked bones and natural cruelty—life's lavatory. (91)

On their next meeting, Evie contrives to have Oliver perform—since such is his lubricity—on an exposed escarpment in full view of Stilbourne and his father's binoculars. The reasons for this public display only become clear—aside from the symbolic value of having Oliver spied upon at the place of his Fall—in this section's concluding coda where the pair chance to meet each other after two year's absence. In the meanwhile, Oliver has gone up to Oxford to study chemistry and Evie goes down to London, having been banished from paradisal Stilbourne because—and this makes the crystal of the social pyramid tinkle—a tiny smear of lipstick was spied on the face of Dr. Jones, the partner of the lofty Dr. Ewan.

As they sit in the Crown's saloon bar, the two reminisce almost affectionately, though Evie feels stifled by the drab weight of the town. Warming to the brown ale and Evie's new sexual briskness, Oliver refers—he thinks with sophistication —to Captain Wilmot; he, then, coarsely toasts her health: 'Bottoms up.' The callous insult is too much for Evie and she loudly declares to the pub's respectable gathering that Oliver had raped her, in the clump, when she was fifteen. Of course, Oliver is convulsed with shame and astonishment and beats a hasty escape to the street. In a sudden explosion of frustration with the abject meanness of the town, its innate snobbery and obscene voyeurism, Evie cries out that she no longer cares if Oliver goes on laughing snidely and 'telling [about] me'n'Dad' (110). We leave Oliver brooding on 'this undiscovered person and her curious slip of the tongue' (111).

The obscuration and apparent contradiction here in the coda follow the habitual ideographic technique whereby we must reconsider our interpretation of the preceding narrative in the light of the new information. Essentially, what we discover is that Oliver's musky obsession with sex and social caste determines his first notion of Evie's lower class promiscuity. Just as he is misinformed about her age—a crucial mistake since her admission in the confrontation scene that 'it' began when she was fifteen makes us assume she has had three years of perverse sexual experimentation—so he is mistaken about her intimacy with Bobby Ewan. As the older Evie remarks, Bobby was simply her 'first sweetheart', an allusion more girlish in tone than her knowing reference to Dr. Jones: 'now there's a man!'

As I understand the coda, Golding wants us to reconstruct— free of the narrator's limited and egoistical point of view— Oliver's moral culpability in shaping Evie's future. What may be of particular importance here is Dr. Jones' flirtation with

Evie, which follows Oliver's seduction. Dr. Jones teaches her
'secretarial skills' when she has finished typing for him; Evie
tells Oliver, at one point, that Jones threatened her with a
beating if she did not attend more carefully to the lessons. If
we reassemble these clues in the light of Evie's remark about
feeling sorry for some man, it is quite possible to see that Evie
had to suffer another loveless manipulation.

The crucial question concerns the beating, however. How
does the coda throw new light on this episode? As we know,
Oliver's formulation is inaccurate, made histrionically out of
his own sadistic fantasies as well as a kind of atavistic loathing
for the misshapenness of a cripple. Golding plants several
clues throughout the story to make us associate brutality with
Sergeant Babbacombe. Very early on, Evie sports a black eye,
presumably inflicted by her father when she returns late after
an escapade. In a much more important scene, later in the
story, Evie hears her father's bray, in the town below, and
inexplicably her desire for Oliver quickens. Passionately she
urges him to take her and 'hurt' her. Perhaps the concluding
remark about 'me'n'Dad' is meant to indicate this depraved
relationship. The welts on her body would, then, be the ugly
marks of an incestuous congress.

We know from *The Spire* that ambiguity in Golding's fiction
is always instructive and designed to demonstrate the spiritual
complexities inherent in any human situation since it is his
conviction that paradoxically many explanations may be
simultaneously 'true'. By such a strategy of ambiguous
indirection, Golding tries to test the moral imagination of his
readers, leaving it open to one's private set of priorities which
explanation one will choose to adopt. Here in *The Pyramid*, I
believe, there is another explanation for Evie's demonstrable
masochism. Quite possibly she has been punished physically
for her disobediences so often that she comes to need love to be
expressed in some sadistic manner. From this perspective, her
father has not sexually molested her, but certainly he has
warped her capacities for tender love. The ghastly marks on

her thighs could, in this view, be another example of her father's tyranny. Finally, there may be another explanation for the welts which Golding hints at by way of Jones' curious suggestion that Evie would enjoy being hurt were she to be punished for inattention. Imagine the irony implicit in having the socially—and, therefore from Stilbourne's point of view, morally—impeccable gentleman inflict such gruesome talismans.

Conceivably, Evie's 'slip of the tongue' at the conclusion of the episode could represent no more than a lament that the securely situated Olivers of the world—the rich with their bathrooms and Oxford-promised futures—find the socially inferior—with their poverty and cockroaches—contemptible, ridiculous, and worthy of hilarious gossip. Like the puzzle which closes *Free Fall*, Evie's riddle here about 'me'n'Dad' is not so much an explanation as a means by which Golding forces the reader to inspect his own spiritual values. And we can see that, in a real way, the title of the book could well have been *The Pyramid, Or As You Like It*.

We need not examine the other two episodes in this kind of detail. In the second Oliver returns from a first term at Oxford several months after his baptismal fire. His mother bullies him into performing in a banal light opera which brings about his second initiation. In a long besotted conversation at the Crown with Evelyn De Tracy, the foppish director down from London, Oliver dimly comprehends Stilbourne's sterilities. In a torrent of words, he cries out:

> Everything's—*wrong*. Everything. There's no truth and there's no honesty. My God! Life can't—I mean just out there, you have only to look up at the sky—but Stilbourne accepts it as a *roof*. As a—and the way we hide our bodies and the things we don't say, and things we daren't mention, the people we don't meet—and that *stuff* they call music— (147)

Provoked by the youth's demand for honesty, Evelyn presents
a set of photographs of himself dressed as a ballerina. But the
classbound Oliver is again inadequate to the moment's
revelation and he can only roar with laughter—as earlier
with Evie—at this private display of frustrated love.

In the third, more elaborately structured, episode, we
watch an adult Oliver returning to Stilbourne; in an extended
reverie he explores moments in his past and its slow, mean
metamorphosis under the twin gods of class prejudice and
longed-for prosperity. Brooding upon the grave of his eccentric
music teacher, Bounce Dawlish, he relives his gradual
abandonment of music, an imaginative repudiation associated
with Bounce's frustrated pitiful love for Henry Williams, now
Stilbourne's most prosperous garageman. In an agony of
remembering Oliver recalls one day when Bounce in a
grotesque bid for Henry's attention stepped into the town
square decorously dressed in hat, gloves, shoes and 'nothing
else whatsoever' (207). The memory of her massive, ungainly
nakedness pitches Oliver back to the present. Suddenly he
knows that, though Stilbourne prevented him from admitting
this to himself, he had loathed the pathetic woman.

> I caught myself up, appalled at my wanton laughter in
> that place. . . . For it was here, close and real . . . that
> pathetic, horrible unused body. . . . This was a kind of
> psychic ear-test before which nothing survived but
> revulsion and horror, childishness and atavism, as if
> unnamable things were rising around me and blackening
> the sun. I heard my own voice—as if it could make its
> own bid for honesty—crying aloud.
> 'I never liked you! Never!' (213)

Here again we are presented with a confrontation scene.
What seems new about it is that for the first time in Golding's
fiction we watch a protagonist developing through time and
frustration, change and professional success. The three

outsiders—Evie, Evelyn De Tracy, and Bounce—try to help Oliver to transcend the limitations imposed by the town. As the two codas indicate, Oliver partially learns to unharden his heart (the lesson the epigraph from the *Instructions of Ptah-Hotep* instructs: 'If thou be among people make for thyself love, the beginning and end of the heart') and observe the pain in others which we have watched grow infinitesimally as the years pass.

The method of narration is very accomplished indeed, particularly in the Bounce episode where Golding employs but transforms the elements of the ideographic structure. For there are two perspectives to which the reader has access here throughout the developing story. Oliver sees events with the immediate eyes of childhood—'primary, ignorant perceptions' (165)—with the eyes of 'gradual sophistication' as adolescence sharpens class prejudices and in retrospect, with the eyes of middle age. The third episode opens with the successful Oliver, armoured by his car of 'superior description' (159)[10] returning to the Old Bridge, 'gliding down the spur to all those years of my life' (158). It closes with his driving back over the Old Bridge towards the motorway and 'concentrating resolutely on my driving' (217). Here the fusion of the developing point of view with the developed point of view is accomplished by the protagonist-narrator through the device of recollection and meditation. As Oliver looks Henry 'in the eye; and saw my own face' (217) (another reorchestration of the confrontation scene), the reader discovers simultaneously with Oliver that the latter has paid the same price of love for success as Henry. And such an insight is an appropriate concluding lesson to draw from the stillborn world of *The Pyramid*.

VI

A patch of land no bigger than a farm—a handful of apes left high and dry by the tide of men—too ignorant,

*too complacent, too dimwitted to believe the world is
more than tens miles of river—'*

— Golding, *The Scorpion God*

Golding's most recent book, *The Scorpion God*, (1971) consists
in three long novellas, one of which, 'Envoy Extraordinary',
appeared some fifteen years before, and another of which,
'The Scorpion God', was apparently written between *Free Fall*
and *The Spire*, though it remained unpublished. The third,
'Clonk Clonk' was written just before its publication.
Perhaps this hiatus explains why, though there is thematic
consistency of a sort, the method of the three is dissimilar.
In all three, however, Golding seems to be preoccupied with
those crucial moments in history when consciousness changes
unpredictably and finds itself constructing its own moral
evolution. *The Hot Gates* told us, of course, that Golding was
much absorbed by history and pre-history; several of its
essays concern themselves with man's painful yet triumphant
capacity to make intellectual and intuitive leaps beyond his
immediate situation. Here in *The Scorpion God* the stories cut a
similarly wide and assured sweep into the historical past—as
The Inheritors so richly reveals in its creation of Neanderthal
life, Golding possesses a stunning ability to imagine—and,
then populate—remote, obscure times.

In the title story we are immediately thrust into the stern
sun of an ancient Egypt: 'There was not a crack in the sky, not
a blemish on the dense blue enamel. . . . Out of this sky, heat
and light fell like an avalanche so that everything between the
two long cliffs lay motionless as the cliffs themselves' (9).
A figure with cross and flail emerges from this flat, silent
stillness, almost as though the pharaohs on *Free Fall*'s fag-cards
had been twitched into action. He is running. Described from
a distant perspective which detaches us from (rather than
engaging us in) the activity, this first dislodging of motion-
lessness sets in motion the story's theme and a plot whose
several episodes move swiftly in one direction. Gradually, we

discover our place in an Egypt of the late Middle Kingdom where the sacred King—believed to support the sky and cause the Nile to rise and fall annually—is called Great House, a literal translation of the hieroglyphic *per-ass*, or pharaoh.

As always in Golding's fiction, though we are not so much informed as forced to infer the situation, a crisis is at hand. The river's water-level is dangerously low. A rivalry seems to be developing between Great House's favourite Fool, the Liar, and the powerful Head Man, the key member of the priesthood which, at this time, effectively ruled the kingdom. As to the great Pharoah, his obesity and beer-lethargy prevent him from performing the obligatory copulation which will validate his royal daughter, Pretty Flower.

Nor can the dynasty depend on his degenerate heir, the son born to his former wife/sister, since the boy is a weepy ten year old, possibly going blind. It is left to the Liar to inject what vitality he can into this moribund court by whispering what amount to obscene lies. There is a white land where water becomes as hard as stone, he insists. There, men as pale as peeled onions marry across 'the natural borders of con-sanguinity' (55). To a civilization which believes that correct sexual relations involve incest, which conceives of the earth as a disc centred in the flat plains of Egypt and is surrounded at its extremity by foreign lands, these whispers are indeed blasphemous.

Of course, the Liar is considered mad. And a political and religious heretic when later he, inexplicably, refuses to join Great House's retainers—baker, brewer, potter and jeweller —who joyfully sip poison along with the Pharoah as he prepares to be translated to his 'motionless Now'. In death, he becomes a living power: 'So the Sleeper woke and Great House stood and stared through his family of his motionless Now, in life and health and strength' (39). Everyone else believes, since such is the religious certainty, that the river's troublesome immobility will cease when the Pharoah fortunately enters 'Eternal Life'. But the rationalist savagely dismisses such

belief as mumbo jumbo: 'I won't, I tell you! I don't want to
live! I won't!' the Liar screams and his revolutionary commitment to this life amounts to a rip in the fabric of things.

What is original about the confrontation of two worlds
depicted here in *The Scorpion God* is that our conventional
expectations are ironically reversed—at least the ones we
normally employ with a Golding story. Rather than *The Spire's*
spiritual mystic, it is the free-thinker—the man who explodes
religious orthodoxy—who emerges as the spokesman for the
imagination. It is the Liar—he who tells stories—who carries
Golding's important theme that if a civilization has not vision
it will perish. For the river starts to rise and indeed rises far
past the Notch of Excellent Eating, through and past the
Notch of Utter Calamity; the people believe that when the
Sleeper 'wakes into his Now' he will be able to send the
swollen water back. But the flooding does not abate. Only the
Liar has the mechanical insight to suggest they should climb
the cliffs away from the flooding Delta. He, then, makes the
intuitive jump that he could well be the new god Pharoah.
Etched against the brazen sky he stands at the story's close,
stinging like a scorpion, gesticulating 'the mechanics, the
necessity of survival'.

At first reading, 'Clonk Clonk' seems to share the primitive
locale of the world of *The Inheritors* but as the coda hints, without stating so explicitly, the scene of the action must be Africa,
near a Hot Spring, some hundred thousand years ago. My
speculation is that Golding has in mind the Olduvai Gorge in
Tanzania where *Australopithecus* was discovered and where,
it is claimed, man the hunter emerged. If so, Golding sees the
origins of society in the aggressive bonding and ritual displays
of the male hunters—he calls them the Leopard Men—and the
practical but more knowledgeable hearth-tending of females.

Again, as in *The Inheritors*, the novella makes luminously
vivid a crucial stage in social evolution; however, the confrontation here involves not two species but the two sexes.
Furthermore, it is a hilarious, if richly frivolous, encounter—

especially the confrontation scene where an uninitiated brave is overwhelmed by several women, orgiastic and lusty at full moon. Though, indeed, there is a descent into warm, wet darkness, his fear—*vagina dentata*—holds little of the nightmarish desperation of such encounters in the earlier fables. It seems deeply, even comically, characteristic of Golding's imagination that he should explore our contemporary preoccupation with the nature of the sexes by casting the fabulist's eye upon the possibilities and probabilities of sexual dimorphism in a remote Stone Age community.

Not that the story lacks ethnographic authenticity; the naming of infants, for example, is a female prerogative and Palm, the tribe's Head Woman, bears this august responsibility. In contrast, the warriors' volatile, profoundly narcissistic, and fantasy-ridden virility is expressed in their adoption of new names. These names are associated with their changing moods as well as the degree of masculine authority the group decides they possess. Thus, the main character, a flautist with a weak ankle and miserable conviction of failure, starts the hunt as Charging Elephant. When he trips during one foray, he is taunted with the name: Charging Elephant Fell On His Face In Front Of An Antelope. Later, he is banished from even the periphery of the group which snuggles together in contented sleep; now he is dubbed Chimp.

Terrified by solitude, whimpering with humiliation and misery, he limps back through the moondrenched forest to the campsite where, unknown to the absent warriors, the women celebrate the full moon, deep in drink and rich contempt for their infant-menfolk. Here, a drunken Palm wickedly and wonderfully ensnares Chimp; she flatters and soothes his male vanity and the next day declares to the returning hunters that he is now her Leopard Man, 'who goes to my hut when he wills!' (113). And the group with male solidarity and dimwitted devotion thump the ground in approval. 'Water Paw, Wounded Leopard', they name him, as they sing out what they take to be his astonishing triumph.

As the graceful lyric introducing the story makes clear:

Song before speech
Verse before prose
Flute before blowpipe
Lyre before bow

Golding prefers this almost hunter to the commanding
executives of the hunting tribe. In fact, Chimp is a symbol of
the male group itself: tender, touchy, and preposterously
adolescent in its displays of bravery and conquest. Not that
their violence is romanticized; as in *Lord of the Flies* we come
to share in the visceral excitement of the hunt when whirling
bolasses and sharpened spears join prey and predator: 'An eye
might go, or teeth . . . or even a smashed skull. Then . . . there
would be a kicking hysterical thing threshing about in the
grass and a line of light brown men closing in on it' (82). At
the same time, our responses are filtered through an ironic
screen. Golding seems to have special fun in mocking them by
using—as a comic motif throughout—the hoot, '*Rah! Rah!*
Rah!', familiar to every Englishman as schoolboys' rugby chant.
Less successful is the facetious aside which occurs when Palm
flings at the disrobed Chimp the insult, 'you naked ape'; the
comic introduction of Desmond Morris' best selling title
tends to trivialize Chimp's attractive ineptitude in an irritating,
jeering way.

'Clonk Clonk' celebrates, above all, the wisdom of women,
in particular the ripening, if drink-needy, maturity of the
Head Woman. Females here, like the characters in Barrie's
What Every Woman Knows, are matter of fact, cautious, devious
in hiding their deceits, and outrageously skilled in their
flattery of male vanity. On the other hand, they know about
birth and death since only they attend to these ultimates; unlike
the men who populate nature with demons and goddesses, the
women think instrumentally without personification. Palm,
for example, has to chide herself when turning towards a

mountain which looms in its own smoke she starts to feel, 'ungraspable as water,' uneasy and menaced: 'a mountain is a mountain! Palm, you think like a man' (71).

It is she, finally, who gives this novella its ironic warmth and restrained humour. Under her deliberate attention, cold moonlight and hot springs, child-labour's hooting and the howling of hunters, the fantasies of bravery and the bitter cynicism of knowledge, all these opposites are brought into reconciliation. The coda comes, then, not as a reversal of this balance, but as a distant judgment upon the real significance yet deep insignificance of that time's momentary harmony. 'So everything ended happily and all changes were for the best . . . though the mountain's eruption overwhelmed the spa that had grown up round the Hot Springs, by that time there were plenty of people in other places, so it was a small matter.' (114).

Though minor Golding *The Scorpion God* is written—as is *The Pyramid*—with acute sensitivity and penetration, written movingly, gently, even genially. Looking back from *The Pyramid* to *Lord of the Flies* which is another book about England,[11] we can see that the latter's stark, fierce, implacable, even luminous denunciation is in a profound sense untrue. For Golding too, since the darkness of man's heart has modulated into a central opacity, good as well as not-good. At the moment it is Golding's major and overriding intention to write a novel about England; 'not about Britain, about England' he remarked. For this reason my case for William Golding's fiction must rest suspended. But unlike the five fables, *The Scorpion God* and *The Pyramid* seem to me to go a long way towards suggesting that such a work may be accomplished with the complex, wondering sense of the potential richness of life, and also of opportunities irrevocably—antiquely, because that is the nature of the universe—destroyed. One trusts here in a final glance for just such a vast book, bearing on its surface 'the print of a more than human thumb.'[12]

CONCLUSION—NOTES

1 Golding, 'The Writer and His Age', *The London Magazine* (May 1957), p. 45.
2 Golding, 'The Condition of the Novel', *New Left Review* (January–February 1965), p. 34.
3 Golding, 'The Writer in His Age', p. 45.
4 Golding, *The Pyramid* (London: Faber and Faber, 1967), p. 213.
5 Golding, *Talk: Conversations with William Golding*, p. 31.
6 Golding, 'Tolstoy's Mountain', *The Hot Gates*, p. 125.
7 Kermode, 'The New Novelists, An Enquiry', *The London Magazine* (November 1958), p.25.
8 Golding, 'On the Escarpment', *Kenyon Review* (June 1967), pp. 312–400; 'Inside a Pyramid', *Esquire* (December 1966), pp. 165–169; 286–302.
9 Leighton Hodson, *William Golding*, Writers and Critics (Edinburgh, 1969), p. 103.
10 Change in Stilbourne over the years is subtly documented by the introduction and growing significance of the car. It is not irrelevant that Henry Williams, Bounce's chauffeur, shows his inadequate affection for Bounce by polishing and attending to her car. The commercial success of his garage (and the means by which he climbs the slippery pyramid) comes to alter the face of Stilbourne, 'the small huddle of houses by a minimal river—a place surprised by the motor road' (157) in ways completely irrevocable.
11 Golding claims that *Lord of the Flies* was first and foremost intended as a novel about England, an intention most criticism has not considered.
12 The phrase is Golding's in 'Tolstoy's Mountain'. I use it here in the conclusion in just the eulogistic sense in which Golding applies it to Tolstoy.

BIBLIOGRAPHICAL NOTES

Works by William Golding

'The Anglo Saxon'
London *Queen Magazine* (December 22, 1959), pp. 12–14.
The Brass Butterfly
London: Faber and Faber, 1958.
The Genius of the Later English Theatre, ed. Sylvan Barnet, Morton Berman, and William Burto. New York: New American Library, 1962.
'Break My Heart'
British Broadcasting Corporation Third Programme, February 3, 1962 (unpublished play).
'Clonk Clonk'
The Scorpion God. London: Faber and Faber, 1971.
New York: Harcourt Brace & Jovanovich, 1972.
'Envoy Extraordinary'
Sometime Never: Three Outstanding Tales by William Golding, John Wyndham, and Mervyn Peake. London: Eyre & Spottiswoode, 1956.
Sometime Never. . . . New York: Ballantine, 1962.
The Scorpion God. London: Faber and Faber, 1971.
New York: Harcourt Brace & Jovanovich, 1972.
Free Fall
London: Faber and Faber, 1959.
New York: Harcourt, Brace & World, 1960.
The Hot Gates
London: Faber and Faber, 1965.
New York: Harcourt, Brace & World, 1966.
The Inheritors
London: Faber and Faber, 1955.
New York: Harcourt, Brace & World, 1962.
'Inside a Pyramid'
Esquire (December 1966), pp. 165–169; 286–302. Revised and enlarged as Chapter III, *The Pyramid*, pp. 157–217.
Lord of the Flies
London: Faber and Faber, 1954.
New York: Coward-McCann, 1955.
'Miss Pulkinhorn'

Encounter, XV (August 1960), pp. 27–32.

> *An Introduction to Literature*, ed. Sylvan Barnet; Morton Berman, and William Burto. New·York: Little, Brown & Company, 1961.
>
> *Best Stories of Church and Clergy*, ed. F. Bradley and J. E. Ridler. London: Faber and Faber, 1966.

'Miss Pulkinhorn'

> British Broadcasting Corporation Third Programme, April 20, 1960 (unpublished play).

'On the Escarpment'

> *Kenyon Review* (June 1967), pp. 312–400. Reprinted as Chapter I of *The Pyramid*, pp. 11–101.

Pincher Martin

> London: Faber and Faber, 1956.
>
> New York: Harcourt, Brace & World, 1957 (published under the title *The Two Deaths of Christopher Martin*).

Poems

> London: The Macmillan Company, 1934.
>
> New York: The Macmillan Company, 1935.

The Pyramid

> London: Faber and Faber, 1967.
>
> New York: Harcourt, Brace & World, 1968.

'The Scorpion God'

> *The Scorpion God*. London: Faber and Faber, 1971.
>
> New York: Harcourt, Brace & Jovanovich, 1972.

The Spire

> London: Faber and Faber, 1964.
>
> New York: Harcourt, Brace & World, 1964.

Articles by William Golding

'A Touch of Insomnia', *The Spectator* (October 27, 1961), pp. 569–571. Reprinted in *The Hot Gates*, pp. 135–139.

'Advice to a Nervous Visitor', *Holiday* (July 1963), pp. 42–43; 93–97; 125–126.

'Affection for Cathedrals', *Holiday* (December 1965), pp. 35–39.

'All or Nothing', *The Spectator* (March 24, 1961), p. 410.

'Androids All', *The Spectator* (February 24, 1961), p. 263–264.

'Astronaut by Gaslight', *The Spectator* (June 9, 1961), pp. 841–842. Reprinted in *The Hot Gates*, pp. 111–115.

'Before the Beginning', *The Spectator* (May 26, 1961), p. 768.

'Billy the Kid', *The Spectator* (November 25, 1960), pp. 808–811. Reprinted in *The Hot Gates*, pp. 159–165.

'Body and Soul', *The Spectator* (January 19, 1962), pp. 65–66. Reprinted in *The Hot Gates*, pp. 145–151.

'Children's Books', *The Listener* (December 5, 1957), p. 953.

'The Condition of the Novel', *New Left Review* (January–February 1965), pp. 34–35.

'Copernicus, A Universe Revealed', *Holiday* (January 1964), pp. 56–61; 150; 152. Reprinted in *The Hot Gates*, pp. 31–40.

'Crosses I Bear', *Holiday* (December 1963), pp. 12, 14–21. Reprinted in *The Hot Gates*, pp. 21–30.

'Delphi, The Oracle Revealed', *Holiday* (March 1963), pp. 60; 87–88; 90; 150.

'Digging for Pictures', *Holiday* (March 1963), pp. 86; 99–105. Reprinted in *The Hot Gates*, pp. 61–70.

'Egypt and I', *Holiday* (April 1966), pp. 32; 46–49. Reprinted as 'Egypt from My Inside', *The Hot Gates*, pp. 71–82.

'English Channel', *Holiday* (November 1961), pp. 32; 40–47. Reprinted in *The Hot Gates*, pp. 41–50.

'Forward', in Jack I. Biles, *Talk: Conversations with William Golding*. New York: Harcourt, Brace & Jovanovich, 1970, pp. lx-xii.

'The Glass Door', *The Spectator* (November 24, 1961), pp. 732–733. Reprinted in *The Hot Gates*, pp. 140–144.

'*Gradus Ad Parnassum*', *The Spectator* (September 7, 1962), pp. 327–329. Reprinted in *The Hot Gates*, pp. 152–156.

'Headmasters', *The Spectator* (August 12, 1960), p. 252. Reprinted in *The Hot Gates*, pp. 116–120.

'In My Ark', *The Spectator* (September 16, 1960), p. 409. Reprinted in *The Hot Gates*, pp. 102–105.

'In Retreat', *The Spectator* (March 25, 1960), pp. 448–449.

'Irish Poets and Their Poetry', *Holiday* (April 1963), pp. 10; 16–19.

'Islands', *The Spectator* (June 19, 1960), pp. 844–846. Reprinted in *The Hot Gates*, pp. 106–110.

'It's a Long Way to Oxyrhnchus', *The Spectator* (July 7, 1961), p. 9.

'The Ladder and the Tree', *The Listener* (March 24, 1960), pp. 531–533. Reprinted in *The Hot Gates*, pp. 166–175.

'Letter Fragment Answering John Peter's Queries', 'Postscript', in William Nelson, *William Golding's 'Lord of the Flies'*, *A Source Book*. New York: Odyssey Press, Inc., 1963, p. 34.

'Man of God', *The Spectator* (October 7, 1960), p. 530.

'No-Nonsense Verse', *The Guardian* (February 17, 1967), p. 8.

'On the Crest of the Wave', *Times Literary Supplement* (June 17, 1960), p. 387. Reprinted in *The Writer's Dilemma*. London: Oxford University Press, 1961, pp. 42–51. Also reprinted in *The Hot Gates*, pp. 126–132.

'Our Way of Life', British Broadcasting Corporation Third Programme, December 15, 1956 (unpublished article).

'*Pincher Martin*', *Radio Times* (March 21, 1958), p. 8.

'Prospect of Eton', *The Spectator* (November 25, 1960), pp. 856–
857.

'Raider', *The Spectator* (June 10, 1960), pp. 844–846.

'The Rise of Love', *The Spectator* (February 10, 1961), p. 194.

'The Scum of the Sea', *The Guardian* (December 9, 1972), p. 23.

'Shakespeare's Birthplace', *Holiday* (May 1962), pp. 82–83; 151–153.
Reprinted in *The Hot Gates*, pp. 51–60.

'Surge and Thunder', *The Spectator* (September 14, 1962), p. 370.

'Thermopylae—A Walk Through History', *Holiday* (September
1962), pp. 50–51. Reprinted under the title 'The Hot Gates',
The Hot Gates, pp. 13–20.

'Thin Partitions', *The Spectator* (January 13, 1961), p. 49.

'Thinking as a Hobby', *Holiday* (August 1961), pp. 8–13. Reprinted
in *Modern Essays*, ed. Russell Nye. Chicago: Scott Foresman &
Co., 1963.

'Through the Dutch Waterways', *Holiday* (January 1962), pp. 58–
59; 91–96; 100.

'Tolstoy's Mountain', *The Spectator* (September 8, 1961), pp.
325–326. Reprinted in *The Hot Gates*, pp. 121–125.

'The Well Built House', *Authors Talking*. London: BBC Broadwater
Press Ltd., 1961, pp. 18–19.

'Wiltshire: The Rural Retreat', *Venture* (September–December
1966), pp. 19–26.

'The Writer in His Age', *The London Magazine* (May 1957), pp.
45–46.

Interviews and Questionnaires on William Golding

Anon. '*Lord of the Flies* Goes to College', *The New Republic* (May 4,
1963), pp. 27–28; 29–30.

Anon. 'Portrait', *Time* Magazine (September 9, 1957), p. 118.

Aldridge, John W. 'Mr. Golding's Own Story', New York *Times
Book Review* (December 10, 1961), pp. 56–57.

Biles, Jack I. *Talk: Conversations with William Golding*. New York:
Harcourt, Brace & Jovanovich, 1970.

Davis, Douglas M. 'A Conversation with William Golding', *The
New Republic* (May 4, 1963), pp. 28–30.

——. 'Golding, the Optimist, Belies His Somber Pictures and
Fiction', *The National Observer* (September 17, 1962), p. 4.

Dick, Bernard F. ' "The Novelist is a Displaced Person'', An Interview with William Golding', *College English* (March 1965), pp. 480–482.

Dolbier, Maurice, 'Running J. D. Salinger a Close Second', New York *Herald Tribune Books* (May 20, 1962), pp. 6; 15.

Keating, James. 'The Purdue Interview (of William Golding)', Purdue University (May 10, 1962) in Baker and Ziegler's *Casebook Edition of William Golding's 'Lord of the Flies'*, pp. 189–195.

Kermode, Frank. 'The Meaning of It All', *Books and Bookmen* (October 1959), pp. 9–10. Transcript of interview edited from BBC Third Programme, August 28, 1959 (part unpublished).

Webster, Owen. 'Living with Chaos', *Books and Art* (March 1958), pp. 15–16.

——. 'The Cosmic Outlook of an Original Novelist', *John O'London's* (January 28, 1960), p. 7.

Critical Books on William Golding

Babb, Howard S. *The Novels of William Golding*. Columbus: The Ohio State University Press, 1970.

Baker, James R., and Arthur P. Ziegler, Jr. (eds.). *Casebook Edition of William Golding's 'Lord of the Flies': Text, Criticism, and Notes*. New York: G. P. Putnam's Sons, 1964.

——. *William Golding A Critical Study*. New York: St. Martin's Press, 1965.

Dick, Bernard F. *William Golding*. New York: Twayne Publishers Inc. 1967.

Gregor, Ian, and Mark Kinkead-Weekes. *William Golding, A Critical Study*. London: Faber and Faber, 1967.

Oldsey, Bernard S., and Stanley Weintraub. *The Art of William Golding*. New York: Harcourt, Brace and World, 1965.

Nelson, William. *William Golding's 'Lord of the Flies', A Source Book*. New York: Odyssey Press, Inc., 1963.

Pamphlets on William Golding

Biles, Jack I. 'A William Golding Miscellany', *Studies in the Literary Imagination, II*. Georgia State College, 1969.

Broes, Arthur T. 'The Two Worlds of William Golding', *Carnegie Series in English, No. 7*. Pittsburgh, Pa., 1963.

Dewsnap, Terrence. *Golding's 'Lord of the Flies', Monarch Study Notes*. New York: Monarch Press, 1964.

——. *Golding's 'The Inheritors' and 'Free Fall'*, Monarch Study Notes. New York: Monarch Press, 1966.

Elman, Paul. *William Golding, A Critical Essay, Contemporary Writers in Christian Perspective*. Eerdman Publishing Co., 1967.

Handley, Graham. *William Golding's 'Lord of the Flies'*, Notes on Chosen English Texts. Bath: James Brodie Ltd., 1965.

Hodson, Leighton. *William Golding, Writers and Critics*. Edinburgh: Oliver Boyd Ltd., 1969.

Hubbard, Ed., and Alfred Sundel. *'Lord of the Flies', A Critical Commentary, A Study Master*. New York: American RD Corp., 1963.

Hynes, Samuel. *William Golding, Columbia Essays on Modern Writers*, 2nd edn. New York: Columbia University Press, 1968.

Livingston, James C. *Commentary on William Golding's 'The Spire'. Religious Dimensions in Literature*. Scadbury, 1967.

Moody, Philippa. *A Critical Commentary on William Golding's 'Lord of the Flies'. Macmillan Critical Commentary*. London: Macmillan's Press, 1966.

Pemberton, Oliver. *William Golding*. London: Longmans Green, 1969.

Whitley, John. *William Golding: 'Lord of the Flies'*, London: Edward Arnold, 1970.

Criticism on William Golding

The following represents a selected bibliography of articles and reviews considered generally useful. Items noted already in the bibliographies of B. F. Dick and L. Hodson which were useful but not directly relevant to this study have not been included. For a more complete bibliography see V. Tiger entry below.

Adriaens, Mark. 'Style in William Golding's *The Inheritors*' *English Studies* (1970), 16–30.

Allen, Walter. 'Recent Trends in English Literature', *English* (September 1969), pp. 2–5.

——. *Tradition and Dream*. London: Phoenix House, 1964, pp. 288–292.

Ali, Masood Amjad. '*The Inheritors*: An Experiment in Technique', *Venture* (April 1969), pp. 123–31.

Anderson, Robert S. '*Lord of the Flies* on *Coral Island*', *The Canadian Review of Social Anthropology* (February 1967), pp. 54–69.

Amis, Kingsley. *New Maps of Hell*. London: Gollancz, 1964, *passim*.

Axthelm, Peter M. *The Modern Confessional Novel*. New Haven: Yale University Press, 1967, *passim*.

Baker, James R. 'The Decline of *Lord of the Flies*', *Southern Atlantic Quarterly* (Winter 1970), pp. 446–460.

Barnet, Sylvan, Morton Berman, and William Burto (eds.). 'Introduction to William Golding's *The Brass Butterfly*', *The Genius of the Later English Theatre*. New York: New American Library, 1962, pp. 439–442.

Berger, Hélène Croux. 'L'Allegorie du Mal dans l'Oeuvre du William Golding', *Critique* (April 1966), pp. 309–320.

Bird, Stephen B. 'Natural Science and the Modern Novel', *English Record* (February 1966), pp. 2–6.

Blake, Ian. '*Pincher Martin*, William Golding and Taffrail', *Notes and Queries* (August 1962), pp. 309–310.

Boyle, Ted E. 'A Denial of Spirit, An Explication of William Golding's *Free Fall*', *Wascana Review* (1966), pp. 3–10.

Bradbury, Malcolm. 'A Near Myth', *New Statesman* (October 29, 1971), p. 594.

Braybrooke, Neville. 'Two William Golding Novels: Two Aspects of his Work', *Queens Quarterly* (September 1969), pp. 92–100.

Broberg, Britta. 'Connections Between William Golding's First Two Novels', *Moderna Sprak* (1969), pp. 1–24.

Bufkin, E. C. 'The Novels of William Golding, A Descriptive and Analytic Study' (unpublished Ph.D dissertation). Vanderbilt University, 1964.

Burgess, Anthony. 'Golding Unbuttoned', *The Listener* (November 4, 1965), pp. 717–718.

——. *The Novel Now*. London: Faber and Faber, 1967, pp. 63–65.

Byatt, A. S. 'Of Things I Sing', *The New Statesman* (June 2, 1967), pp. 761–764.

Campbell, Archie. 'William Golding's *Pincher Martin*', *From the Fifties*. London: BBC Sound Radio Drama Series, 1962, pp. 30–35.

Clark, George. 'An Illiberal Education: William Golding's Pedagogy', *Seven Contemporary Authors: Essays on Cozzens, Miller, West, Golding, Heller, Albee, and Powers*. Edited by Thomas Whitbread. University of Texas Press, 1966, pp. 73–95.

Corke, Hilary. 'The Maggot and the Chinaman', *Encounter* (February 1957), pp. 79–81.

Cox, C. B. *The Free Spirit*, London: Oxford, 1963, pp. 172–184.

Crompton, D. W. '*The Spire*', *Critical Quarterly* (Spring 1967), pp. 63–79.

Davies, Cecil W. 'The Novels Foreshadowed: Some Recurring

Themes in Early Poems by William Golding', *English* (Autumn 1968), pp. 86–89.

Delbaere-Garant, Jeanne. 'From the Cellar to the Rock: A Recurrent Pattern in William Golding's Novels', *Modern Fiction Studies* (Winter 1971–2), pp. 501–512.

Diericlx, J. 'La Thème de la Chute dans les Romans de W. Golding', *Etudes Anglaises* (July–September 1963), pp. 230–242.

Donoghue, Denis. 'The Ordinary Universe', *New York Review of Books*, December 21, 1967, p. 9.

Drasdo, Harold. 'William Golding: From Darkness to Blackout', *Anarchy* (February 1965), pp. 35–38.

Ely, Sister M. Amanda. 'The Adult Image in Three Novels of Adolescent Life', *English Journal* (November 1967), pp. 1123–31.

Epstein, E. L. 'Notes on *Lord of the Flies*', *Lord of the Flies*. New York: Capricon Books, 1959, pp. 188–192.

Fackler, Herbert, V. 'Palaeontology and Paradise Lost: A Study of Golding's Modifications of Fact in *The Inheritors*', *Bull State University Forum* (1969), pp. 64–66.

Fleishman, Avrom. *The English Historical Novel.* Johns Hopkins Press, 1972, *passim.*

Forster, E. M. 'Introduction', *Lord of the Flies*. New York: Coward-McCann, 1962, pp. ix-xii.

Fraser, G. S. 'The Novel in the 1950's', *The Modern Writer and His World*. Middlesex: Penguin, 1964, pp. 171–172.

Frye, Northrop. 'The Voice and the Crowd', *Media* (Autumn 1966), p. 42.

Furbank, P. N. 'Golding's *The Spire*', *Encounter* (May 1964), pp. 59–61.

Gallagher, Michael P. 'Human Values in Modern Literature', *Studies* (Summer 1968), pp. 142–153.

Gindin, James. *Post War British Fiction.* Berkeley: University of California Press, 1962, pp. 196–206.

———. 'The Fable Begins to Break Down', *Wisconsin Studies in English Literature* (Winter 1966), pp. 1–4.

Gordon, Robert C. 'Classical Themes in *Lord of the Flies*', *Modern Fiction Studies* (Winter 1965–1966), pp. 424–427.

Green, Peter. 'The World of William Golding', *Transactions and Proceedings of the Royal Society of Literature*, 32 (1963), pp. 37–57.

Gregor, Ian, and Mark Kinkead-Weekes, 'Introduction', *Lord of the Flies*. London: Faber and Faber, School Editions, 1962, pp. i-xii.

———. 'Introduction', *The Inheritors*. London: Faber and Faber, Educational Edition, 1964, pp. 11–18.

Herndl, George. 'Golding and Salinger, A Clear Choice', *Wiseman Review* (Winter 1964–1965), pp. 309–322.

Hoagland, Edward. 'The Scorpion God', New York Times *Book Review* (February 6, 1972), p. 5.

Josipovici, Gabriel. *The World and the Book, A Study of Modern Fiction.* Standford University Press, 1971, pp. 236–255.

Karl, Frederick. 'The Novel as Moral Allegory: The Fiction of William Golding', *A Reader's Guide to the Contemporary English Novel.* New York: Noonday Press, 1962, pp. 254–261.

Kermode, Frank. 'The Case for William Golding', *The New York Review of Books* (April 30, 1964), pp. 3–4.

———. *Puzzles and Epiphanies.* London: Routledge and Kegan Paul, 1962, pp. 198–213; 214–218.

La Chance, Paul R. '*Pincher Martin*: The Essential Dilemma of Modern Man', *Cithara* (May 1969), pp. 55–60.

Lederer, Richard H. 'Student Reactions to *Lord of the Flies*', *English Journal* (November 1964), pp. 575–579.

Lewis, R. W. B. 'The High Cost of Piety', New York *Herald Tribune Book Week*, April 26, 1964, pp. 1; 10.

Littlejohn, David. 'The Anti-Realists', *Daedalus* (Spring 1963), pp. 250–265.

Lodge, David. 'William Golding', *The Spectator* (April 19, 1964), pp. 489–490.

MacClure, Millar. 'William Golding's Survivor Stories', *Tamarack Review* (Summer 1957), pp. 60–68.

McGuiness, Frank. 'Selected Books', *The London Magazine* (August 1964), pp. 84–88.

MacNeice, Louis. *Varieties of Parable.* Cambridge: Cambridge University Press, 1965, *passim.*

Malin, Irving. 'The Elements [sic] of William Golding', *Contemporary British Novelists.* Southern Illinois University Press, 1965, pp. 36–47.

Marcus, Steven. 'The Novel Again', *Partisan Review* (Spring 1962), pp. 171–196.

Merren, John. '*Lord of the Flies* as an Anatomy', *Conference of College Teachers of English.* University of Texas (September 1966), pp. 28–29.

Michel-Michot, Paulette. 'The Myth of Innocence', *Revue des Langes Vivantes* (1962), pp. 510–520.

Mitchell, Charles. '*Lord of the Flies* and the Escape from Freedom', *Arizona Quarterly* (Spring 1966), pp. 27–40.

Mitchell, Juliet. 'Concepts and Techniques in William Golding', *New Left Review* (May–June 1962), pp. 63–71.

Niemeyer, Carl. 'The Coral Island Revisited', *College English* (January, 1961), pp. 241–245.

Nossen, Eron. 'The Beast-Man Theme in the Work of William Golding', *Bull State University Forum* (September 1968), pp. 60–69.

O'Hara, J. D. 'Mute Choirboys and Angelic Pigs, The Fable in *Lord of the Flies*', *Texas Studies in Literature and Language* (Winter 1966), pp. 411–420.

Peter, John. 'The Fables of William Golding', *Kenyon Review* (Autumn 1957), pp. 577–592.

Phelps, Gilbert. 'The Novel Today', *The Modern Age*, *The Pelican Guide to English Literature*, ed. Boris Ford. Middlesex: Penguin, 1961, pp. 475–496.

Pritchett, V. S. 'Genesis', *New York Review of Books* (February 24, 1972), pp. 12–13.

———. *The Living Novel and Later Approaches*. New York: Vintage Books, 1967, pp. 309–315.

Quinn, Michael, 'An Unheroic Hero, William Golding's *Pincher Martin*', *Critical Quarterly* (Autumn 1962), pp. 247–257.

Plimpton, George. 'Without the Evil to Endure', New York *Times Book Review* (July 29, 1962), p. 4.

Podhoretz, Norman. 'A Look at Life', *New Yorker* (September 21, 1957), pp. 177–178.

Quigly, Isabel. 'New Novels', *The Spectator* (September 30, 1955), p. 428.

Rexroth, Kenneth. 'William Golding', *Atlantic* (May 1965), pp. 96–98.

Roper, Derek. 'Allegory and Novel in Golding's *The Spire*', *Wisconsin Studies in English Literature* (Winter 1967), pp. 19–30.

Rosenberg, Bruce A. 'Lord of the Fire-flies', *The Centennial Review* (Winter 1967), pp. 128–139.

Rosenfield, Claire. 'Men of Smaller Growth, A Psychological Analysis of William Golding's *Lord of the Flies*', *Literature and Psychology* (Autumn 1961), pp. 93–101.

Servotte, Herman. 'Sterfelijkheid en Licht., *Dietsche Warande en Balfort* (1964), pp. 590–595.

Smith, Patrick J. 'Typology and Peripetia in Four Catholic Novels' (unpublished Ph.D dissertation). University of California, 1967.

Steiner, George. *Language and Silence*. New York: Atheneum 1970, pp. 288–294.

Stern, James. 'English Schoolboys in the Jungle', New York *Times Book Review* (October 23, 1955), p. 38.

Sternlicht, Sanford. 'A Source for Golding's *Lord of the Flies, Peter Pan?*' *English Record* (December 1963), pp. 41–43.

Stinson, John J. 'The Uses of the Grotesque and other Modes of Distortion, Philosophy, and Implication in the Novels of Iris Murdoch, William Golding, Anthony Burgess, and J. S. Donleavy' (unpublished Ph.D dissertation). New York University, 1971.

Sullivan, Walter. 'The Long Chronicle of Guilt: William Golding's *The Spire*', *The Hollins Critic* (June 1964), pp. 6–12.

——. 'William Golding, The Fables and the Art', *Sewanee Review* (Autumn 1963), pp. 660–664.

Tanner, Tony. 'Fables of an Ancient Egyptian', *New Society* (December 2, 1965), p. 185.

Taylor, Harry H. 'The Case Against William Golding's Simon-Piggy', *Contemporary Review* (September 1966), pp. 155–160.

Thomson, George H. 'The Real World of William Golding', *Alphabet* (November 1964), pp. 26–33.

——. 'William Golding: Between God-Darkness and God-Light', *Cresset* (June 1969), pp. 8–12.

Tiger, Virginia. 'An Analysis of William Golding's Fiction' (unpublished Ph.D dissertation). University of British Columbia, 1971.

Townsend, R. C. '*Lord of the Flies*: Fool's Gold', *Journal of General Education* (July 1964), pp. 153–160.

Trilling, Lionel. '*Lord of the Flies*', *The Mid Century* (October 1962), pp. 10–12

Veidemanis, Gladys. '*Lord of the Flies* in the Classroom, No Passing Fad', *English Journal* (November 1964), pp. 569–574.

Wain, John. 'Lord of the Agonies', *Aspect* (April 1963), pp. 56–57.

——. 'The Other-Worldly Eye', *The London Observer* (June 4, 1967), p. 11.

Walters, Margaret. 'Two Fabulists: Golding and Camus', *Melbourne Critical Review* (1961), pp. 18–29.

Watson, Kenneth. 'A Reading of *Lord of the Flies*', *English* (Spring 1964), pp. 2–7.

Weintraub, Stanley. 'A Certain Significance', New York *Times Book Review* (March 27, 1966), p. 8.

White, Robert J. 'Butterfly and Beast in *Lord of the Flies*', *Modern Fiction Studies* (Summer 1964), pp. 163–170.

Wilson, Angus. 'Evil in the English Novel', *Kenyon Review* (March 1967), pp. 167–194.

INDEX